W9-BKF-382

TRAVELERS' TALES

THE

BEST
WOMEN'S TRAVEL
WRITING

2006

TRUE STORIES
FROM AROUND THE WORLD

T RAVELERS ' T ALES

THE BEST
WOMEN'S TRAVEL
WRITING
2006

TRUE STORIES
FROM AROUND THE WORLD

Edited by
LUCY MCCAULEY

Travelers' Tales
Palo Alto

Art Direction: Michele Wetherbee/Stefan Gutermuth
Interior design and page layout: Melanie Haage using the fonts Nicolas Cochin, Ex Ponto and Granjon.

Distributed by: Publishers Group West, 1700 Fourth Street, Berkeley, California 94710.

ISBN 1-932361-35-9
ISSN 1553-054X

First Edition
Printed in the United States
10 9 8 7 6 5 4 3 2 1

For my mother, Elisita McCauley,
and my sister, Elizabeth McCauley.

Certainly, travel is more than the seeing of sights; it is a change that goes on, deep and permanent, in the ideas of the living.

— MIRIAM BEARD

Table of Contents

Introduction

 A number of years ago I volunteered on an archae-
ological dig at Assos, on the western coast of
Turkey. My days were spent sifting dirt in a cemetery
from a distant time, sarcophagi open all around me—
hundreds of them—many broken, strewn about like
cracked treasure chests. Warm winds carried the scent
of mint and thyme and sounds from the village nearby:
a rooster's crow, the hollow clang of goat bells.

We dug our trenches yards and yards deep, through a
palimpsest of eras, all the way back to when the ancient
city was at its height of glory, in the period just after
Homer. I would use my fingers to break open the larger
clumps of earth, feeling like the blind for what the eye
couldn't see: a pottery fragment or coin when it is caked
with centuries of dirt. Mostly, though, I found bones,
small ones, perhaps the bones of fingers.

I had never visited Turkey before, yet the country and
the site of the dig, especially, felt deeply meaningful for
me: a little more than a century before my arrival there,
my great-great Uncle Frank had excavated the very
same ancient city. He later married in Turkey and spent
the rest of his life moving between his Boston home and
his wife's home on the Dardanelles Strait.

Stories of Uncle Frank's adventures in Turkey filled
my childhood. And there was also the tale of his journey
by sailboat, when he was just twenty-two, down the

Rhine and Danube rivers and into the Aegean Sea. All of this—the sailboat trip, the excavations at Assos—Uncle Frank documented in several volumes of journals filled with lively prose and meticulous drawings. As a child, sitting on the floor of an aunt's house, I would pore over those volumes, sometimes becoming so immersed in my ancestor's words and sketches that I would lose all track of time. Something that my uncle possessed resonated profoundly with the child I was and the adult I would become: the desire to travel, not just for its own sake, as an occupation or a compulsion or as a way of moving away from things, but rather a wish to dwell in the journey itself—to travel as a way of bringing you back to yourself.

Those are the reasons that I believe my uncle was a traveler, and why I would grow up to be a traveler, too. When, many years after those afternoons spent immersed in Uncle Frank's journals, I found myself working on the same dig and retracing his footsteps through western Turkey, it felt like nothing less than the gathering of pieces of myself. I had come upon a particular memory of who I was and what I'd come from, of a family legacy of adventure, of choosing to live in a different way, outside the boundaries that life normally prescribes for us.

In *The Book of Laughter and Forgetting*, Milan Kundera describes this aspect of reclaiming parts of ourselves through the act of journeying. "Memories are scattered all over the world," he wrote. "We must travel if we want to find them and flush them from their hiding places." For women, I think this idea of gathering memory through travel rings especially true—and feels critically important. It doesn't necessarily have to mean travel to a place where we have a direct link to the past, as I did in Turkey—or as Patricia Hampl does in her story in this collection, "The Art of the Wasted Day," in which she travels to Prague and connects with her Czech heritage. Rather, simply by sallying forth to where we are drawn, by journeying away from our domestic routines and the ways that other people define us, we come to recall our most authentic selves.

Travel allows us the anonymity and solitude of the wanderer; it opens a place of suspended time that enables us, for a while, to be neither here nor there. To happen upon experience through the act of putting one foot in front of the other, inviting insight and inner meandering. Through travel we discover parts of ourselves whose outlines are usually obscured by the veneer of daily life. In moving from this periphery outward—in the journey away from the selves that we cultivate in our everyday lives—we come, paradoxically, to our center. We remember, then, what we've always known, connecting with memory that resides in our bodies, hearts, unconscious, and the part of ourselves that exists out of time.

More than anything else, I think that what the women in this collection do is to tap *memory*—in ways that are wise and funny, poignant and startling. The book opens with Anita Kugelstadt's very funny "Packing Light," a story that helps us remember both the distinctive rush and the apprehension of embarking on a journey. Later, in "Saving Face and Smoking in Italy," Maya Angelou travels to an art colony during Thanksgiving and is reminded of her own childhood feasts—and how "a respect for food and its preparation could obliterate distances between sexes, languages, oceans, and continents." And Anne Lamott's "Cruise Ship" recounts the author's first shipboard vacation, which taps hilariously into the visceral memory of some of her own deepest fears, including group hugs and platters of cream puffs.

Several authors are forced in their travels to remember their courage and strength. Karla Theilen in "The Man Who Came in from the Cold" helps a frostbitten hunter search for his lost companion on a mountain; Kari Bodnarchuk in "Awash in the Jungle" is awakened in the night by a flash flood while camping in Malaysia. But other authors find that travel ignites the memory of their most feminine selves. Sharon Balentine's "In the *Hamam*" describes her reconnection with her own beauty during a visit to an Istanbul bathhouse, where "we women lay out in a circle dreaming and luxuriating like great cats" on a hot slab of marble. Similarly, Marguerite Rigoglioso's "Eruptions" recounts how, on a visit to Sicily, a live volcano and a delightful young man helped the author recall—and stoke—her own internal fires.

The book ends with two stories that poignantly remind us of other unique gifts that journeying offers. Ruth Kear's "Oaxaca Care" describes a trip the author promised herself to mark her return to health after a long illness. And finally, Daisann McLane in "Point, Shoot, and Remember" muses on how photography during our travels can create memory itself—even if, as she points out, some of our best photographs are the ones we'll never see.

These are just some of the stories in this volume, the "best" that we editors at Travelers' Tales have seen over this past year in the sense that they each relay, in an authentic and enticingly readable way, some aspect of that most profound promise of travel—as a threshold onto a space where we might rediscover ourselves. And, as I experienced so tangibly during my own Turkish travels to the echoing ruins where my Uncle Frank had worked and dwelled, such journeys serve as passageways to our deepest memories and longings, to that which makes us human and ultimately underlies our connection to all being.

—Lucy McCauley
Somerville, Massachusetts

※ ※ ※

Pack Light

Leave room for the unexpected.

"Pack light," he said, overlooking the fact that I was a university student who had until recently slept on a foam mattress and could move households assisted by a few garbage bags and a friend with a bicycle. I lived light and it never occurred to me to reciprocate with the same command, or define "light," or snoop through his luggage before we left. Had I only shown some sort of initiative.

But I hadn't, so a few days into the trip, I was a woman changed: disheveled, a bit pongy, displaying a dismaying interest in food-stain design. His unending supply of crisp new shirts and command of Spanish left me wondering how he explained my mucky presence at his side to the small-town inhabitants we spoke with while traveling dirt cheap down the west coast of Mexico.

The room cost us less than one fast food meal at home. At that price, of course, the *cucarachas* were both included and copious. "They're vegetarians. They're vegetarians," I chant, trying to calm myself and find a bond, if not for friendship, at least for amicable co-existence. I try to picture them as smaller, less hairy cows. I am a farm girl and in my experience, bovines deserve confidence.

My partner has left our room in search of a glass. I turn on the tap to wash my hands and feel a strangely powerful tingle scurry up both my arms into my chest. Travel, I reflect as I look wide-eyed into the cracked mirror, is exciting. Staying at home never sent frissons of energy through me like this.

My partner comes back with a glass. The owner, met with such a simple request, had begun an enthusiastic search, only to come up empty-handed. But when his eyes lit upon his own half-filled glass, he dashed its contents to the floor, gave the inside a quick wipe with his shirttail, and handed it over with a triumphant smile and modest dip of his head. Back home such a report would have left me open-mouthed and aghast. Now I smile gratefully at our host's creative generosity, and pour myself a liberal shot of Kahlua.

Avoiding the tourist crowds, we press against bodies in teeming streets, buoyed by the lyrical Spanish chatter of people out for the evening. Supper consists of beans, chicken and rice, too many *cervezas*, and a burgeoning, next-door-to-maudlin attachment to a joyful and generous populace.

We make our way back to our economical digs and I engage in one of my favorite fantasies, one that is only possible when I don't understand a word being spoken around me. Each conversation is a gem of intellectual prowess. People discuss love and beauty and truth. No one is alluding to the size of a woman's hooters or how they overcharged the dumb sap with the bad brakes. Of course, to make this fantasy work I must carefully look away from nose-pickers or men who believe that repositioning their "pride and joy" is a fundamental duty in which they must engage at regular intervals.

Back home, anxious to ensure my best chance to sleep despite the cockroaches that I fully expect to construct major roadways across my face, I decide on a refreshing shower.

I advance gingerly into the shower. Priority one: do not step on a cockroach. I realize that they move fast enough to break the sound barrier, and that I'd probably need steel boots to actually crush one, but I am unwilling to take any chances at harming one of their number. The thought of millions of vengeful family members inspires in me a caution well-suited to space walks or neurosurgery.

As it turned out, I needn't have worried about the little beasties. I have, as the saying goes, bigger fish to fry.

Naked, wet, I cannot let go of the taps. I am in every aspect—thought processes, panic level, comically bulging eyes—like a drunken mariner seizing the ship's rail during a colossal storm, except considerably more undressed. Electrical current courses through my arms down to my feet. "Naaauugh," I holler, in neither Spanish nor English, reverting to the language of our neolithic ancestors.

My boyfriend yells helpfully from the other room, "They don't bite!"

"There's electricity! In the bathroom!" Clearly the electroshock has diminished what little intellectual capacity the Kahlua and *cervezas* have left me. Only basic instincts for self-preservation permit me to liberate my hands. Torn between averting possible death and regaining a modest level of hygiene—well, I am a woman—vanity wins the day. My head is not smoking, I reason, and as long as I don't touch the taps, the current remains safely in the wall.

Clean and pondering my next move, I call out, "There's a current of electricity when I touch the taps!"

"You're imagining things."

Tell me and I shall forget. Show me and I will remember. Involve me and I will understand. A little something I learned while getting an education degree.

"How about a shower?" I offer magnanimously. "I'll leave it running for you."

A few days later, an effective truce having been negotiated, we amble along a deserted beach, searching for a place to spend the morning. Moving past tampon applicators, syringes, and other disturbing detritus, we remain hopeful of finding a pristine little corner. Luck is not yet with us and we give a dead dog wide berth.

A bit farther along, a dead seal. Long dead. We carry on, confident it cannot get worse.

Two people approach from the other direction. An exchange in Spanish follows. I watch everyone's mouth, trying to arrange my face to reflect growing comprehension, and convinced—knowing the giving nature of these people—that my partner is gaining knowledge of a secret paradise, not far down the beach.

Grimly, my partner thanks the two men, takes my arm, and turns me back the way we've just come. "It's a dead person. About a hundred yards down."

We have, throughout our trip, been extolling the wondrous beauties of nature along the Mexican coast. But when nature washes up on the beach in the form of dead bodies, we opt for the security of town. We decide to visit a fish market that some of the locals have told us about.

Our keen sense of direction fails us once more, and we approach the fish market from the rear. We're still yards from the market but we see—and mama do we smell— tons of fish. Four tons, to be exact. Fish heads and fish guts bursting from the back of a four-ton truck.

Imagine your living room, packed to the ceiling with the parts of fish no one will eat. Now envision a baking sun. Add 500 or so seagulls swirling overhead. Seagulls incapable of exerting any semblance of control over their beaks. Or their backsides.

The deluge of fish, in one form or another, is almost biblical. And you are without a hat.

But looking at our visit from a guidebook point of view, it was free, and I'd never seen anything like it before. Shrimp the size of my forearm. Worth a detour.

We board a bus. There is another bus, constructed after—rather than long before—I was born. This other bus travels a smooth, modern toll highway. But this other bus costs quite a bit more, and it will be full of tourists. We want to travel as the Mexicans do. Of the fifty or so people who will share this adventure with us, only two others are not native.

We exchange proud looks as we find a seat. A look of the virtuous. A look of the staggeringly but blissfully ignorant.

An old woman falters down the aisle, hand out, her collapsed mouth mumbling. Every single person on the bus, besides the two athletic-looking blond Americans, drops a bit of change into her palm. "What is she doing?" I ask. "We already paid for our tickets."

"She's praying for us," my partner informs me. "May your souls complete the journey to your destination. May the wheels of this bus stay on the road. May you not perish in a fiery explosion in some deep and forgotten ravine." I believe that he is only exaggerating slightly. This woman knows how to work a crowd.

Next comes a young girl, handing out candies. I examine mine. Two rewrapped throat lozenges and a green thing I cannot recognize. Gum? A suppository? The two Americans, I notice, are happily consuming their pre-flight extra.

I am still staring at the offering in my palm when the girl walks back up the aisle. She takes the candy out of my hand along with the few coins my partner has given her for his delicacies. The Americans are now gaping at the girl, confused, helpless. My partner explains to them that they are expected to pay. She is not a flight attendant.

"All of our money is on our bikes, tied to the back of the bus!" This particular situation with the young girl aside, leaving all of your money outside the bus just doesn't seem like a prize-winning idea. My partner pays for them, and we have two new friends.

In an explosion of sound and stench, our bus lurches into traffic. Out on the highway, our driver and the ticket collector carry on a lively conversation which involves much gesticulation and eye contact. Never have two people, people without breasts I might add, had so much to say to each other. The driver commemorates each glance at the road with a merry honk of the horn.

To call the road twisted, or to characterize the ditches as impossibly steep, would be like calling indoor plumbing a development not worth mentioning, or Ebola a trivial nuisance. We seem to be carried ahead by centrifugal force, like water at the bottom of a circling bucket. How many bus wheels are actually on the road, I cannot be sure, but I would bet my life—I may, in fact, be doing so—that some fraction would be accurate.

Only the two Americans and I watch the road. When we are not lurching left or careening right, we are rigid in white-knuckled horror. Most of our fellow passengers have paid their insurance to the old woman and rest easy, peacefully surveying the panorama of mangled cars heaped far below and the colorful roadside shrines dedicated to souls lost en route. Some close their eyes and enjoy their throat lozenges.

After ninety minutes or so the bus is half empty and I come to the conclusion that it's tricky to maintain the high alert essential to truly believe in your own immediately pending death. I start to relax. It helps to laugh at our poor new friends. The man—I shall call him Milquetoast to protect his identity—has moved to the driver's side of the bus by an open window. He explains that he may have time to exit the window if the bus starts going over. He laughs, but he's not joking.

His girlfriend, Nervous Nellie, sticks with our side of bus, unwilling to tempt fates by moving. She too is laughing by now, in a high-pitched way one usually associates with the unhinged.

They yell back and forth across the aisle, mostly making plans to cut short their trip and cycle through their native Oregon instead, but sometimes crying sharply and pounding a window when they spot the carcass of a bus in the ravines below. When we arrive at the small town which is our goal, our new friends embrace us happily, bonds forged in the face of death. We have told them about the other buses, on the toll highway, and we know where they will be by the end of the day. They have promised themselves to come back, without the bicycles.

Perhaps it was the electricity, or perhaps the bowel-constricting bus ride. I do not know, but the situation is this: I am the only person I know actively courting Montezuma, drinking the water, soliciting his help. My partner, who I believe was conceived on an airplane and delivered straight into a piece of luggage, cannot muster the sympathy I would desire for my circumstances. Forget the beautiful architecture, the generous people, the palms swaying under a friendly sun. What I want is a mixing bowl full of prunes. My thoughts turn enviously back to the seagulls.

Getting around in a larger city means taking a mini-bus, a van converted for public transportation. At the driver's right hand is a shrine to the Virgin Mary. Red velvet is puddled on the console, held in place by statues and pictures of Mary, a rosary, and a few homemade crafts. There is also a big pile of change, to which we add our fare. There are perhaps fifteen of us crammed into this van, along with dozens of bags and, although I cannot see them, I can hear chickens.

I am pinned beside the driver. My first thought is to hope that his standards for body odor are lax. But then it occurs to me that in my slovenly state I am a walking metaphor for much of what we have encountered. Grimy, shambolic, perhaps a bit fearsome on the outside; benevolent, optimistic, and, at the risk of sounding immodest, fetching within. I needn't apologize, for anything. I am doing the best that I can in challenging circumstances. Looking around me, I believe that everyone sharing this van understands.

We stop at a red light. Beside us is a small pickup truck, whose driver leans over and begins to yell at our driver who throws open his window and hollers back. They exchange heated words I do not understand. Suddenly, our driver grabs a fistful of change from the shrine, and heaves it mightily through the truck window, much of it bouncing to the street below.

The light turns green, and he floors it. Tires squeal, he clutches the steering wheel like a man possessed, or like a woman being quietly electrocuted in a shower, and it slowly dawns on me that we are racing the truck beside us.

We lose, but not without a fight. A couple of passengers beside me smile heartily at the driver, who appears proud of his showing, his honor intact.

I look down at the Virgin Mary, who seems unfazed by this strange turn of events. Then I recognize that given Mary's background, this would hardly qualify as strange. It also occurs to me that I don't find this particularly outlandish anymore either. And I realize that this is why I travel—the guidebook highlights are lovely, often breathtaking, and I wouldn't want to miss them. But it is the smelly, bowel-twisting, wacky experiences that help me widen the narrow parameters of my safe existence. It's good advice, pack light, and I always will. Doing so gives me a better chance of fitting more into my head and heart for the journey home.

Plus, it really goes without saying, a lighter backpack is more convenient when you need a seagull umbrella.

❧ ❧ ❧

Anita Kugelstadt caught the travel bug in the safety of her own home, from a roommate who financed her world travels by dressing as Mr. Kool-Aid. After that, her career as a teacher seemed to make more sense. The kids might make anyone crazy, but the holidays cannot be beaten, and the crazy part often helps, depending on where your flight lands.

ЖФ ЖФ ЖФ

Saving Face and Smoking in Italy

Far from home, a beloved American writer
helps cook a Thanksgiving feast to remember.

*T*he Rockefeller Foundation's Study and Conference
Center was a large mansion snuggled into the hills
above Bellagio, Italy. Fifteen artists at a time from around
the world were invited to the enclave. Selected artists with
companions had to make their way to Milan airport, and
then magically they were swept up by tender arms and
placed in a lap of luxury that few popular movie stars or
rich corporate chiefs even dreamed existed. A chauffeured
car picked up the invitees and drove them carefully fifty
miles north to Bellagio. There they were deposited at the
Center, which stood atop a high hill. Its buildings were
low-slung and meandered over carefully tended acres only

a few miles from the Swiss border. Within those elegant walls, forty-eight employees cared for thirty guests and the retreat center's director and wife. Each artist had a commodious suite.

Once ensconced in this graciousness, the artists were informed of the regimen. Breakfast was ordered nightly and served each morning by footmen. Lunch was served informally at midday. Artists could sit at will in a casual dining room and choose food from an elaborate buffet. The time could have been passed off as an ordinary lunch save that each table sported a handwritten menu of foods offered and the company was served at the buffet table by the uniformed head waiter and the tailored butler.

The artists were addressed as *dottore*, which meant that their scholarship was respected. They were told that dinner was formal, and that was an understatement. Dinner was an event of meticulous structure. Guests were expected to dress each night and were directed where to sit by a placement, which lay on a hall table at the door of the drawing room. There must have been an exemplary social statistician in the Center's employ because in the four weeks when I was a resident, no one ever once sat twice between the same two people.

Jessica Mitford and I were invited and found ourselves to be the only female artists. We had brought along our husbands, Robert Treuhaft and Paul du Feu, but the staff, so unused to female scholars, could not bring themselves to address us as they addressed the thirteen male scholars. So they called us *signora* and our husbands *dottore*.

One evening during a lull in the ten or twelve conversations plying the table, the director reminded the guests that Thanksgiving was approaching. He then asked if anyone had a good recipe for roast turkey and corn bread dressing. I waited, but no one moved. I said, "I do, I have a recipe." I spoke it before I thought.

Everyone beamed at me except my husband, Jessica, and Robert. In a second, their faces told me I had done the wrong thing. Company never volunteers, never offers. Nonetheless, the director said the butler would come to my suite mid-morning to collect my recipe.

I broke my writing schedule to recall and write the recipe. I handed the missive to the butler. Within minutes he returned and said the chef wanted to see the *dottore* who had sent him the recipe. I followed him down a flight of dark stairs and, without a hint of change to come, stepped suddenly into a vast noisy, hot, brightly lit kitchen, where a fleet of white uniformed cooks were stirring steaming pots and sizzling pans. The butler guided me over to meet the head chef, who wore a starched white toque. His surprise at seeing me let me know that he had expected Dottore Angelou to be a white male, and, instead, a six-foot-tall daughter of Africa stood before him ready to answer his questions. He did shake my hand, but he then turned his back rather rudely and shouted to another cook, "Come and talk to this woman. I don't have the time."

The second cook tried his English, but I told him we could speak Italian. He said, "Signora, we want to follow your recipe, but we have never made corn bread or corn bread dressing. We need your help."

I asked for cornmeal, only to be offered polenta. I asked for baking powder and was told they didn't even know what that was. When I described the work of baking powder, I was shown a large slab of moist yeast.

The polenta was an orange powdery meal many times brighter than American yellow cornmeal.

During the Easter seasons, my mother always used yeast to make hot cross buns. I figured I could use it as the riser for my corn bread.

I gave my jacket to the butler and listed the other ingredients I needed. He put men to work, and in seconds I was able to put a pan of polenta corn bread into a hot oven and the turkey's neck, gizzard, liver, and wing-tips to boil. I added celery, onions, a stick of cinnamon, and garlic to the pot.

When the bread came from the oven, hot and smoking, the head chef was standing near me. We both looked at the orange brown crust. His eyes widened. He said, "*Bella.*"

I said, "This is the bread my people eat."

The chef asked, "Who are your people?"

I answered, "African Americans. My ancestors came from Africa to America."

The chef said, "Every person in America except the Indians had ancestors who came from some other place."

I couldn't argue that.

He asked, "What makes you different from other Americans?"

I said, "My skin is black. That tells me and everyone who sees me who I am."

He raised his voice. "Roberto, Roberto, come."

A small dark-skinned cook came from the rear of the kitchen.

The chef said, "Here is Roberto. He is from Sicily, but because of his color should I call him an Afro-Italian?"

There was a burst of loud laughter. We had been

speaking in Italian and everyone had heard our conversation and enjoyed the fact that the chef was putting me on.

I decided to stop the razzing and get on with the cooking. I quickly diced an onion and sautéed it in a large pan. I drained the stock and mixed some with the onion and crumbled corn bread in a large bowl. No one offered to help me, so I took the raw turkey and stuffed it with the dressing. I laced the turkey's cavity and placed it into a roasting pan. I cut the oven down and set the turkey to roast.

I finely diced another onion and sautéed it and made gravy using the cut-up meat and the rest of the stock. I put a drop of the gravy on my thumb and tasted it for seasoning.

When I looked up, I realized the chef had been watching me for the past twenty minutes. His face told me he had been watching with approval.

He asked, "Would you like a smoke?"

I said, "Yes."

His nod told me to follow him. He shouted to the cooking staff, "Watch her sauce, and keep an eye on the turkey in the oven."

We walked out into an alley. He gave me a strong French cigarette and lighted his own and mine. He breathed in deeply and exhaled loudly, and although he never said a mumbling word I knew his invitation to me to join him in a smoke was his way to show his approval.

That night when the exclusive intellectual assemblage had gathered around the dining table, the chef entered followed by his sous chef, who carried a fine brown turkey.

The sous chef lifted the platter and bowed to the chef, who gave a small bow, then reached out his right hand to me and asked me to stand. All the scholars and their mates and the director applauded the turkey, the chef, and me.

I learned that day that a respect for food and its preparation could obliterate distances between sexes, languages, oceans, and continents.

ᔥ ᔥ ᔥ

Maya Angelou is an author, poet, historian, songwriter, playwright, dancer, stage and screen producer, director, performer, singer, and civil rights activist. Best known for her autobiographical books, including All God's Children Need Traveling Shoes *and the National Book Award nominee* I Know Why the Caged Bird Sings, *she also has written many volumes of poetry, such as* Just Give Me a Cool Drink of Water 'fore I Die, *which was nominated for the Pulitzer prize. This story was excerpted from her book* Hallelujiah! The Welcome Table: A Lifetime of Memories with Recipes.

❧ ❧ ❧

Kalidou's Horse

A horse chosen to ride across Senegal
has to be special indeed.

*T*onight, a sky of stars so luminous that clouds appear
as dark shadows against the light. The animals are
rustling in their pens, crouched before the dead-dark
plains, where embers of outside fires swim away in the
wind.

People come barefoot from the night to Kalidou's
doorway, stepping onto its lip, bending their heads. The
young girl, Jarry, begins the tea preparation in long
elegant purple-and-green cloth, purple scarf wrapped
across her hard forehead, kneeling with long straight
back, all movements measured and fine. She seems
barely conscious of us, whispering. She was fourteen
when she married Kalidou.

Tonight, all of us are in this small hut. The children

smell of milk, and Maimoun, the plump, giggling sister-in-law, is breastfeeding her little baby, Baid. She has a small red leather amulet tied to the braids at the back of her head. Mariama, Hamat's wife, has thick silver rings on the second toes of each foot. Hamat, Kalidou's brother, is tall and humorous, with sparkling eyes, and the neighbor men are murmuring as they pull out their pipes from deep under layers of blue and black cotton. There are two small boys, solemn in the presence of men. The warmth of these people, always laughing.

Kalidou reclines beside me while I write, asking me, in the French he once learned from tourists in Nouakchott, to teach him English, starting uproars of laughter.

His Afro hair and tufted beard, blood-shot, smiling eyes, tunic and harem pants, blue veil now draped on his neck, bag of tobacco and bone pipe in hand. He is both comedy and humility, like he was today at Thilé market where we met.

Mr. Kalidou Bâ, herdsman and Mauritanian refugee, became my interpreter among the herdsmen and children, lighting his pipe, following as I went to check horses' hooves and teeth.

He led me to horses, a red-roan, a dark brown, a small gray, three whites with pepper markings, scarred, gaunt, some with good heads and bad knees, good feet and wild eyes, some listless, sleeping, gathered at the back, in the shade of trees, or tied to the posts of doorways and sheds, or bound to their tilted carts.

Kalidou saw my face, the days of markets passing through my mind, Bokhol, Niassante, M'Pal, walking among crowds of buyers and sellers, past sacks of grain and charcoal, watermelon, electronics, clothing, to the space of land where the dust is raised by herds of cattle, and spotted goats are led like dogs by blue herdsmen, and men are watering their cart horses down at the troughs, hides glistening. They refused to sell me their good horses, and every bush taxi meant to take me home in the evening was forever sitting in the sand, would roll forward a few millimeters, then roll back, and stop, motor droning, hovering on that edge of come or go, waiting, waiting, waiting.

Not once has he asked me: Why do you want a horse to travel this sand-swept land? His brother, Hamat says I must buy a cart. Otherwise, how far could I get? Kalidou pretends to agree. But he is teaching me Peulaar and the ways of the plains. He seems to know that every journey needs a point of departure, a home, a gathering of purpose. He said I must go back to my rented room in Dagana and fetch my luggage, that he would find me a horse.

Now, the men are talking about when the Moors drove the blacks out of Southern Mauritania in '89. Kalidou's people fled R'kiz, the beauty of the immense jade lake in the desert, and lost their homes, their herds. There was a story of a man who swam his only horse across the river at midnight into Senegal.

This small refugee camp of thatch and clay is nestled on the sand slopes before the open plains like it has drifted here on the wind, in pieces of husk and twigs, as I myself have come.

When I was a child I had a horse with a diamond on his brow. We used to ride along the escarpment and I would look down on the valley, at fields and fences, highways and roads, housing developments crawling ever closer. I wanted to keep riding. Where was a place where you could ride free, a land of no fences?

In the morning the neighbors brought a mare for me to look at: sharp-boned, and ragged, one eye of dark purple and blue light, the other eye gone. She was a racehorse, they argued, capable of taking me all the way to Mali, but she rode like a strange dream.

At breakfast, Kalidou was still trying to convince me that I could not go wrong with the one-eyed horse. I was looking at him, wondering if he had lost his mind. He lay back while I drank my tea, and began filling his pipe, twirling the tobacco between his thumb and fingers. He made me an offer: his own gentle white stallion with yellow brush mane and bandy legs, full-boned and healthy, now nestled in the hay of its pen like a lamb, the one he thought he could never sell.

When I agreed, he said, in a kind of quiet, pensive way, *"Maintenant, on est entré dans quelque chose..."* Now, you and I have entered something.

The knotted cord around the horse's neck was an amulet that he had paid a sheep for in Barkevi village. He wouldn't take it off, because the horse was going to me. But he made me promise that I would keep the amulet, and bring it home to Canada, later, long after the journey.

We took the horse and cart down the tarmac, five kilometers or so, to Bouane village where I bought a saddle from an old Marabout. Kalidou said the man once walked to Mecca in a year. He was *"un ancien combattant,"* a veteran, who had served with the French in North Africa in the Second World War.

He appeared in velvet black fez and long white-and-red striped tunic, with a metallic gold case amulet that hung heavily at his neck. He gestured for us to sit on his blue prayer mat in the shade of a crumbling old house while he went to get the "*hirq*." It was the closest thing I had yet seen here to an American western saddle, with embossed dark leather, pommel horn, and low seat, but it was threaded with web and dust, brittle, and torn. He held it in place with his hands on the sharp spine and sunken ribs of his old horse.

He brought out his leather satchel and a cardboard book of prayers and made an amulet, a piece of paper on which he spent a long time writing in Arabic lettering and symbols. He then folded it many times into a small triangle and gave it to Kalidou. He said a blessing over the saddle, wrote a word in the sand and erased it.

When we walked over to the cart he made a sound of praise and put his hand on the horse and looked him over. He seemed to feel the whole thing was possible now. He was laughing with Kalidou. I watched the old man get down on the earth and begin doing push-ups, a memory of his days in the army.

We rode away laughing, along the sand track into the bush to see M'bour Mountain. Kalidou kept asking, "Do you see it?" And all I saw was a mere hill of orange sand and green reed grass from which we saw the plain and further, a dark fleck on the horizon. Podor. The mountain, he explained, was not high but long, about fifty kilometers.

He gave me the reins and I let the horse prance slowly homewards. He taught me the sounds in the mouth, how to talk to his horse, the large flickering ears, yellow brush mane waving with wind, the blue X-mark brand on its right hind flank, and the bare thudding hooves in the sand. Kalidou lit his pipe and had a story of an old Moor he once worked for in Nouakchott, and a plotting wife who bribed him for love. Or the time a French family invited him to live with them on the Canary Islands, but the uprising came the day he was to leave. A rush of grass, the heat of noon.

Tonight there are crickets in the hut walls and I am eating peanuts by lamplight with the women. Jarry is making tea crouched in her way, kneeling with one leg under her, the other knee up against her chest, her face lit by the stove, her eyes, her spirit gazing at the coals.

Someone brushes aside the doorway curtain and Mariama comes in from the night balancing a large black calabash bowl on the palm of her hand. She holds it out to me with her hands pressed against the sides and says something in Peulaar, eyes never leaving me, holding back from smiling, wondering what I will do. You know this? The purest white against the black fibrous wood of the bowl, like liquid lead, a few specks of ash or dust, a few floating hairs, but as I drink I taste the warm smell of the herds in the night, the oil in their hides, the foraging of the plains, and the hairs come to lie on my tongue.

Kalidou is out at the pens with the animals. He pulls thorn boughs across the openings to keep in the sheep and goats. We prepare the horse's evening meal of bran with water, mixing it in a basin with our hands. The horse is nickering, night and firelight in his dark eye. The warm sounds and movement, stars and drums, laughter, clapping from down the highway towards Thilé village. A transport truck's headlights are seen all the way from here, a searchlight from a distant world. It is New Year's Eve and our hands are floured with bran. Kalidou asks, "What do you do to celebrate this? You want to go to town?" And I say, "No, this is fine."

Today Hamat hitched up his donkeys and cart and took "the boys" and me to Thilé for market day. He was joking the whole time, playing an old man driven to madness by his sullen donkeys. Each time they slowed down he whined and winced, lifting his stick and making it sting the air, until they awoke, flicking their ears, the whites of their eyes. There was nothing to hold onto but the gaps between the thick cart planks, the donkeys galloping recklessly along the uneven sand tracks, our breathless laughter.

Kalidou led me under rows of hanging harnesses and dry leather halters, strands of black tire rubber, recycled burlap, plastic and iron bits, stalls of fabric, tobacco, peanuts, grain. I bought a halter lined with decorative red plastic, a strand of padded cloth for the saddle girth, lengths of woven nylon for the stirrup straps, a tablecloth, and tea, sugar, beans and bread for the house.

I ate with the men and boys at Hamat's hut. There were three basins of rice and fish. The first basin Kalidou doused with cow oil and it made the rice taste thick, salty, and creamy. The grilled fish lay silver and white across the rice with small hot green peppers.

"Nyam! Ar nyam!" are their words, their insolent cries. "Eat! Eat!" They tease and provoke me constantly, saying that I don't know how to eat, that I don't eat enough.

My hands among their hands, large and small, ringed fingers and bare fingers, grasping at the hot greasy rice, kneading it in the palm, pressing it to the mouth. The savoring sounds in the mouths, the distant looks, no one talks. Grains of rice spill onto the mat, and slivers of bones. And always it is the same. One by one, the men first, then the small boys, shake the rice from their hands over the basin rim and suck their fingers clean and sit back until I am left eating alone, knowing that if I stop they will protest but while I continue I feel gluttonous, and they are waiting. When the second basin is produced they come back leaning in against me. I am already full, but they mean for me to eat, rice and milk and grease, the sustenance of this land, pressing it down inside me until I learn.

I spent all afternoon sewing two meters of checked blue cotton tablecloth into a pocket for the saddle blanket while Kalidou took the saddle to the leather-worker and the blacksmith to attach the girth and fix on three more iron rings. Tea boiled to sugar on the tiny stove and people came. They said, laughing, that I sewed like a sewing machine and should be a tailor.

Later Kalidou's old quiet mother came to offer me her *"gallaye,"* a blue straw-filled pillow for my comfort on the journey. She did not enter the hut, but stood in the long oval door frame in the light, her bare feet on the dust firmly planted, her hands at her side while I held the pillow, in the blue dusty coolness of the room, saying, *"Adjaruma."* Thank you. Now the saddle—washed of its webs and powdered dust, fixed, and oiled—sits perched on her hut roof in the sun.

Tonight, walking to the boutique, Kalidou took my flashlight and clicked it off. He said that the night was so dark the light would only blind us.

"Do you think you can find your way back?" he asked, then laughed. "You lose your way because you're always looking at the stars."

Both the horse and I have come down with colds. I hear him coughing at night from the pen. I told Kalidou we shouldn't wash him in the mornings at the well like we always do. I bought two tins of tiger balm at the market, one for me and one for the horse. Kalidou pasted it in the horse's nostrils, and the animal shook his head furiously, snorting. Only Kalidou could hold him.

Afterward, the horse lifted his lips to the sky. He turned his eye to us. He seemed to glow by his own light. We listened to him grind his teeth, and to the rustling goats in the next pen, and the strange other sounds of the night that came and went like ghost remnants of a song. I wondered how it would begin, this journey into the open, and how I could take this gentle horse away from his nest.

Kalidou lit his pipe. There was a fan of clouds above the horizon that we both watched. The high road on the plains is isolated, he said. There is no water and the villages are too far apart, sometimes sixty kilometers between them. It would be better to follow the river all the way. He told me never to ride at night, always to ask for the village chief, and gave me the names of all the villages he knew, and those to be avoided because of bandits. He said the horse would always lead me home.

I saddled up the horse and rode out on the land and began my journey. The beauty is that the earth comes first, it is all there is, like surface of bone, the slope of it under the sky, iron rock and ash sands brushed across it, bristling tired grasses and thorn limbs clawing their way to the sky. It holds us. We step directly on it. And it is forever. There is nothing to stop me from riding on, taking everything I find and meet along the way only once in my heart, the color of a rock, a termite hill, a bird, the expression of a face, the curve in a path, and not return.

Once I heard voices and for a long time I saw no one, and then they appeared over a rise. Two men on a cart led by a small donkey that seemed to be dreaming. One man was reclining on his elbows, the other was at the front with the long dark reins in his hand, one leg pulled up, the other leg hanging over the edge, and both men were so relaxed I saw the bumps of the cart wheels jostle them, but they let their muscles float. They went silent when they saw me, their faces did not change. I called out, *"djam nyalli,"* good afternoon, and they answered. And we passed each other within a foot, on this one track on the open land of no fences.

The horse was gentle, listened all the time, but he was still a carthorse, threw his strength forward to feel the wheels and the weight behind him. These horses are not like those I have known at home. They do not sweat on the skin and they know only Peulaar and the particular sounds in the mouth I have not been able to imitate.

We moved down towards the river. I heard a loud buzzing in the sky, and a swarm of traveling bees flew over us, so close that I bent my head. I dreamed about honey, and finding it next market day. At the river goats were climbing into the thorn trees, and herds of cattle were being driven down to the water in clouds of dust, smell of metal. I felt the surge of blood in the beasts and wondered how it would affect them if I rode through. I felt it in the horse. He wanted to meet them. He turned his head, his eyes went wide, and the cows spilled alongside us, tilting their heavy bone horns, only wanting the river. The river was milk and turquoise in the heat.

We rode far out across the plains until the sun came behind dark yellow bands of clouds on the horizon, and moved on into the dusk. I leaned my hand on the horse's back and felt the sky on my face, and had no idea where I was. There was a particular quality of distance in the color of the sky, in the high traveling clouds. It had a curve in it, like looking at the surface of a close, hovering, ethereal planet. It made a strange luminosity on the horse's hide, a red light that was active in the air and on the surface of things like electric dust.

Distance in the night is greater. We went on in utter darkness for the longest time, until I began to listen because I could not see. I have never been alone in such an open place. I gave him the reins and he led me on. When a flickering light came into the darkness it seemed only to be a solitary firefly. It blinked out and appeared again somewhere else. The darkness was such an immense presence it took me beyond the idea of being lost. My breath and the steps of the horse were of the same, in and out, back and forth. We were held in a place forever, and then, somehow, we were let go. We moved forward and came into life, into firelight and orange lamps, into a hum of voices, a vibration. It was like approaching a hive.

I rode across northern Senegal that winter on Kalidou's small white barb that I named "Leo Lawal," "Light of the Moon" in Peulaar. He carried me for two months over 800 kilometers, along the river, on cattle trails, cart tracks, and on the open plains. I made it into Mali, only because I was on Kalidou's horse, and I was blessed. He sold it to me, but later, under the iron mountains of Kayes, I dreamed of returning his horse to him, returning to the large hovering sky, fan and funnel patterns of clouds, the plains. The soft, pastoral scene, small homes of clay and thatch, and the smell, the presence of the herds. The slow swaying cattle coming in from the plains, unguided and unbound.

Erika Connor is a painter, writer, and art teacher from rural Quebec, Canada. She has a BFA in studio art and creative writing from Concordia University, in Montreal, where she also won The Irving Layton Award for Fiction in 1991. She has traveled extensively in West Africa, and recently returned from Mongolia where she first worked as a volunteer on a wild horse reserve then bought a white horse and rode to Karakorum, the ancient capital of Chinngis Khan.

෯ ෯ ෯

Cruise Ship

The author overcomes fears of group hugs,
VX gas attacks, and platters of cream puffs to
join friends on a floating vacation.

The aunties have put on weight since our last trip
to the tropics, the aunties being the jiggly areas of
my legs and butt that show when I put on a swimsuit.
I had fallen in love with them five or six years ago, the
darling aunties, shyly yet bravely walking exposed along
the beaches of Huatulco, Mexico. Used to having them
hidden in the dark of long pants and capris and the
indoors, I suddenly understood that they had carried me
through my days without complaint, strong and able,
their only desire to accompany me, on beaches, in shorts,
and to swim in tropical water. I vowed to include them
from then on, to be as kind and grateful as possible.

But that had been nearly fifteen pounds earlier.

Now they wanted to come with me to the Caribbean.

My friends Buddy and Father Tom had persuaded me to go on a cruise with them, shortly before the United States went to war "preemptively" in Iraq. Tom said the trip would be a lot like the cruises I take in the comfort of my own home when the world has gotten me down, left me incredulous and defeated. At those times, I make a nest for my baby self on the couch in the living room. I stretch out with a comforter and pillows, and magazines, the cat, unguents, and my favorite drink, cranberry and soda with lime twist. These are periods of stress and *Twilight Zone* isolation, marked by hypochondria, numb terror, despair, and the conviction that I must go on a diet. Even at—especially at—these times I hate to stop, though I know that to go faster and faster and do more is to move in the direction of death. Continuous movement, I tell myself, argues a wasted life. And so I try to create a cruise ship, to carry me back toward living.

The main difference between my cruise, though, and the one Tom and Buddy wanted me to go on, was that at my house, during school hours, there is no one around to whom I have to be nice, and no one who will see me in a bathing suit. And my cruise takes only two hours, instead of a week. It's unbelievably healing; it resets me. Yet it takes time, at least two hours. You can't rush a cruise ship; you can't hurry doing nothing. After a while, you see the sweetest, most invigorating thing of all: one person tenderly caring for another, even if it's just me taking care of me on my old couch.

Tom and Buddy persisted, and my son Sam was desperate to go, and Tom pulled some strings to arrange for nearly free passage on an Italian cruise ship. He and I would give lectures on faith to a group of sober people, in exchange for a week traveling among Caribbean ports with Buddy, Sam, and Sam's friend Alex.

Sam and Alex and I got up one day at dawn and flew to Fort Lauderdale. I had developed a tic by the time we met up with Tom and Buddy at the dock. I'm the world's worst traveler, afraid of all the usual things—of wars, of snakes, of sharks, of undertows. But I was also worried about group hugs, VX gas attacks, and huge platters of cream puffs. I was afraid I would never be able to stop eating the cream puffs once I got started: I saw myself as Al Pacino in *Scarface*, face down on the plate of cocaine, only I'd be buried in puff pastry, custard in my hair.

I love to swim in warm seas but hate getting there. I cling to the motto of my favorite travel agents, Karl and Carl, who advise, "Trust no one, see nothing."

A thousand people were waiting to board when we arrived at the dock. The predominant adornment—stitched, beaded, embossed, tattooed—was the U.S. flag. There were lots of women with big hair, but as Ann Richards once said, "The bigger the hair, the closer to heaven." My sense, which was confirmed in conversations later in the week, was that these were not people with a lot of money: these were largely people who saved to go on cruises every few years.

Tom was wearing a t-shirt with the Arabic alphabet on it. Buddy had a bag of M&M's, and the five us ate them by the fistful. Tom and Buddy, in their upscale hobo clothes and with the beginnings of beards, stuck out in the bright, cheery crowd. People gave Buddy second looks, because he's the last person you'd expect to find on a cruise ship, besides me. He's in his mid-fifties, and to the untrained eye looks sort of seedy: overweight, with fly-away hair and at least two front teeth missing, as if he'd just gotten out of bed and forgotten his partial dentures.

Tom travels worldwide to lead spiritual retreats and teach English, and very little worries him when it comes to travel. Buddy, in contrast, had not been on a boat since the Vietnam War, and everything waterish scares him. As soon as we were safely onboard, he became convinced that the ship would tip over. Then, after we were shown to our rooms by smiling, handsome young men, he became convinced that a revolution was brewing among the cabin help. And that John Ashcroft was spying on us three adults, because of Tom's shirt, and also because, while standing in line in port, we had accidentally expressed our opinions on George Bush's sobriety and deft diplomatic touch in the Middle East.

Sam and Alex went off on their own, and we went to sit outside and look out at the ocean, which was kindergarten blue. People streamed past us in bright-colored leisure wear and with flags—flag pins, t-shirts, purses, sarongs, swimsuits, baseball caps, fingernails. A woman with a huge blond beehive wrapped in a flag scarf walked by, and Buddy turned to Tom. "The rain and the sun fall on the just and unjust, and while this is offensive, it is true."

I loved my room. It was small and clean and had a porthole—and there was no one else in it. I could have stayed there forever, if I hadn't been in there with myself.

I started to channel Buddy: worried about the ship's tipping over, water pouring through my porthole, shark attacks. I put on some shorts and announced to the aunties that we were going for a brisk walk on the ship's promenade. They are so in love with me, as if I were a gentleman caller. Half the time I am hard on them, viewing them with contempt, covering them in blue jeans when it is hot, threatening to do something drastic one of these days—I'll make them start jogging, that's what I'll do! Or I'll get them some lymphatic seaweed wraps, bandage them like mummies in Saran Wrap, and then parboil them for an hour. Sometimes I catch myself being mean to them, and my heart softens and I apologize, hang my head, and put lotion on them, as if laying on hands. And after periods when I have acted most ashamed of them I adorn them with children's tattoo bandages, with butterflies and wolves.

Sam and Alex became co-conspirators with Buddy on our way to dinner the first night, after he announced to them, *sotto voce*, that he had discovered plans for an uprising among the cabin crew brewing, even as we walked, in the boiler room. After that, the boys would follow him anywhere.

On the way to the dining room, Buddy took us on a tour of the ship's more glaring infirmities: gouges in the wall, various cracks that needed caulking. He showed us to the fancy glass elevators in the center of the ship, from which people were streaming on their way to the dining rooms, past well-appointed shops and bars, ornate columns and marble staircases. When everyone had gotten out of one elevator, Buddy stared inside and clutched his head. He looked at Sam and Alex to see if they had noticed: the handrail had pulled free, and screws stuck out of the walls. "What if the *hull* is like this?" he said. Alex and Sam gripped their foreheads.

I walked to dinner with my arm on Buddy's, like royalty, past the shops, where vendors stood in the doorways and called for us to come in, like the sirens in the *Odyssey*. Buddy, with his missing front teeth and mussed-up hair, pulled me close, protectively. "This woman is *incorruptible!*" he cried to them.

There was way too much food on the cruise, every time you turned around. Half of me wanted to eat it all, and half wanted to go on a diet. I heard my therapist reminding me again and again that diets make you fat and crazy, 95 percent of the time. So I asked the aunties, who get out so rarely, what *they* wanted to eat. They covered their mouths; it was too ridiculous to say. Eventually they chose slices of mango, cocktail prawns, and whole-wheat buns still hot from the oven, and two servings of crème brûlée.

Sam and Alex wore white shirts and khakis to dinner, and the five of us sat with four adults we'd just met. I watched the other adults relate to the boys, who talked away like normal people, making shifty eye contact as they spoke; when others spoke, the boys listened. Every so often Sam looked at me with a vague scorn, as though he thought I was talking too much, but I tried to let him be. I am not here to be his friend. I'm here to be me, which is taking a great deal longer than I had hoped, and I am here to raise him to be a person of integrity and joy. Besides, the kid you know at home is only a facet of the child who lives in the world. His voice, bearing, and vibe change to suit the company, as in those flip books where you can change the hat, head, torso, and legs of the figure, so that an admiral with a spyglass can turn into a pirate, then into a sea monster, then into a sailor or a porpoise. I liked to watch Sam discover parts of himself through other people at the table, the way I have liked to watch him over the years discover Caesar salad, and the Rolling Stones, and even, to some extent, me.

"Why are you eating such weird food?" Sam demanded of Buddy, who had chosen only an appetizer and dessert, pumpkin soup and crème brûlée.

"I'm preparing for the nursing home," Buddy said, opening his eyes wide. It took a moment for Sam to realize Buddy was teasing. "I am! I practice sleeping with a pillow between my knees, so I don't get bedsores."

"Oh, Buddy," said Sam, so affectionately it was as if the flip book had just gone past the spy, past the pirate, past the hoodlum, to a young sweet boy.

I met up with Tom and Buddy for breakfast the next morning. They already had been to the internet café and were filled with the latest evidence that the United States really was about to attack Iraq within days. "The whole world hates us now, and I'm so afraid," Buddy said. "I don't feel there's any hope at all—I feel like one of those goats you see in Indonesia, that tour guides bring along with them, tied to the top of their buses, when they take people to see Komodo dragons. They toss the goats over the cliffs to the Komodo dragons below."

"*Live* goats?" I asked.

"The goats *have* to be alive, because the dragons want to play, and it's more fun for the tourists."

"Maybe the goats don't know what awaits them."

"Of course the goats know," Buddy replied. "The smell of Komodo dragon shit and dead goats gets stronger the closer they get."

"What are we going to do? I mean, seriously."

"I can't speak for you, miss," Tom said. "But I'm

going back to my room pretty soon, and I'm going to stretch out and read all morning. And if there is crème brûlée again for lunch, I think I'll be able to get through the day."

That sounded like a plan. I got into bed with a stack of magazines. Tom had given me *The Nation* and *Harper's* while the receptionist at the spa had lent me *Harper's Bazaar*, and the combination was perversely right.

After a while, though, I went to visit Tom, whose room was next door to mine. He was lying on his back, reading a book about Muslim culture.

"I get so afraid," I said.

"And God delights in you, even when you're scared and at your craziest. Just like God delights in the men in their flag bikinis, with their little units showing."

"I don't get it."

"I'm incredulous, too."

I stretched out beside him on the bed, laughing. "Some of these people seem to be drinking dozens of nice social drinks all day," I said.

"As soon as we're tied up near a beach, we'll have them all thrown overboard. After lunch, before boating. Until then, we'll just be kind and say, 'Hi! How are you doing? Can I get you another crème brûlée?'"

It was beautiful and dreamy up on deck. I lounged on a chair in the shade, in my shorts, studying the people who were lying in direct sun. I heard my father's dermatologist explaining to him, thirty years ago, "A tan skin is a damaged skin," when he was treating him for melanoma. I practiced identifying with a few people nearby, but not the thin, lithe, young, tanned, toned beauties. What was the point? It was like a caribou's comparing herself with a cat, a different species altogether. That's me in twenty pounds, I thought pleasantly, looking at one woman. That's me in twenty years, I thought, watching an old man with Coke-bottle glasses. I closed my eyes and listened to the engines, and to distant voices. I felt as though I were inside a great breathing being, buoyed up by the water in the pool, the pool buoyed up by the ocean, floating on the earth. I remembered learning to swim in the deep end of the rec center pool, when my dad would hold me up until I felt safe enough to rest down into the water and float. In those days, we all spent too much time in the sun—who knew?

I slathered on more sunscreen, pulled my floppy lavender hat down lower, and covered my legs with a towel, even though I was in the shade.

I slept and woke a few times over the next hour. Once when I came to, a bevy of young women was swimming in the pool, so sunlit and Pepsodent and similar that for a groggy moment I thought they were doing synchronized swimming. They stirred my memory of the older girls at the rec center, the thirteen- and fourteen-year-olds, practicing in the deep end while we younger girls paddled nearby, agog, flannel fish sewn to our suits so the lifeguards, would know we could swim. We worshipped the peppy, vigorous older girls in their white tank suits and bathing caps with petals and chin straps, swimming on their backs in perfect circles like a dream, like a wedding cake, suddenly dipping beneath the turquoise water, the pointed stalks of their legs reappearing first, and then the rest of them, as they floated on their backs like skydivers in a daisy chain.

When I was young, I thought that this must be what heaven was like, to be one of those teens. When you're

synchronized, you are all beautiful—Breck girls opening and closing like anemones in time-lapse photography, kaleidoscopically.

I fell asleep again, and when I woke, Buddy was
standing over me, calling my name. Sam was peering at
me with disapproval, as if he'd found me sunbathing in
biohazard gear. Buddy bent down beside me.

"Things are clearly growing uglier down in the boiler
room," Buddy whispered. "We need to be on the lookout for possible security breaches."

"Who's the leader of the uprising?" I asked.

"The revolution is being led by unseen forces. In the
boiler room."

Alex held his finger to his lips. I nodded grimly.

Tom and I were out on deck that afternoon, waiting for Buddy. Everything was more fun when he was
around. Sam and Alex had fallen in with a roving gaggle
of teenagers, had gone off to God knows where.

"Why are you always chewing on ice?" I asked.

"Rage," said Tom.

"I'm worried about what Sam and Alex do after we
go to sleep," I said. "I'm afraid they sneak into the bars.
It's such a mean, scary world. And Sam can be so mean
to me, too."

"He's very different with us from how he is with you.
He's wonderful with us. All kids' behavior makes their
parents a little crazy sometimes. And vice versa. My
ninety-four-year-old mother said something annoying
to me over the phone on Christmas Eve, and I whined
at her, 'I *hate* it when you say that.' So she says it again,
right? I said, 'Please don't say that. It makes me feel
like an eleven-year-old.' And when she said it again,

I slammed down the phone. She's ninety-four! I'm a middle-aged priest—and it's Christmas Eve! I wanted to throttle her over the phone. But I finally figured out that it was my craziness, so I went to see her at the old folks' home, and I brought everyone communion, and it was lovely."

We stood at the railing, our backs to the sea. Even from fifteen feet up, I could see the corrugated skin, the lumps and veins and chicken-skin knees of other passengers. I saw huge guts, bad moles. There were many fat, hairy middle-aged men in teeny bikinis, many matronly middle-aged women with big fallen breasts and poor posture—that which used to be the offering was now the burden. But it's our hearts that weigh us down. Who could even imagine what cargo these people carried? One old woman seemed to be wearing oversize pink-tinted panty hose. They looked like the pink tights we wore for ballet lessons, a room of small girls in black leotards, leaping about the rec center's deeply scratched polished floors. Because I was so thin, my tights were always baggy, but I felt pretty—until I would hear a grown-up ask my mother, "Don't you ever feed her?" and my mother would laugh, as if this was so witty, even though we heard it all the time. But she'd be mad when she told my father later. He always used the word "slender" to describe me. The pink stockings on the cruise ship turned out to be the old woman's own skin. She had grown too thin for her tights, and they were bagging on her.

Saint Bette said that heaven is where people finally stop talking about their weight and what they look like. I feel grateful just to think of Bette Midler's being alive during my years on the planet—just as I do about

Michael Jordan and Nelson Mandela. Gratitude, not understanding, is the secret to joy and equanimity. I prayed for the willingness to have very mild spiritual well-being. I didn't need to understand the hypostatic unity of the trinity; I just needed to turn my life over to whoever came up with redwood trees. And in a sudden moment of clarity, I realized that I also needed to create my own cruise ship again.

I said good-bye to Tom, and stopped at the snack bar for a glass of cranberry juice and soda with lime. I went by the café and asked the aunties what they might like for a snack—bread pudding or fruit salad. They wanted half a sandwich, a lot of bread pudding, and one small whole-wheat bun. I think they would have ordered a bread beverage if they could—beer, with hops and barley, or in the interest of sobriety, a raisin-bread frappé. Bread is as spiritual as human life gets. Rumi wrote, "Be a well-baked loaf." Loaves are made to be eaten, to be buttered, and shared. Rumi is saying to be of service, to be delicious and give life.

The aunties know things.

I went to my room, changed into my swimsuit, slathered on sunscreen, and stopped at the spa for a couple of magazines. I went on deck, where people lay sunbathing. I found a lounge chair in the shade and lay down. At first I used my towel as a blanket, but even in the shade it was hot, and the aunties felt smothered. They love the sun. So I took off the towel, and then my shorts, and ate my bread pudding. I opened a magazine. Every so often, I looked up and smiled at people walking by.

Once again: If Jesus was right, these are all my brothers and sisters.

And they are *so* letting themselves go.

This is not how Jesus would have seen things, but at first I couldn't help it—once again I saw an expanse of walruses, big wet bodies flopped down on towels, letting it all hang out. Some people were sleeping in the sun. I worried about their sunburns and melanomas, as some of them had moles I thought should be looked at when we reached the next port. People were putting cool lotion on their bodies, and on one another. They got up and returned with drinks. They handed one another caps and visors, and covered one another with towels.

I drank my cranberry and soda, and put more lotion on the aunties. They love it out here on deck—the sun, our favorite drink, watching the company onboard. I felt safe with the people around me now. This sense of safety suddenly made it clear to me that, looking at us, God saw not walruses but babies: radiant and befuddled, all these hearts at temporary rest. When you rest, you catch your breath, and it fills your lungs and holds you up, like water wings, like my father in the deep end of the rec center pool.

Anne Lamott's books include the novels Blue Shoe *and* Rosie, *and the nonfiction works,* Bird by Bird, Traveling Mercies: Some Thoughts on Faith, *and* Plan B: Further Thoughts on Faith, *from which this story was excerpted.*

❧ ❧ ❧

Postcard from the Edge

A pilgrim in Tibet celebrates the life that was nearly taken from her by a bus accident.

"One step at a time, one breath at a time," becomes my mantra as I struggle up the snowy 18,700 Dolma La pass, icy wind whistling around my head and searing my lungs. My stomach churns and my head aches from altitude sickness, but my spirits are buoyed by the Tibetan pilgrims who trudge with me on this sacred thirty-two-mile circumambulation of Mount Kailash, the holiest peak in Tibet.

Despite the cold and the blinding snow, we all stop at the crest of the pass to eat lunch and perform rituals. Pungent, rich incense wafts through the thin air. I join the pilgrims in adding to a colorful array of prayer flags that whip so hard in the wind they sound like hooves drumming the ground.

Kneeling, I make an altar that includes photos of my three nieces; the mountain is said to be so powerful that just visualizing loved ones while there will bring them a good fate. Both Buddhists and Hindus believe Kailash is the center of the universe, and circling it is said to cleanse your karma; each circumambulation brings you closer to nirvana. As I move on, I can see pilgrims scattered along the path far ahead and far behind me, some of them not just trekking around the mountain, but creeping along one full prostration at a time.

Even as my lungs labor and my legs protest, I feel a huge wave of gratitude wash over me, a prayer of thanks that I'm alive and that I've recovered the strength to make this journey. Many pilgrims save for years and travel hundreds or even thousands of miles to perform the *kora*, the ritual trek around the mountain. But for me, the *kora* is more than the fulfillment of a fifteen-year dream. Every step is a celebration of the life I nearly lost in a horrendous accident, and a symbol of all the physical and spiritual challenges I've faced in my long, arduous healing.

Four years and twenty surgeries before my Kailash journey, a logging truck screeched around a corner on a remote Laotian jungle road and slammed into the bus I was riding. My left arm was shredded to the bone as it smashed through a window; my back, pelvis, tailbone, and ribs snapped immediately; my spleen was sliced in half; and my heart, stomach, and intestines were ripped out of place and pushed up into my shoulder. With my lungs collapsed and my diaphragm punctured, I could barely breathe. I was bleeding to death inside and out. And it would be more than fourteen hours before I received real medical care.

A practicing Buddhist, I had been headed to a meditation retreat in India, where I had planned to sit for three
silent weeks. Instead, I lay crushed and bleeding at the
side of the road. Struggling to draw in air, I imagined
each breath to be my last. Breathing in, breathing out:
Consciously willing myself not to die, I concentrated on
the life force fighting its way into my lungs.

Along with my breath, pain became my anchor. As
long as I could feel it, I knew I was alive. I thought back
to the hours I had sat in meditation, fixated on the sensation of my leg falling asleep. That discomfort could
hardly compare to the torment from my injuries, but
I discovered that meditating could still help me focus
and remain alert, and I'm convinced it saved my life. I
managed to calm myself, slowing my heart rate and the
bleeding, and I never lost consciousness or went into
deep shock. In fact, I've never felt so aware, so clear-
headed and completely in the present moment.

Unharmed passengers loaded a few of us with the
worst injuries into the back of a passing pickup truck,
which jolted along for almost an hour to a "clinic"—a
dirt-floored room lined with cobwebs, cows grazing outside the doors.

There seemed to be no medical care in the area, no
phones, and almost no one who spoke English. Finally,
a boy who looked to be barely into his teens appeared,
sloshed alcohol onto my open wounds, and, without
painkillers, stitched up my arm. The agony was almost
more than I could endure.

Six hours passed. No more help arrived. Opening
my eyes, I was surprised to see that darkness had fallen.
That's when I became convinced I was going to die.

As I closed my eyes and surrendered an amazing

thing happened: I let go of all fear. I was released from my body and its profound pain. I felt my heart open, free of attachment and longing. A perfect calm enveloped me, a bone-deep peace I could never have imagined. There was no need to be afraid. I knew that everything in the universe was exactly as it was meant to be.

In that moment, I felt my spiritual beliefs transform into undeniable experiences. Buddhism had taught me the concept of "inter-being," the idea that the universe is seamless mesh in which every action ripples across the whole fabric of space and time. As I lay there, I felt how interwoven every human spirit is with every other. I realized then that death only ends life, not this interconnectedness. And that is when my beliefs became truths. A warm light of unconditional love encompassed me, and I didn't feel alone.

Just as I was experiencing this surrender to death, Alan, a British Aid worker, drove up. He and his wife gently placed me in the back of their pick-up truck. Unable to lie flat, I rested my head on the hard metal hump of the wheel well. For the next seven hours, my broken bones jarred against the metal ribbing of the truck bed as we slowly maneuvered over heavily pot-holed roads and into Thailand. "Bless your heart," Alan told me later, "you didn't say a word the whole time."

Instead, I focused on the beauty of a sky full of stars, certain it would be the last thing I would see in this life-time. The feeling that I wasn't alone, that I was being watched over, stayed with me and brought me great comfort.

At 2 A.M, we finally pulled into the Aek Udon hospital in Thailand, where Dr. Bunsom Santithamanoth was the only doctor on call. He was incredulous I'd made it. "Another two hours and I'm sure you wouldn't be here," he said, looking at my X-rays as he prepped me for emergency surgery.

I flat-lined on the operating table, but Dr. Bunsom managed to revive me. For two days I remained on the brink of death in intensive care. Once my condition stabilized, the doctor continued to perform surgery after surgery, slowly patching my body back together. My days passed in a constant fog of unbearable pain that the intense medication hardly seemed to penetrate.

After three weeks, Dr. Bunsom felt it was safe to medevac me back to San Francisco. When he asked if there was anything I wished to do before I left, I realized I wanted to revisit the peace that had always enveloped me at Buddhist temples, and said I would love to visit one. I was touched when he arranged for an ambulance and paramedic to take me to a nearby monastery.

It was my first time outside the safe cocoon of my hospital room, and everything felt surreal. It seemed as though I was looking at everything through a thick pane of glass; I felt much less rooted in the world than everyone around me. Supported by the monks, I made my way to the altar, and joined the Thai families making offerings before the giant gold-leaf Buddha. Being here, free from tubes and machines, I could appreciate just being alive. As I meditated, a young monk approached and invited me to have tea with the abbot. After all my trauma, it was a comfort simply to sit with them, absorbing their quiet kindness.

In the first days after the accident, I received hundreds of well-wishing e-mails and prayers. During my years of travel in Asia, working as a documentary photographer (including books on Tibet and the Dalai Lama), I'd developed an extensive network of friends. As soon as they heard the news, my friends contacted monks and lamas who began performing around-the-clock religious pujas (religious ceremonies) for me. Even the Dalai Lama had been notified. (Not a bad guy to have on your side when you get hit by a bus.) Those first few weeks made me a believer in the power of prayer and positive thoughts.

But this first outpouring of support was just the beginning. In a way, my return to San Francisco was like coming to my own funeral and realizing that I was loved more than I had ever known. That discovery turned out to be the greatest gift of all, but it took me some time to adjust to how much I'd had to rely on that gift. I have always been a fiercely independent person, and it was immensely humbling when I arrived in San Francisco and realized that for a long time I'd have to depend almost completely on my friends. And not just for shopping, cooking, cleaning, and rides to medical appointments: I couldn't walk or even feed myself.

Despite all the support, my transition back to America was abrupt. The first thing the doctors wanted to do was cut off the Buddhist protection string that the Karmapa Lama had given me in Tibet. I had worn around it around my neck for all my surgeries, and I was adamant about keeping it on. It had gotten me this far, I reasoned. The doctors in San Francisco, who called me the miracle kid, didn't have a better theory. They admitted they weren't sure they could have saved me even if the accident had happened right outside their hospital.

Even with the full arsenal of American health care available to me, my recovery seemed glacially slow. I've always been athletic, and all my running, trekking, kayaking, and yoga practice had kept me fit and strong. I'm sure that storehouse of health helped me survive the initial trauma of the bus accident and its aftermath. But it could only take me so far.

I spent my first four months back in the States bed-ridden and in such a morphine-induced haze I began to fear I'd suffered brain damage. Still barely able to hobble, I grew angry at the lack of encouragement and support from my doctors. The final straw came the day my back specialist told me I'd probably never walk properly again. He suggested I reconsider what I was going to do with my life now that my former career and activities were beyond me.

I came home and feverishly started scrubbing the dried blood off my camera bag. And for the first time since the accident, I began to cry. With tears of frustration running down my face, I decided I hadn't come this far just to give up. Maybe my doctors were right, and I'd have to forge a new life that wouldn't include scuba diving, rock climbing, or adventuring around the world to document both beauty and injustice with my cameras. But before I accepted that, I had to know I'd done everything I could to reclaim the life I loved.

First, I needed my mind back: strength of mind for strength of body. I ceremoniously dumped my arsenal of painkillers—Percocet, Vicodin, Morphine—down the toilet and turned to alternative healing. I started weekly treatments of traditional Chinese medicine, including acupuncture and the ancient art of applying heated cups to the body, and bodywork, including massage, chiropractic, reflexology, and more. As in those first moments in Laos, I used meditation to help manage my pain—focusing on it, breathing into it, observing it. I read medical books to comprehend the repercussions of my surgeries, and bombarded my doctors with questions at every visit.

I knew my mental attitude mattered most of all. I changed doctors and physical therapists, finding ones who believed I could recover. "Tell me what I can do, not what I can't do," I begged my new physical therapist, Susan Hobbel. She pushed me to the point of tears in each session, and soon had me back at my gym, working with a trainer. Slowly, first with crutches and later with a cane, I forced myself to walk to and from the hospital for my therapy sessions, two torturous miles each way. Focusing on small goals like this gave me the power to go on, avoiding the chasm of fear always ready to suck me into its dark abyss.

I would be lying if I said I didn't have my bouts of self-doubt—was this a good pain or a bad pain? Was it O.K. to push myself this hard or was it making things worse, causing permanent injury? Should I just accept that this is the damaged person that I am now? But with it came the realization that fear is just a thought, and with that came a more powerful belief within myself. I could get through this.

As my physical healing progressed, I continued to experience surprisingly intense emotions. On one hand I felt euphoric, reborn, able to appreciate people and experiences more deeply. The world seemed vibrant and electrified, and my heart felt more open. My life was one giant postscript. The taste of death was a touchstone, reminding me of what seemed truly important—family, friends, a desire to give something back to the world through my work. I felt a new empathy—with the subjects I photographed, with all those who suffer—that still informs my ongoing projects: a book called *Faces of Hope* about children in developing countries; another book on poverty in the United States; my photographs documenting the tsunami devastation in Asia.

On the other hand, it was difficult to resume the ordinariness of everyday life after surrendering to death. Perhaps I'd never fully appreciated life until it was nearly taken away from me; at any rate, I was determined to stay in touch with my hard won sense of its sacredness. Yet I also discovered that sometimes I had to let it go a bit just to function again and get through the day. Even as life drew me back into its busy world, though, my meditation practice helped me to return to that sacred place; the window pane between it and the mundane didn't look so thick anymore.

Of course, I also had dark moments, grappling with the pain and frustration of my slow recovery; after all, it was more than two years before I could walk properly again. I struggled with bouts of self-doubt. Was I making things worse by pushing myself so hard? Was it time to accept that the damage to my body was irreversible, and start a new and different life? But when those thoughts arose, I would remember what I'd learned about fear on that dirt floor in Laos, as well as everything I'd already been through. My doubts would recede before a more powerful belief: Whatever the future brought, I could get through it.

My biggest adjustment was letting go of who I was before the accident and learning to measure my progress in much smaller increments. An athletic, hard-driven person, restless to return to my active life, I struggled to accept this new timeline. My yoga practice helped me enormously, not only in reclaiming my flexibility but also in reconnecting with my body exactly as it is each day and in sitting with my limitations. At times, I'd become so stymied that I'd dissolve into tears. But as I progressed, I came to think my tears were not just from frustration; they seemed to release the pain and fear buried in parts of me traumatized by the accident. Yoga continues to give me a new awareness and respect for my body, which has seen me through such adversity. Instead of getting angry at its limitations, I now marvel at and encourage its healing capacity.

I'm learning, as my yoga teacher has often told me, that tension doesn't always come from the body; it can come from the heart and mind as well. As I continue to recover, I find myself curious about just how open these parts of me can become. That curiosity motivated me to finally realize my dream of traveling to Mount Kailash.

As I circled the base of that powerful snow-covered pyramid, I felt a force growing within me, a strength I never would have found without the challenges of the previous four years. Each day as I trekked around the mountain, visualizing all the people I cared about, I could feel my heart expanding, embracing all the beings knit together with me in the web of life. Over and over, I remembered my revelation at the moment that I thought I was dying: Nothing is more important than this inter-connectedness. The commitment the Tibetans around me brought to their devotions suddenly had a new resonance. I found myself grinning at the next group that straggled past me. We were all in this together, all companions in the pilgrimage of life.

Alison Wright is the photographer and author of The Spirit of Tibet, Portrait of a Culture in Exile, A Simple Monk, *and* Faces of Hope. *She is currently photographing poverty in the United States for the book* Third World America. *Her web site is www.alisonwright.com.*

🕉 🕉 🕉

The Art of a Wasted Day

How to enjoy the slow life.

*J*n May 1975, lilac time, during one of the chilliest of the Cold War's many frosty seasons, I first traveled from Minnesota—alone, with backpack, without a credit card, without "contacts"—to Prague. I landed on the far side of the moon—and instantly knew I was home.

It really *was* home. Sort of. My grandparents had emigrated from Bohemia at the end of the nineteenth century, and I was born in a Czech immigrant enclave in St. Paul. But the instinctive recognition I felt on that first two-week visit wasn't the embrace of ethnic identity, and I never did locate any relatives. It was the gloomy gold of Mitteleuropa that grabbed me.

I sat in coffeehouses blue with smoke and watched the world before me become a black-and-white photograph. Communism, it appeared, was a form of stasis. There was a bleak poetry to its worn visage, especially to a child of the heated-up consumer culture I'd traveled from. I fell in love with dreaminess, with laziness, in this most unlikely place—"behind the Iron Curtain," as we said with shivers for decades.

Yet I never expected to return to Prague. It was impossible for an ordinary American to live there, and difficult, potentially dangerous for the few Czech friends I made in the city to maintain contact with me.

The Cold War creaked along in its dreary—and as we all thought, eternal—way. Then, late in 1989, came its astonishing collapse, and Prague became a hip destination, another place on the map you could rack up frequent flier miles getting to. I went right back—and have gone back every summer since, still crazy after all these years, as the old song says.

Yet what captivates me in "the new world order" of brightly painted Mozartian pastels on buildings that once were begrimed with anthracite dust and neglect is what claimed me from the start: a luscious ease—call it laziness, but say it with respect. This is the sloth the Czechs concocted as a secret weapon against political oppression and still employ against the more beguiling tyranny of the free market.

I remain magnetized by the modesty and relish the little pleasures that my friends, good people—decent in the Cold War, decent now in the sometimes even tougher market economy—have managed to sustain against all the odds. They refused to sell their souls (which is to say their time) to the false angels of socialism or, more recently, to the devils of raw capitalism. Thanks to them—especially my friend Anna (and her terrier, Dyn)—I've been studying the sweet discipline of wasting time every summer.

It started, really, in the early post-Cold War summers when, every weekend, we piled into Anna's old two-cylinder Polish Tuzka with Dyn, and hit the road. It was like touring in a Mixmaster, putt-putting along in the beat-up yellow Mr. Magoo car, narrowly missing disaster as new BMWs and Mercedes flashed by, driven with mad aggression by gleeful Praguers with freshly-minted drivers' licenses.

We had many close calls. The free-market bullies nearly forced Anna's little car into the ditch. They shook their fists at us as they hurtled past. Clearly, to them, *we* were the hazard, tooling around in our ridiculous socialist excuse of a car. We were the dead-end past; we didn't deserve to live.

Finally, ten years after the Velvet Revolution, Anna gave in and got herself a second-hand VW-made four-cylinder Škoda. "I couldn't take it anymore," she said, looking glumly at her improved vehicle with a hint of defeat.

The Škoda took us further afield on the weekends than the Tuzka did. Anna wanted me to see everything. We stayed one July weekend at a fairy-tale hunting lodge just opened to the public. Like many such choice spas and retreats, it had been reserved in the former regime for Party members. We ordered wild boar and drank thimbles of Becherovka which is like sipping essence of forest. Dyn moaned tenderly over his delicate dish of boiled bones under the table (the Czechs, like the French, maintain a civilized hauteur about American rules against dogs in restaurants).

We were sitting next to a beautiful old hunter-green art nouveau-tiled oven. I noticed a small figure, a bronze statuette, stuck in the back of the stove, consigned, it seemed, to a dark corner of hell. It looked like Lenin.

"Yes," the waiter said, nodding in the direction of the figurine, as if at a common weed, "it's Lenin. We found him in a cabinet when we opened the lodge. We decided this is the place for him—in the fire." He didn't laugh, didn't work the joke. It was a deadpan Czech moment, the sort of remark I'd come to relish during the Cold War when a Czech poet I met would murmur with ironic relish, "Kafka, Kafka" every time we encountered yet another bureaucratic absurdity.

"Perfect," Anna said of the waiter's remark as she mopped up the last of her *knedliky* with blackberry sauce, looking contentedly at Lenin in his hotbox and at her laconic countryman who had placed him there. Capitalism hasn't been easy for her or her friends, but she has no desire to go back.

The next year we made a tour of the Moravian wine cellars ("an older wine culture than France," Anna said, allowing herself a little civic pride). One year we went in search of the blighted territory in north Bohemia so Anna could show me how far behind the Czechs are in environmental policy. She wants me to see everything, she says, good, bad, in between.

But our destinations out of Prague are usually not to edifying places but to visit her Prague friends who scatter north, south, east, and west to their summer cottages. In winter they gather in each others' flats in Malá Strana and Old Town, small apartments still shabby from the Socialist years though now shockingly valuable real estate in the tourist center.

But in the summer to be a Praguer is to be a country person, at least on the weekends. We dip off main roads, following turns and pathways barely wide enough for a line of cows, till we come to one of her friends' sum-

mer cottages, the beloved *chata* every Czech lives for or
wishes for, the little country residences Anna presents to
me as a series of wrapped packages, weekend after summer weekend. She believes these cottages were part of
the unlikely glue that held the country together during
the Cold War when fixing up a *chata* was the only bit of
private ownership the regime allowed.

Most summer Sundays we spend with her friends,
sitting in the musty coolness of old cottages or former
farmhouses, drinking red wine at wobbly tables covered
with patched embroidered linen. We gather black lilac
for tisanes from garden hedges that scribble themselves
along flowery meadows where beehives are stacked like
filing cabinets.

We move beyond the margin of the meadows and
hike into the charcoal-dark woods, bestirring ourselves
to hunt for mushrooms, cackling over our plush finds,
returning to our gingerbread cottage for dinner and a
long night of talk as dusk gathers itself in violet folds.

One thing about the threadbare Socialist regime,
grafted onto the old Czech bourgeois heritage: it supported a culture of time-wasting which is, after all, the
essence of friendship, or how friendship is sustained.
This life, still licking at the margins of the new world
order, feels old-fashioned, deeply relaxing, as little in
contemporary life does.

It's possible that the country was sustained over the
long haul of Communism by its relish for homemade
consolations tended by a population denied the big satisfactions of foreign travel, of home ownership, and all the
lovely greeds that grease the gears of a consumer society.
Theirs was—and to a great extent still is for the aging
middle generation formed by post-war Socialism—a life

of little pleasures, coffee and berry coffeecakes baked in smoking woodstoves, served on chipped blue-and-white china, young red wine we drink from unmatched jam jars. Anna's generation—already middle-aged at the time of the Velvet Revolution—was too old to make a fresh start in the new system, and too young to retire on the tiny pensions of the socialist yesteryear. They persist at the margins, sustaining a modest way of life, holding fast to their passion for art and music, for the theater and opera—not that they can afford tickets much anymore. "Everything's for the tourists now," Anna says. Just after the Velvet Revolution, I remember, she used to call them "our visitors." But now she sees they're never going home, these tourists who have taken over her once sleepy city.

The people you wasted time with during the Cold War were, by definition, people of your sort, not because of economic status or even profession. They had the same moral code, the same view of life, so akin it didn't need to be argued. They belonged to the intelligentsia, a class category impossible to translate into American terms. It doesn't mean "intellectuals" (though they share the passionate book reading and music-making associated with the educated anywhere). The intelligentsia was comprised of those who ran the civic and cultural and, of course, political show in the old bourgeois republic, during and after the Hapsburg Empire, before Hitler, before Socialism. Vaclav Havel, son of a famous architect, belonged to this class—and was denied a university education as a direct repudiation of this lineage.

The intelligentsia was, humanly speaking, the Czech heartland, the educated and the exiled within their own homeland. It was as if during the Cold War, especially after 1968 when the Warsaw Pact troops rumbled into Prague, the intelligentsia really did let themselves eat cake—and it helped.

Anna thinks that the notorious Czech male pattern of marital infidelity (read your Kundera, read your Klíma) was the dark side of this Cold War life of small satisfactions: ambition, outside the Party (and even within it), was impossible. At least a man could display his prowess as a lover.

It's a theory of repressed ambition emerging as libido instead of, in the standard critique of the driven American overachiever, stifled libido coming out as workaholism. But, I would insist, isn't this attitude toward eros more generally in Europe? What about the French, how they snigger at Americans for trying to impeach a president because he was a cheating husband?

Anna shakes her head. Infidelity was different here, she maintains, just as alcoholism was different: it wasn't wholly personal but partook of the lethargy of a numbed, hermetically sealed, and controlled culture.

I have become addicted (such an American word for pleasure) to these lazy weekends in cottages all over the country and to the long evenings in the old Prague flats of Anna and her friends—an art conservationist whose father was an important theater director, a French teacher, a potter, a weaver whose father was a diplomat. The intelligentsia.

The kitchen suppers at Anna's Kozí Ulice (Goat Street) flat near the medieval St. Agnes Kloster in Old Town, her "salons" where music students play on her mother's old Bechstein, and especially on long summer nights the picnics in the weaver Vlasta's bower-of-bliss garden tucked below the Hrad—any near the British

Embassy—they're all part of the conspiracy of deliciously frittered away time that feed the soul.

A genius of ease presides, and we talk late, late into the night, the afternoon tea in the onion-pattern Meissen cups giving way to glasses of homemade wine, and finally, in the dark of the evening as the crickets come out, small lead-crystal shot glasses of slivovitz, the distillation of plums bringing the bright day to a finish in a burning transparency.

I come back to St. Paul every fall exulting about these long-into-the-night days, the sheer joy of companionship from these parties that refuse to end, that aren't exactly "parties." Anna and her friends—now my friends—aren't part of the economic gold rush that has swept through the old Hapsburg realms, "the Kondike" as the Czechs call the raw free marketeering of their country.

They live as they lived before, getting by, entertaining each other. They can't afford to go to the old *vinárnas* in their own neighborhoods anymore—only tourists can afford that place, Anna will say with contempt, as if she never wanted to go there anyway, though it was once her pub where she could get a glass of Velkopopovický Kozel for a dime.

Last year when I got back to Minnesota I was trying to explain to Jarda, my Czech (now American) friend whose Malá Strana apartment I sublet every summer, how much I love this quality of Czech life.

I notice his frown deepens as I carry on—the crumbly berry cakes, the sharp stab of slivovitz as the stars start up in the navy sky, my list of heartfelt pleasures I've freighted with great intercultural significance.

"Then can you tell me," Jarda says severely, obviously warming to a pet subject, "why you—all these Americans—go to Czecho now, and you come back saying how you love this Czech life, you love Czech drinking and talking all night long. Then people invite you over for dinner here and—you look at your watch, it's eleven o'clock! Oh-oh, everybody better go home! Can you explain this?"

I cannot. I can't even explain why it's never occurred to me that it is, after all, possible to do this delicious time-wasting in America—isn't it?

It wasn't an Iron Curtain, but a more filmy cultural scrim that made it all seem impossible. It still does, long after that political fabric has rusted away.

Jarda was waiting for an answer. But I could only shrug, bow my head, momentarily baffled, and plot once again to return next summer for more of that elixir I seem to require, whether it's plum brandy or black lilac tea, I can't say for sure.

Patricia Hampl is the author of two books of poetry and four works of literary nonfiction, including A Romantic Education, *a memoir of her Czech-American girlhood and her travels to Prague before and after the Velvet Revolution. Her most recent book is* I Could Tell You Stories, *essays on memory and imagination.*

இ இ இ

Traveling Heavy

For some, packing is part of the journey.

I travel heavy. This is probably something of a surprise, since you might well assume that someone who travels as much as I do would be the sort to throw a t-shirt and a toothbrush into a paper bag and go. Unfortunately, this is not the case. I deliberate endlessly before I travel; I pack and repack; I am shamed by how much I've packed, and then, as penance, I force myself to remove a few items; then I capitulate, put everything back in, add one or two more things just to be safe, and at last, burdened and beaten, limp to the airport or the train station or the parking garage with my gross overload. Why do I do it? I've decided that it is a sort of passage I have to make before making my true passage—it's my ritual of clinging to the familiar before entering the unfamiliar, my resistance to leaving the comforts of home for the displacement of travel, of being a stranger embarking on exploration.

This might make me sound like a reluctant traveler, but I'm not at all; I'm only a reluctant packer. I'm a passionate voyager, and as soon as I can force the locks shut on my overstuffed suitcase, I'm eager to head out the door. I love the jolt you get from travel. I love the freshness and surprise of being in a new place, the way it makes even the most ordinary things seem extraordinary and strange. It makes me feel extra-alive. The things that are routine in a familiar place are thrilling somewhere new; things I don't notice at home jump out at me when I'm traveling. As soon as I get out of town, I love stopping for gas so I can poke around the gas station minimarket; besides the usual, ubiquitous junk food and cigarettes, there are always odds and ends that reveal the character of the place. Those serendipitous discoveries are my addiction. I found a real raccoon-skin Davy Crockett hat for sale in a gas station in Tennessee; a hand-printed pamphlet—the biography of a famous local giant—among the mass-market magazines in a convenience store in Florida; homemade barbecue beside the Doritos and Slim Jims in a minimart in Missouri. These are little tokens of what make all journeys seem so promising, so loaded with possibility—full of the yet unseen, the impossible to imagine, the still unknown.

I'm a sucker for going places that sound wonderful, of course, but I'm even enthusiastic about places that don't. This quality sometimes vexes the people around me. Years ago, I had some reporting to do in Houston. I was, as usual, excited about the trip. I mentioned it to a friend of mine who had lived in Texas for a few years, and he warned me that Houston was a drag. I said that

I couldn't imagine how it could be, since it was a major city in an interesting state full of interesting industries like oil and gas, and in my opinion that guaranteed that it would be a great place to explore. My friend was disgusted. "Believe it or not," he said, "there *are* places in the world that even you wouldn't find interesting." I will confess that he was almost right: Of all the places I've been, Houston was one of the hardest to love, but its blankness and shapelessness fascinated me and made a great backdrop to the story I had gone there to see.

To be honest, I view all stories as journeys. Journeys are the essential text of the human experience—the journey from birth to death, from innocence to wisdom, from ignorance to knowledge, from where we start to where we end. There is almost no piece of important writing—the Bible, the *Odyssey*, Chaucer, *Ulysses*—that isn't explicitly or implicitly the story of a journey. Even when I don't actually *go* anywhere for a particular story, the way I report is to immerse myself in something I usually know very little about, and what I experience is the journey toward a grasp of what I've seen. I picture my readers having the same expedition, in an armchair, as they begin reading one of my pieces and work their way through it, ending up with the distinct feeling of having been somewhere else, whether it's a somewhere physically exotic or just the "somewhere else" of being inside someone else's life.

The farthest I've ever gone for a story was Bhutan, which is on the other side of the world. In fact, since it is literally on the other side of the world, I used one of my trips there to satisfy a lifelong desire: Instead of doing a round trip there and back, I flew around the entire world, stopping in Bhutan in between. The closet "travel" story I've ever done is the piece called "Homewrecker," in which the roles of visitor and visitee were reversed—it is a story about how someone (almost) made a journey into my own home, which was a peculiar experience for someone like me, whose professional life involves going into other people's houses. The most difficult trip I've ever taken for a story was probably one that was just a few blocks from home, to Martin Luther King Jr. High School in Manhattan. Even though the person I wrote about—the president of the student body—was a buoyant and witty young woman, the school struck me as a harsh, hard place, ground down and depleted, and what made it difficult was reconciling this with the fact that is was just a few blocks from my very comfortable apartment. The easiest trip I've taken for a story, hands down, was the one I took to visit three lavish spas in Thailand. I prefer going on my reporting trips alone, and since I often go to unglamorous places like Midland, Texas, and Jackson, New Jersey, I rarely have to fend off friends and family who want to keep me company. In the case of the spa trip to Thailand, though, I had a waiting list of volunteers who told me they were very, very concerned about my taking such a long, difficult trip all alone.

A few years ago I was asked to speak on a panel about travel writing. A week or two before the panel, the catastrophic attacks on the World Trade Center took place. During the weeks and months that followed the attacks, nothing seemed to matter—or at least nothing except those things that could be shown to matter even through the heavy shroud of that event. The panel on travel writing went on as scheduled, and one of the first questions we were asked was what we thought would happen to travel writing in the new world that 9/11 seemed to have brought forth. I thought it was a legitimate question. Should anyone write about—or read about—what it's like to snowshoe through Alaska or raft in Costa Rica when the world seemed to be falling apart? Would anyone in his or her right mind have any interest in leaving home when the universe seemed so threatening? What I said then, and still believe, is that human beings are stubbornly and persistently curious and that I can't imagine we will ever lose our desire to know about what lies beyond our immediate horizon. At a time when the world feels chaotic and frightening, writers who go out to see it and describe it seem more important, not less. Even fluffy, expository stories about pretty places matter if people are less inclined to travel, since then the writer acts as the reader's proxy, bringing back the world that most people might be reluctant to go out and see for themselves. At the most elemental level, the world's troubles are the result of people turning inward and turning away from whatever and whoever is different and unfamiliar. If a writer can make even one reader feel more open to someone or some-place new, I think he or she has accomplished something well worth doing.

What do you get for all this travel? Lots of frequent-flier miles, of course. I've ended up with a passport that is stamped, ink-stained, dog-eared, creased, and in need of supplemental pages to accommodate the piling on of seals and visas. Also, I am seized repeatedly by epiphanies (or what I mistake for epiphanies) about how to travel well: how to conquer jet lag (stay up until the proper time to sleep, no matter how bad you feel); how to master suitcase selection (I'm now very big on wheelie bags and down on soft luggage); how to pack (never go anywhere without a sweatshirt, a string of pearls, and a big, elegant scarf, which can be used as a dress, a shawl, a skirt, a shrug, a blanket, or a tent, and try, try, *try* not to overpack); and how to find my bearings in a new place (hang out in a coffee shop, strike up a conversation with anyone willing to talk, read the local papers, spend a day walking around downtown, stop in at garage sales and open houses and flea markets and fairs). Travel quietly.

Probably the most valuable lesson I've learned after these years of travel is how to bear being lonely. There is nothing that has quite the dull thud of being by yourself in a place you don't know, surrounded by people you don't recognize and to whom you mean nothing. But that's what being a writer requires. Writing is a wonderful life—a marvelous life, in fact—but it is also the life of a vapor, of floating in unseen, filling a space, and then vanishing. There are times when I'm traveling, when I'm far from home, that I am so forlorn that I can't remember why I chose this particular profession. I yearn to be home so fiercely that I feel as though my heart will pop out of my chest. And then I step out and see the world spread out around me. I know where I'm heading: I am heading home. But on the way there, I see so many corners to round and doors to open, so many encounters to chance upon, so many tiny moments to stumble into that tell huge stories, that I remember exactly why I took this particular path. The journey begins again; the story starts over; I gather myself and go out to see what I can see and tell it as best I can, and the beckoning of home is always, forever, there, just over the next horizon.

ॐ ॐ ॐ

Susan Orlean is a staff writer for The New Yorker *and author of such books as* The Orchid Thief *(which inspired the movie* Adaptation*),* The Bullfighter Checks Her Makeup: My Encounters with Extraordinary People, *and* My Kind of Place: Travel Stories from a Woman Who's Been Everywhere, *from which this essay was excerpted.*

AMY WILSON

ß, *ß*, *ß*,

What They Taught Me

What the eye sees, the heart never forgets.
—Malawian proverb

After three months of Peace Corps training, I am sent to live and work at Mchoka, a village in Malawi, Africa, where I will serve as an AIDS extension worker. When I first arrive I wander around the parched, red-dirt landscape searching for people who might listen to the AIDS speech I've been taught to deliver.

In front of the village chief's mud hut sit a circle of women rubbing dried corn cobs together, the speckled kernels falling into open baskets: tap, tap, tap. When they see me they start to laugh and talk in quiet voices.

"Oh, Onani apo, azungu nenepa kwambiri." Oh, look at *that very fat white woman.*

At five-foot-eight and 140 pounds, I am not a small woman, but no one has ever called me "very fat."

In our training they told us, "Your task is to forge connections and alliances with the villagers." Without these connections, I can do nothing. So I walk to the edge of the circle and say, in Chichewa, *"Moni nonse, ine ndi Ami."* Hello, everyone. My name is Amy.

More polite laughter.

"I want to chat with you about AIDS."

The laughter stops. Heads look down. Hands become busy.

"Would you like to chat?"

One woman directs her gaze to the right of my head: in this small East African country, it is impolite to look someone straight in the eye. The woman sitting next to her jabs her in the side. She puts her head down and does not raise it again.

Since I don't know what else to do, I launch into my prepared monologue. With each phrase I recite, I feel more uncomfortable. The women listen obediently, adults transformed into children. We are not "connecting."

I later learn that most of the villagers already know what white people have to say about AIDS. Although they listen respectfully, in practice they disregard it.

I spend many nights alone at my house, a cement box with a corrugated tin roof. I think a lot about sex. Why? Because I am here to teach the villagers about a disease that is spread through intercourse. Because I live alone in an isolated village. Because I am twenty-three years old.

Peeling blue and white paint marks the Mchoka Health Center. From nine to five every day, Nurse Saidi sits in a rolling chair with a broken wheel and attends to her patients. In the labor-and-delivery room, the same steel buckets that catch the white embryonic fluid and blood of childbirth are also used to mop the floors. The medical supply room contains only aspirin and a dusty box of expired condoms. There is no bathroom, no electricity, no running water.

I have followed Abambo Banda, the man who sells bananas at the Tuesday market, to the health center. He carries his grown daughter on his back. She is so thin that her thighs are like sticks. People sit, stand, and sprawl all over the gray hallways and floors. Many display the characteristic signs of AIDS: cataracts in the eyes and ulcerated skin. A man with cholera lies in a puddle of clear, rice-water diarrhea. I watch the liquid pour out of the top and bottom of his pants. It smells sour, like vinegar.

A woman lying on the floor grabs my leg. Her cloudy, unfocused eyes are a symptom of malaria. "Give me... give me," she says, squeezing my leg with her hot hand. I reach down to remove it.

Abambo Banda circumvents the line and tries to walk straight into Nurse Saidi's office. The waiting patients protest, and Nurse Saidi steps out to investigate the noise, her mouth tight, as if she's just bit into a lemon.

Nurse Saidi is the only practitioner for 16,000 villagers. She arrived at Mchoka Health Center a few weeks ago. Before then, the center was closed, because there was no one to staff it. Nurse Saidi has fled her abusive husband and left behind five young children: In Malawi, under all circumstances, the children belong to the father.

I asked her once if she misses her children. "Of course," she told me. "But I'd rather they live without me than watch me get beaten."

Now she yells, "Stop it, everyone! Stop it! I do not like all of this noise."

Abambo Banda approaches her with his daughter, who looks as if she has fallen asleep or passed out. Her eyes are closed, and a stream of pasty, white saliva rolls down her chin. Nurse Saidi looks at the girl, feels for the pulse on her neck, and announces, "She's dead."

Abambo Banda begins to wail: a deep, throaty howl that makes me think of curdled milk.

Nurse Saidi tells him to go outside. Then she attends to the next person in line.

I stand facing a queue of Malawian women with babies strapped to their sides and backs. Behind me are white plastic bags—labeled "World Food Bank" in blue—full of soy-corn flour. Together with two Malawian health-care workers, Mercy Kuzimva and Mrs. Kazembe, I am distributing the flour to the mothers. Mrs. Kazembe, who is older than Mercy and I, gives the orders. The three of us are wearing brightly colored sarongs to cover our knees. (In Malawi, knees are sexually suggestive; breasts are not.) Many of the women are shirtless and shoeless. Their bare breasts hang like pancakes, and the exposed heels of their feet are cracked and crusty, like stale brown bread. The parched earth beneath us cannot produce enough food to feed everyone who lives on it. The sparse vegetation—hollow baobab trees, arthritic bushes, too thin stalks of new corn—sticks out of the ground with exhausted persistence.

The midday sun burns the sweat off the women's bodies; salty white trails line their faces and necks. I know many of them by name. In the mornings and evenings, I fetch water from the well where they congregate to scrub their pots and bowls with their bare hands. I buy goods from them at the Tuesday market—matchbooks and bars of hot pink glycerin soap.

To more efficiently give away the food, Mercy, Mrs. Kazembe, and I split up the tasks: Mercy determines which babies are malnourished enough to qualify for food aid. After each mother unwraps her child, Mercy lifts the infant's arm, leg, or eyelid to search for signs of malnourishment. If a baby qualifies, the mother is sent over to Mrs. Kazembe, a sinewy woman with a square patch of greasy hair that glints in the sun like damp steel wool. Mrs. Kazembe shovels two scoops of flour—roughly the amount in a box of cereal—into the mother's open bag. I prepare the big bags of soy-corn flour: dragging each one from the storage shed, shaking down the contents, and opening it by pulling on the string along the top. I've just finished opening the last six bags. The line of waiting mothers stretches away from us for almost a quarter mile.

The mother at the head of the line, an obese woman named Amayi Banda, steps forward and shows Mercy her child. Amayi Banda sells fried potatoes, called "chippies," at the Tuesday market; her own frequent consumption of chippies has given her an unusually large body. Mercy searches her baby boy for signs of malnourishment: Is he suffering from a deficiency of protein in his diet? Is he starving?

Mercy holds up one of his fat, dimpled arms and announces, in Chichewa: "This baby looks fine. You don't need food."

Amayi Banda shakes her empty bag and demands, "*Ndipatseni. Ndipatseni.*" *Give it to me. Give it to me.*

"No," Mercy says.

The waiting women start to cluck their tongues in disapproval. I can't tell who they're unhappy with: Mercy for refusing to provide food, or Amayi Banda for demanding it. The two women stare at each other for a moment, and then Amayi Banda yanks her empty bag to her belly, pulls her baby boy to her bosom, and walks away with steps so heavy they raise clouds of red dust around her feet.

While Mercy waits for the next mother to step forward, she pulls on her long, braided hair and picks at the chipped red polish on her fingernails. I wonder if Mercy is intentionally flaunting her good fortune—a diet nutritious enough to produce shoulder-length hair and long fingernails. Most of the women in line have short, brittle hair and paper-thin nails.

The next mother unties the cloth holding her baby to her back and presents him to Mercy. The baby's body is distended, and his enormous head—two or three times the normal size for a child his age—floats, as if filled with helium, at the top of his neck. His tiny features are almost lost in the middle of his puffy face: a nose, a mouth, two eyes sealed shut by yellowish pus. This child has kwashiorkor: his internal organs are swollen, and his body is full of toxic fluid. I reach a hand out toward him. The skin on his swollen arm crumbles beneath my touch. When I pull my hand away, his skin sticks to my fingers and falls to the ground in dry flakes. Mercy indicates to the mother that she will receive food.

As Mrs. Kazembe scoops the flour into the mother's green-and-orange cloth sack, she yells at the mother in Chichewa: "He's going to die! You have not fed your child. I will give you this food, but you probably won't even give it to your child. You'll feed your husband, yourself, and your older children. Won't you? Won't you?"

The mother simply keeps her head bowed low and repeats, over and over, *"Zikomo, zikomo."* Thank you, thank you.

Mrs. Kazembe is right. If the child is near death from malnutrition, then the rest of the family must also be hungry. According to Malawian custom, the husband eats first, then the wife, and then the children, in order of age. Often no food is left for the youngest.

Mrs. Kazembe finishes pouring the second scoop of flour, and the mother, still hunched over, walks away.

Earlier in the day, I asked Mrs. Kazembe why she shouted at the women.

"It's my job as a health worker to educate them," she told me.

I also asked Mercy why so many children starved in Malawi.

Mercy said, "God misses them so much that he wants them back."

Now Mrs. Kazembe turns to me and says, "Amy, come here."

She motions for Mercy to back away, and I find myself facing the next mother. The determined lines of Mrs. Kazembe's lips and brow inform me that it is my turn to decide which babies are most in need of food.

The next mother, a slight woman named Amayi Sokho, shows me her sleeping child. The baby looks like a bird, her tiny body all bones. She starts to fidget and rolls her head back and from side to side. Her lids flutter up, and her blind eyes wander around in their sockets.

They don't name the newborns here for several weeks or months. Those who die are buried in unmarked graves. The mothers aren't supposed to mourn their unnamed children.

I take a long deep breath and nod to the mother: *Yes, your child needs food.* With the plastic shovel I heave two large scoops, more than the other women received, into her bag. I do not look at the mother. I do not look at the child. When I am finished and the mother has sealed her bag and left, I turn and walk away. Mercy and Mrs. Kazembe shout to me, asking where I'm going, telling me to come back. I do not answer.

I walk directly to my house. Once inside, I use duct tape to hang two skirts over my windows, securing all the edges so that no one can see in. Then I dig into my duffel bag and take out the cardboard box my grandmother sent me. In the box are ten packages of Reese's peanut-butter cups, a bag of Hershey's miniatures, four bags of Pepperidge Farm Goldfish crackers, and a bag of Fritos.

In breathless bites, I eat it all.

I don't even look at my hands as they work to cram the food into my mouth; instead, I stare at the corner of the ceiling, at the place where the three white walls merge together in a box-like shadow. I focus on this nearly blank space until all of the food is gone. Then, I crawl under my green mosquito net and lie flat on my back on the cement floor to wait for the comfort of sleep.

Malawi taught me about the force of suffering. In its demand for acknowledgment, it often reduced me to acts of shame. Eventually, however, the Malawian people showed me how to draw strength from a deeper place: one that could hold the pain, and more.

ℒ ℒ ℒ

Amy Wilson is a freelance writer living in Oakland, California. She also works as a literary escort, shuffling authors around town when they're in San Francisco on book tours. In the past, Amy's been a stockbroker, a writing teacher at a homeless shelter, a bookseller, a waitress, and an antique rug archivist. Currently, she is working on a series of pieces about the impact of climate change on indigenous communities.

DEBORAH J. SMITH

🎵 🎵 🎵

The Barber's Beads

A traveler learns that the ritual of bargaining
doesn't end when the purchase is made.

One afternoon in Lebanon I came upon a barbershop
in the small town of Juneih. A glass case inside,
filled with beautiful prayer beads, caught my eye as gifts
to bring home. But it seemed strange to stop in a barbershop, point at prayer beads, and just crassly *buy* them.
There had to be some other way to do this.

The barber soon appeared. He spoke French and
Arabic, so we chatted about the weather, where I was
from, how I liked Lebanon. As I moved to the case,
complimenting him on his prayer beads, stones in nearly
every color of the rainbow glittered and shone. They
were really lovely. Before I knew it, I was bargaining—
something I hadn't yet done in the Middle East.

Bargaining isn't all about price. It's a conversation, a

flirt with numbers, a way of cleverly communicating what you are willing to offer or accept—a dance with currency attached. Somewhere in the midst of it, you forget price and simply enjoy the art of making a deal with someone

"These are very nice," the barber said, holding up a set of lapis blue beads the color of deep water. "I can make you a very good price."

"Those are pretty." I pointed to a green jade pair.

"Yes, and you like colors? I have all sorts." He pointed to larger beads on the wall.

"No, I really like the smaller ones."

"If you buy ten, I'll make you a good price for ten."

"But I don't need ten. I just want two pair."

We negotiated back and forth. I began to add up numbers, which changed incrementally depending on how many I'd agree to buy. Finally, after comparative additions on the calculator before us, I could see what dealmakers got out of this. It was exhilarating. The barber was beaming. It was a slow afternoon in Juneih and he was having more fun than he'd had all day. I was getting a great price and enjoying the banter.

I pointed out two pair of beads: one was rock crystal, shiny and transparent. The other was mother-of-pearl, the gleaming, milky inner lining of seashells.

He quoted a price I thought was a little too high. Looking into my wallet, hardly registering what was in there, I said; "I don't have that." We waited, I admired, the price dropped some more—now, buy. Agreeing on a price, I handed over my money as he put the prayer beads into gift bags. My friends were thrilled to get them for Christmas.

When I returned a second time to Lebanon, I told the barber how much the gifts were appreciated. He pulled out a set of rosewood beads in response and let me smell them. Rosewood looks brown and plain, but it contains oils that give the wood a pleasing fragrance. Soon—you guessed it—we were back at the case admiring beads.

I didn't drive as hard a bargain this time. He offered a good price, so I made my choice—a set of yellow agate prayer beads and another mother-of-pearl.

I left briefly to get cash from the ATM up the street. On my return the barber was sitting near the mirrors at the back of the shop, a drawer open before him. He waved me over to the barber chair. At dusk on my last day in Lebanon, we sat and chatted.

It still surprises me how much I can manage to understand, even though my spoken French is abominable. Even without a shared language, we communicated amazingly well. I listened and from other cues I could understand most of what the barber was saying, or I could pick up the general topic. I couldn't speak French, but he understood English enough to figure out what I meant. We talked about his family and mine: he in French and I in broken Arabic and English. He pointed at photos of his relatives in the shop as he told me about them. I pulled my small pack of family photos from my wallet.

Then the barber opened the drawer a little and exhibited new prayer beads he had—he needed to attach the silver ends to them before putting them on display. Like the others, they were gorgeous. Rich red gleamed from a pair of ruby beads, while another pair shone in royal blue. He had turquoise ones, and a set of black prayer beads with silver filigree embedded into them. These last black beads, I assured him, would be a treat I'd buy for myself when I returned to Lebanon in the fall.

I left the barber thinking of an Arabic proverb I'd heard: "Hell is life without people." Appreciative of visitors, the Lebanese enjoy sharing their love of country and family with others. It's not over when a purchase is done. They'll continue talking, and ask about your family or how you like the country. They'll shoot the breeze, drink coffee with you, and pass the time of day, even with their prayer beads in hand. They are looking for life *with* people. Perhaps, for Heaven.

❧ ❧ ❧

Deborah J. Smith is a faculty member with Empire State College's International Program in Lebanon, where she teaches the course "Stories of Food and Culture." She has written about travel, food, and faith for various publications including Tastes of Italia *magazine, the* Rome Italy Tourist Portal, *the* Berkshire Women's Times, *and other Travelers' Tales anthologies. Smith is a native of Troy, New York, and her work is frequently broadcast on Northeast Public Radio.*

Rudolph for Newlyweds

On a journey across Mongolia, the author
encounters goat breakfasts, drunken guides,
and a "national" wedding reception.

*I*t is Day 11 of our Mongolian trek and my pony is the happiest yet because I have officially surrendered all hope of exerting my influence on his speed and his dinosaur antics. I've ridden horses since childhood, but never one pretending he lives in Jurassic Park. We six struggle with our various mounts, teetering along the border of Siberia, looking for reindeer herders, shamans, a slice of inner peace, an escape from personal crisis, adventure, who knows? But by Day 11 we are primarily preoccupied with how cold and uncomfortable we are, and I have begun to hallucinate about Starbucks Frappuccinos.

When my friend Don asked me if I'd be interested in accompanying him on a month-long trek in north-

ern Mongolia I didn't hesitate. It made perfect sense
at the time. To gain perspective on my fracturing life I
would obliterate all distraction by retreating to the most
remote location feasible. I would redesign my role on
this planet in my own vision and return home anew.
When I announced my decision to take this trip to my
girlfriends, they each responded by feverishly pushing
that book about the so-called "quarter-life crisis" on me.
They were so adamant that I suspected they were getting a commission to do so. Of course, I was insulted that
these women who knew me so well would attribute my
job woes, love-life drama, and identity crisis to growing
pains and a mass-market trend.

The book they were pushing would have been
remarkably cheaper than the plane ticket I eventually
bought. But I was able to justify it all with my life-long
fascination with Mongolian ponies, a fetish documented
since childhood. At age five I kicked Barbie out of her
Dream House and plotted a Mongol invasion of her
property that subsequently replaced her and some of her
furniture with two-dozen My Little Ponies. Barbie slept
outside in her big pink convertible while the rubbery,
multi-colored Mongolian steeds with florescent manes
galloped through her living room and ate her house-
plants. Even Ken was no match. Ken had always been
so useless.

By the time I actually questioned my decision to take
such a trip I was already on my fifth or six breakfast of
freshly killed goat, eating it in the cold with my blue
bandana fastened securely on my head. I had never
worn a bandana before in my life. Trips through Mexico,
Morocco, Korea didn't call for a bandana the way
Mongolia does.

By early afternoon on Day 11 of our ride our head horseman, Tuksa, passed out drunk along the edge of the woods, curling up peacefully on the ground, his horse grazing an inch from his face. Nap time. He points east and motions us to keep going, mumbling a faint command into the moist earth. He has set a poor example for the younger horsemen, who are also drunk but at least still riding, which may actually be worse. While the closest Starbucks is thousands of miles away, oblivion is just around the corner.

We follow one of the young horsemen many miles to a yurt—a *"ger"* in Mongolian. I'm closely following British Mark because he rides out here like someone decidedly in search of peace, leisurely weaving his pony off the slightly beaten path and through a meadow dense with flowers. He has nothing to prove, unlike the older guys on the excursion who seem completely unimpressed by how many days travel they'd have to endure to reach any kind of medical attention. Alan is seventy-five and risks the remaining decade of his life every day, enacting scenes from old American Westerns and gallivanting through the steep terrain like the stunt version of himself.

When we reach the *ger*, a customary pile of dried curd sits looming in a bowl on the rug in the small dwelling and the hosts wait for us to eat it. Dried reindeer curd is not an acquired taste. It cannot win you over later in life. If you grow up with it, you may not notice that it is awful. If you are encountering it for the first time as an adult, you already know better. Mark politely pretends to put a piece of it in his mouth and surreptitiously places it on the dirt floor behind him, later digging a little hole for it with his finger and burying it forever.

This particular *ger* in the middle of a vast and vacant expanse is tended by nomads but equipped with a satellite dish, and the Mongolian family within is glued to the Oscars—six months late and dubbed in Mongolian—on a small black-and-white TV. Our translator, Arunya, is not paying attention to the curd being passed and the attempts at avoiding it because *Lost in Translation* is winning an award. She expresses that she's very interested in seeing the film when she gets back to Ulann Bataar, and we all think this is ironic because we've been lost in *her* translations for eleven straight days. When Antoni asked her where we'd be camping that night, for instance, she answered, "Yes, two horses." Arunya begins her answers with "yes," which simply means that she is conscious. "Yes" is sometimes followed directly by "no" and then by something that generally has no connection to the question. Everything after "yes" is a crapshoot on the one hand and a Zen koan on the other. We sit quietly with her responses, awaiting enlightenment.

The eventual ruckus outside is our sobering guide galloping from out of nowhere like a character in *Crouching Tiger, Hidden Dragon*. He's a quick fix, nearly remedied by his three-hour nap and somehow informed of a wedding reception a few miles away.

"National wedding reception," says Arunya to the group.

"*National*," the tourists collectively whisper before politely thanking our hosts and tacking up our horses. "National" is one of Arunya's favorite words to say in translation, and everywhere we go she alerts us to *national* foods and songs and clothes. She also announces when something is special but she pronounces it like "spatial," so for the first few days we're under the impression that foods and games and national songs in Mongolia are spread really far apart. Now we whisper "*national*" after each one of her pronouncements. Not to mock her, just for something to do.

It is impossible to miss us coming. There are fifteen horses in our entourage, one for every rider, cook, and assistant and several pack horses. Luckily the newlyweds know our horseman well or they'd suspect an attack. The young couple readies a bowl of curd for us, not wanting to disappoint. Arunya, the head horseman and the six of us tourists all cram inside the newlyweds' first *ger* as a united couple, remembering to walk clockwise and sit in order of age, which puts me right in middle and directly behind the big steaming pot of reindeer milk tea.

"National tea," says Arunya, pointing into the steam. "*National,*" we whisper carefully, so as not to freak out the newlyweds.

"Did you notice we stepped over someone's grandmother on the way in?" Canadian Antoni asks me. I *did* notice but wasn't clear if I should be concerned. She's face first in the dirt by the opening of the *ger*, and she appears to be about eighty. What might be a crime in some countries is just par for the course in a Mongolian wedding reception; Granny got shit-faced so she sleeps in the bed she made—or didn't make. And we're next.

In Mongolia, when guests drop by, what exists in terms of vodka or fermented mare's milk is forced upon the visitors until entirely consumed. The young bride starts passing a bottle of Ghengis Khan Vodka and a shot glass, initiating the first round of many.

"Do you think she's happy?" Alicia whispers in my ear before taking her first shot, referring to the young and silent bride. It's hard to say. She looks like a terrified fifteen-year-old girl, but perhaps it's us. I'm terrified of us, too, this motley crew of strangers. And I'm terrified of my horse, who thinks he's a velociraptor or some other Cretaceous predator.

"Time for songs for bride and groom," Arunya says authoritatively, and the male family members and horsemen stand up one by one to sing heartfelt, meaningful hymns. We ask for translations and are told that the last song told how marriage will never change a child's bond with her mother. Evidently this does not apply to grandmothers because the bride's Nana is still face down in the doorway.

Then Arunya sings and does a damn good job. "Cheers!" we say, and bottle three comes around, faster than expected. We have now taken off as many layers of clothing as we've had rounds of vodka because the *ger* is getting hotter and hotter by the minute from the boiling tea and the booze-filled bodies squeezed tightly together, contributing to an overwhelming sense of delirium. There is a long, awkward pause in the *ger*. Everyone is looking at the tourists lining the wall, ordered by age. We look at the adolescent bride and groom. They silently stare back at us.

What?

"Time for you to sing song. All of you at one time," Arunya says, translating the silence and then staring at us intensely. Panic. Take six people spanning generations and continents, get them drunk, and then make them find a song they all know the words to. There ensues a pause that a playwright might describe as a "long beat" while the characters mentally scramble to squirm out of this choral obligation.

"Guys, c'mon there has to be *one* song. They won't know the words, could be anything," I whisper, a sense of drunken urgency kicking in. Mark and I propose Neil Diamond songs because we love Neil Diamond—a fact we bonded over early in the trip—but we don't even know all the words to Sweet Caroline, and Don flat-out refuses. Of course he does.

"Look Don, I like opera, too, but now is not the time. If you want to pull something from *Carmen* out of your ass tonight around the campfire, fine..." I have no boundaries with Don anymore and I'm aware that it's a problem, but he asks for it. We had a blissful friend-ship back in Boston but it has since been tested out here, camping with nomads in northern Mongolia, and it has failed.

Antoni is perfectly happy to teach us the words to the Canadian anthem but we don't have that kind of time. No one knows the "Star Spangled Banner" except for Don and me, and we are not about to go in on anything together. Leave it to sweet Alicia to think of Christmas carols—brilliant. And up here with the reindeer herd-ers nothing makes more sense than "Rudolph the Red-Nosed Reindeer."

Don and Alan insist they don't know the words to Rudolph.

"How is that possible?" I whine, desperately. "How *helpless* are you?"

"I'm Jewish," Don snaps.

"Don, it's not like you grew up on a kibbutz. What kind of childhood did you have for Christ's sake?"

Mark is over it. "Just pretend, mates. Just pretend."

We all rise. Mark begins, everyone follows.

"Rudolph the red nosed reindeer (we sound awful) *has a very shiny nose* (this poor couple!) *and if you ever saw it, you would even says it glows."* Alan is still on the line *and*

if you ever saw it while Antoni has accidentally gotten ahead of the lyrics, slurring them occasionally in French. We are likely a curse. There will be nothing but winter from now until eternity once we are done grinding this song into a pulp.

Just as we get to *they never let poor Rudolph,* the shaman appears, as if out of nowhere, hovering in the doorway. We have heard that she is 115 years old and stands only four feet tall, and we've been hoping for a glimpse of her since we arrived on this mountain. Now here she is, waving her amulets, and we're blowing our moment, singing Rudolph. Alicia elbows me and I nod in understanding. *Play in any reindeer games* ("It's her!" she says. I know!)

Our tenuous composure cracks deeper yet when a young, naked hermaphrodite peels in through the doorway—a toddler with bows in her hair and a penis. It's a little much for six drunken tourists and it makes me panicky. I go to sit but the mob mentality of caroling keeps me standing until it's over. We are gasping for air. The *ger* is spinning. I think we are done but suddenly no one seems sure if there is one more verse. More vodka comes around. Someone passes Mark the crusty bowl of curd and he hisses under his breath, *"Get that fucking thing away from me!"*

"Did you see what I saw?" I ask him, as we decide it's over and shamefully bow.

"Oh I saw all of it."

We have barely caught our breath when the newly-married couple asks for a translation of the song. Everyone seems so pleased. Our translator didn't understand the majority of our ballad, and who could blame her? So the entourage simultaneously turned to me for the song recapitulation. Because in eleven days' time everyone is able to spot the biggest bullshitter in a group.

"Well, it's actually a song about a famous reindeer herder," I begin, tentatively. Arunya translates this to the Mongolians and the newlyweds smile.

"The reindeer herder," I said "wears fantastic red robes and once a year takes his flying reindeer into the sky." I look upward for effect, and everyone follows my gaze, staring through the small opening at the top of the *ger* where strips of meat hang drying in the sun. Now I'm running with it.

"One year, the reindeer herder gets caught in a very foggy night sky on his way to deliver presents to…all the newly married couples in the village, and one of his reindeer lights up the sky with his nose. He becomes a very famous reindeer." The Mongolians are delighted. Antoni is trying so hard not to be hysterical that he starts to chew on the dried curd, which works every time. Don rolls his eyes twice because he doesn't think I saw him do it the first time, but I did.

Evidently this is good enough for them. The shaman nods her head and leaves. The hermaphrodite skips out after her. Grandma is just where we saw her last, and we step over her again on the way out. And we're free.

Riding drunk is not quite like driving drunk. It's much safer to some extent, except perhaps for this full-blown gallop we are approaching. My steed is insistent on tearing up the earth with his claw-like hooves, galloping well ahead of our guides. I close my eyes because I'm less scared than usual, thanks to the vodka, and I pretend my horse is not a dinosaur but Rudolph, leading the way through a foggy sky, showing me the way to a

Starbucks just beyond the horizon. I laugh out loud like a crazy person and pat him on the neck. For a moment, but just a moment, Mongolia is home.

D'lynne Plummer is a marketing coordinator for an architecture firm and a freelance writer. She contributes art reviews to several regional papers and magazines, and in her spare time, when she is not trying to skip off to remote places, she gives public readings of her memoirs. She is working on a one-woman show, "Renovations 3:21," *about her close encounter with faith and spirituality when a contractor sent from Hell attempts to renovate her home. She lives in Brookline, Massachusetts.*

To Dresden with Tears

Forced to flee Germany as a child,
the author makes a poignant return.

I probably would never have returned to Dresden if I had not heard that voice in my ear at my mother's funeral in Knoxville, Tennessee. For just when her coffin was lowered into the ground, a faint but clear voice said: "Send your book to Dresden."

I knew, of course, that the book the voice was referring to was my memoir and family history. It was a slim volume that had taken me many years to write. I had called it *On the Way to Feed the Swans* because one day in the early 1930s, when my mother and I were walking towards the *Grosse Garten*, Dresden's palatial public park, to feed the swans—we saw Hitler. He was standing near us on top of a black sedan shouting. My mother pulled me away and we continued toward the swans.

They were gliding amidst lotus blossoms on the smooth surface of the pond, making nary a ripple.

I was born in Dresden and the first ten years of my life there were as undisturbed by ripples as the quiet pond with the swans. Yes, we had one day seen a man with a swastika armband standing on top of a car shouting. But what did this have to do with us? At that moment in time, we could never have imagined what happened to us only five years later when we were fleeing for our lives, leaving everything behind.

Everything embraced a lifestyle—not just of ease but also of courtliness. Not that we were members of the aristocracy—Jews could not be that—but we were very comfortable, and the city of Dresden, with its emphasis on art and beauty, had cast its spell.

I think certain places cast spells, particularly when they come under protections. And Dresden, since the sixteenth century, enjoyed a unique municipal protection from members of the House of Wettin, who were the Electorates of Saxony and made Dresden into their diadem. August the Strong, for example, had much to do with this. He was responsible for integrating the river Elbe into the city planning concept and for envisioning Dresden as the "Venice of the North," inviting renowned artists to design exquisite churches, museums, promenades, weather vanes, clocks—in short, beautifying things large and small. This emphasis on the arts and artisans lasted until February 1945, to be exact, when in two nights the city's center was destroyed and 200,000 people were killed there by Allied fire bombs. Hence, my hesitation to ever return.

So these were my thoughts as I placed a copy of *On the Way to Feed the Swans* into an envelope c/o the Mayor's

Office, 01001 Dresden, Germany, and mailed it at my
local post office in New York City.

Two years went by without a word. Then one day I
received a letter from an organization in Dresden working on a Memorial Book. The writer, Lilli Ulbrich, said
she had found *Swans* at the Mayor's office and could
not thank me enough for having written it. She said she
had been working for over ten years to piece together
the names of the Jewish families and individuals who
had lived in Dresden until 1938, the year the Jews were
sent to the camps. There were some 6,000 of them. But
no personal book-length accounts or memoirs had been
found in Dresden. Mine was the only one.

> *I remember the day in November 1937 when I saw*
> *Stitterich outside the school building standing at the side*
> *of the car.*
>
> *What was he doing here? I wondered.*
>
> *I had never been chauffeured home from school, but*
> *always took the tram. When I asked him why he had*
> *come, he said, "Get in!" He slammed the doors, stepped*
> *on the accelerator, and drove much faster than was his*
> *usual habit.*
>
> *"We are driving home," he said. I was to get my*
> *things and then he would drive me across the border.*
> *Nothing unusual about that part of it, I thought. It was*
> *Friday, and my family often crossed into Bohemia on the*
> *weekends to enjoy the woods and nature walks. But there*
> *was one thing that was exceedingly unusual: my parents*
> *had already left.*
>
> *The feeling that something was odd, even ominous,*
> *was substantiated when we arrived at Bergstrasse Number*
> *16. Gertrud, our maid at the time, was in a highly*

nervous state. She, too, was standing waiting for me. And now all she was doing was telling me to hurry. "Quickly, quickly! Mach schnell, mach schnell!"

I ran to my room. There, everything was packed. Why? I obviously didn't need all these things for a weekend trip. And then I knew.

"You think I'm never coming back?" I screamed. "Well, I will! You wait and see! I will! I'll be back before you know it!"

I opened my suitcases and threw everything on the floor.

"I'm not taking all this junk!" I yelled. "I don't need it. I'll take my toothbrush and that's all!" Then I got into the car and drove off, with Gertrud standing at the door, tears in her eyes, trying to show that she knew, too."

Lilli Ulbrich's letter was followed by a second one. She announced that her Memorial Book co-workers had taken up a collection to send her to New York. It would be an opportunity for her to interview some who had been children at the time and who were now living in the United States. Soon, Lilli and I met in a New York restaurant and immediately became friends. And over time, I was able to imagine myself returning to Dresden and walking the streets with her. And so, on August 27, 2004, my daughter Elizabeth and I boarded Lufthansa Flight 410 for Dresden, with a change of planes in Frankfurt. Dresden, which had come under forty years of East Germany's Communist rule after the firebombing, had not yet established enough commercial clout to warrant direct flights.

We did not expect anyone to greet us at the airport. But there was Lilli with flowers and tears in her eyes.

As our taxi crossed the river Elbe, I could see that famous Dresden panorama on the other side of the river, which had attracted eighteenth-century painters whose works are still in the collections of major museums. Baroque steeples of churches and municipal buildings, now carefully buttressed and continually in the process of restoration, appeared to me dark and fragile and singed with trauma.

Now having crossed the bridge, the scene changed as we neared the Gewandhaus Hotel. I had chosen it because it was not a newly gleaming highrise, of which Dresden has several, but a genuine restoration of the original Gewandhaus, which had served as an eighteenth-century trade fair building. Painted a soft yellow on the outside, it had become a Radisson hotel.

The next morning, we treated ourselves to an exceedingly sumptuous array of breakfast choices, which were spread in a help-yourself-style on many surfaces. As I dipped my spoon into fresh varieties of berries, I took note of a small group of leather-jacketed skinheads seated at a table. My guidebook informed that Dresden, so famous for its opera and classical music, also now hosts the second largest Dixieland festival, right after New Orleans. The guidebook also pointed out that in addition to Dresden's eighteenth-century royal trendsetters, its regular Saxon inhabitants were practical folk, responsible for many inventions. They produced the first mouthwash (1893); the first coffee filter (1908, thanks to Frau Melitta Benz); they were the first to manufacture condensed milk; and in 1895 they patented the first brassiere (thanks to Fraulein Christina Holt, who obviously recognized a need).

Well, after second helpings of smoked salmon, cheeses, and marmalades, the time to get serious had come. The mission for my trip to Dresden was to search for the two houses of my childhood. Actually, one house, Bergstrasse Number 16, was more important to me than the other. It had been my grandparents' house.

It was the house my father went to every morning. Up the marble-faced entrance foyer; up the carpeted stairway flanked by pots of fresh azaleas, or tulips, or whatever was in season; up to the second story with floors so well polished, one had to be careful not to fall. There, the Elbschloss Malzfabrik, the family malt house, had its home office. And there, in a suite of rooms, secretaries with cork-screw curls typed letters on clanky manual typewriters, and bookkeepers wearing green visors to shade their eyes from the glare of electric bulbs, penned careful entries into heavy ledgers.

There, Opa Brach, as I called my grandfather, walked with my father up and down the garden paths richly strewn with white gravel. Their crunchy steps passed the private bowling alley, the espalliered fruit trees, the artificial pond with a nymph holding a shell that spewed fresh water into the fountain's basin.

Opa Brach had commissioned the nymph from the sculptor who lived in a former carriage house at the rear of the main house. The carriage house served both as a garage and as the sculptor's studio. Occasionally, I would leave my cousins in the garden sandbox to walk back there, passing the "kitchen garden" and the berry bushes, just to watch the sculptor work. I would stand in the arched doorway watching him take wet clay out of a large bin, slap it onto the piece he was working on, and shape it with a tool that looked like a butter knife. His pieces were

*large, nude and female, and I learned just from watching
how a sculptor adds, molds, shapes, and pares away.*

*I always stood quietly and he never spoke to me. But
I knew that a blond woman who was tall and thin and
wore sandals was living with him upstairs in their loft. I
did not think she was his wife.*

*Well, as I said, Opa Brach liked to talk business while
walking. Hands folded behind his back, he strode in his
park-like garden with my father and other lieutenants like
a head-of-state.*

*There, Oma Luise, as I called my grandmother, sat in
the Wintergarden, the glass-enclosed veranda surrounded
by palms, cacti, and rubber trees, embroidering a pillow
slip and talking to my mother about servants. To Oma
Luise, servants were not a status symbol, but an essential
crew for the maintenance of property at its optimum
perfection. If, on the second floor, Opa Brach was in
charge of business, Oma Brach, downstairs, was definitely
in charge of everything else, including the well-being of
her husband, the head-of-state. Her salon/music room
was bathed in yellow, its golden hues were interrupted
only by a large black Steinway Grand. Mealtimes were
always announced by striking a muted gong and calling
in French, "Ã table! Ã table!" Apples were never bitten
into, but served on fruit plates and sectioned with mother-
of-pearl-handled fruit knives. This was woman's work,
done at the table. Men never peeled or cut their own fruit.
Opa Brach favored a certain apple, the Calville. It arrived
from Merano, Italy, in wooden crates in October.*

*A born administrator, at a time when administra-
tion could hardly go beyond her home, Oma Luise ran
her household as if it were an official residence, ready
to receive important dignitaries from around the world.*

*Actually, no one like that ever came to Bergstrasse
Number 16. All activities, business and social, involved
relatives only. If my grandparents wielded great influence, it did not go beyond the family. Of course, I did
not realize that at the time. To me, Opa and Oma Brach
were like a king and queen, and Bergstrasse Number 16
was a great seat of power. Everything seemed to me to be
happening there. Nothing happened anywhere else.*

Now, Lilly led the way to find the street and then the house.

In Dresden, as in most European cities, people do a lot of walking, and if they are not on foot, they ride bicycles or use streetcars. We followed Lilli on foot to the Prager Strasse, which I well remembered to have been the "Fifth Avenue" of Dresden. It had been so devastatingly destroyed by the firebombs of 1945 that nothing could be salvaged, and the good citizens of Dresden decided they would start from scratch and "modernize" this former elegant shopping avenue, by making it into a long mall with global concessions offering standard brands.

Lilli was leading the way at quite a clip, but when we passed an H&M, we asked if we could just for a minute run inside to compare the styles with what is sold by H&M in New York. Finding them to be exactly the same, we quickly re-joined Lilli and marched on.

Next, Lilli led us to the railway station whose black-ened stone exterior still showed severe damage sixty years later. But like a strong tree that had been struck by lightning, life was teeming at its base inside and trains were running on time! We used the station to enter, cross, and then exit to the left.

When we emerged, something began to feel familiar.

I could tell that we were close. And there it was! We had found the street. Would you believe it? Bergstrasse still existed! The white letters on the blue enamel street sign clearly spelled the name. I knew that Number 16 would not be far. But where was it? Number 17 belonged to a small villa that seemed to have slept through everything. The trees were old and nothing stirred. What about Number 16? Should it not just be across the street? But there, where it should have been, was a half-block long row of modern apartment houses. I blinked. No, this could not be. Let's go to the back. Number 16 was set back from the street, I said. But no, the back of the apartment houses showed laundry lines and grass. Bergstrasse Number 16 was no longer.

Bayreutherstrasse Number 32 was the second house we came to find. I had lived there on the second floor with my parents, and when I was old enough to go to school, I had walked from that house to my first grade. Above us lived a well-known German painter by the name of Otto Dix. Now, as we stood in front of Bayreutherstrasse 32, which had been nicely restored and seemed fully occupied, we noticed that it had become a landmark. It was now called "The Otto Dix Haus."

And then I remembered something and rushed to the back. Yes, there it was! The swing! The only difference were the ropes. They were blue plastic, not the stringy rope I had remembered. I felt a surge. Out of my way everyone! And I plunked myself on the wooden seat, which seemed a bit narrow now. But never mind. Never mind anything. I had come back and this was my swing!

And I swung, and I swung, and I swung.

❧ ❧ ❧

Hannelore Hahn's books include On the Way to Feed the Swans; Remember the Magic: The Story of the International Women's Writing Guild in Celebration of its 25th Anniversary; Take a Giant Step; *and* Places: A Directory to Public Places for Private Events and Private Places for Public Functions. *She is Executive Director of the International Women's Writing Guild, which she founded thirty years ago and whose conferences and workshops, particularly its annual summer conference at Skidmore College, are attended by women from around the world*

♫ ♫ ♫

Tibetan Truths

A journalist working in the People's Republic
of China explores ways of seeing.

*T*he weather-beaten woman took a contemplative
step, raised her arms high above her head, clasped
her hands together, and swept them forward like a diver
entering the sea. The full expanse of her small frame
embraced the dusty pavement, from her head and shoulders to her knees and toes. After holding this submissive
position for an extended moment, she picked herself up,
took a second step, and repeated the process again and
again, slowly inching her way around the perimeter of
the sprawling Jokhang Temple with hundreds of other
pilgrims rippling like waves beside her.

She called to mind the women I'd seen at the Shrine
of the Virgin of Guadalupe in Mexico City, crossing
the holy grounds on their knees. Their devotion had

similarly transfixed me: hundreds of women wrapped in shawls with rosaries wound between their knotted fingers, sobbing as blood seeped through their skirts. But while this Tibetan woman threw herself upon the pavement time and again, she didn't wince and she didn't bleed.

Tibetans are no strangers to pain. Violence has marred most of the past fifty-plus years. When the Red Army invaded their land a year after seizing power in China, the Tibetans' ill-equipped troops hardly stood a chance—they were outnumbered more than eight to one. Their spiritual leader, the Dalai Lama, was forced into exile in 1959 and by 1970, an estimated 100,000 Tibetans had joined him. Of those who stayed, hundreds of thousands more perished under the stringent Chinese rule.

Yet a year of working as a journalist in Beijing taught me there were no clear-cut answers or simple conclusions. As I explored Tibet's river valleys and rugged rural villages, I tried to keep the passionate perspectives of my Chinese friends in mind:

"They were living in the Dark Ages before we got here."

"Under the Dalai Lama, the Tibetans were serfs in their own land. Just look at that palace he lived in!"

"We liberated the Tibetans from the Dalai Lama just like Mao liberated us from the emperor."

There was some truth to these comments. Before China's takeover, there were few roads and virtually no electricity in Tibet. Health care and education were only available to religious leaders. Thanks to the Chinese, Tibetans now had public schools, medical facilities, transportation systems and—in Lhasa—internet cafés and karaoke bars.

But still I found myself wondering: Was modernization worth the price of religious freedom?

I decided to clear my thoughts and seek a fresh perspective on my questions one morning by renting a bicycle from a hostel and pedaling out of town. An hour into my journey, I stumbled upon a monastery more than half a millennium old. The front gate was draped with a strand of prayer flags that had been bleached into pastels by the sun. I parked the bike and entered the crumbling edifice. Its corridors were dark and damp; incense and yak wax lingered heavily in the musty air. The walls were shrouded with fading *thangkas*—paintings depicting Buddhist deities. It seemed I was alone until I noticed a monk sitting near a window, his round face illuminated by a thin stream of sunlight. He didn't appear much older than I—twenty-five or so. I greeted him in Mandarin, but he responded in English as he strode over to join me. I asked about the eleven-headed deity whose mural adorned a nearby wall and he explained it was Chenresig, the Bodhisattva of compassion.

The tour that ensued lasted nearly three hours and took us deep into the labyrinths of the monastery. Afterward, we shared a lunch of bread, yogurt, and milk tea—a buttery cocktail of boiled yak milk and curly yak hairs—on a terrace overlooking Tibet's rock- and yak-strewn landscape. The monk asked how I came to his part of the world. I rarely admitted I was a journalist in China, as most Chinese instinctively distrusted the media. But how can you lie to a monk? I confessed my profession and he gazed off into the distance.

"I've never spoken to an American journalist before," he murmured.

He let this piece of information tumble in his mind a

few moments before quietly asking if I knew what the Chinese had done to his land. Was I aware that, in the past year alone, several monks had "disappeared" from this very monastery?

My stomach tightened as my eyes darted around the terrace. I had a thousand questions to ask. But what if our conversation was overheard? Chinese secret police had been known to pose as Tibetan monks. What if one was listening? It seemed too great a risk—for both our sakes, but especially his. I changed the subject instead. "Do you speak Mandarin?"

"I can, but I don't," he said, then switched the topic of discussion again. He had an English class to teach and needed to go. Taking that as a polite invitation to continue my day solo, I stood up to leave.

"No," he said, his face brightening. "I want you to come with me."

The only light source in the classroom was the sun streaming through the windows. The floor was packed dirt and the whitewashed walls and ceiling were earthen, but a shiny blackboard stood up front with chalk that resembled chunks of pumice. A troop of five- to twenty-year-old monks with neatly shaved heads soon filed in. They were rambunctious in their violet-red robes, but stopped short the moment they saw me. I greeted them in English, which they found hilarious. Their teacher, however, snapped them to a quick attention. Motioning for them to open their workbooks, he conducted a lesson on colors.

"Red, green, yellow, orange, blue. Red, green, yellow, orange, blue," he recited as a chant.

"Red, grin, yell-o, arnge, bloo," the students rocked back and forth, murmuring as one.

I started wondering whether the students even knew what the words meant beyond some bizarre, foreign mantra when the teacher began a new color scheme: "Pink, purple, black, white, brown." He pronounced the last word hesitantly as "brune" and glanced my way for help. When I corrected his pronunciation, the littlest monk giggled and—when I looked at him—turned his head shyly, stealing my heart in the process. The teacher posed a question in Tibetan and the class once again erupted in laughter. He looked at me, smiled, and handed over his workbook. "Will you lead our class?" he asked.

I leaped to the front of the room and pointed at my shirt. "Black!" I enunciated carefully. The monks looked surprised. "Black!" I repeated.

Whispers. A cough. Silence.

Then, from the corner, a monk who was about half my age decided to take the lead. "Blllek," he mouthed.

"Good!" I clapped.

Confidence was won. "Blllek!" the other monks chimed in.

After I took his students on a guided tour of the color wheel, the class ended and the monk escorted me back to my bike. It was nearly dusk, and the golden dharma wheel that crested the monastery's roof glowed in the sunlight. We exchanged addresses, but he warned that it might be a while before he wrote me. "I can only mail letters through Western tourists, and they don't come by so often," he sighed.

As he spoke, I thought about the reason I had set out on my bicycle journey in the first place: to find a kernal of truth about Tibet and try to draw some conclusions.

"I feel so confused," I confessed. "I don't know who or

what to believe in all of this, and how can I be a journalist if I cannot..."

He placed his hand on my shoulder. "There are many
ways to look. Trust what you see," he said quietly. And
then he turned and walked away, his red robe flowing
behind him.

*Stephanie Elizondo Griest has belly danced with Cuban rumba
queens, mingled with the Russian Mafia, and edited the propaganda
of the Chinese Communist Party. She is the author of* Around the
Bloc: My Life in Moscow, Beijing, and Havana, *and her work
has also appeared in* The New York Times, Washington Post,
Latina Magazine, *and several Travelers' Tales books. She once
drove 45,000 miles across the nation in a beat-up Honda, documenting alternative U.S. history for a children's website. You can
visit her own website at www.aroundthebloc.com.*

JUDY COPELAND

🐦 🐦 🐦

A Tale of a Journey Deferred

A seeker learns the truth about love
and about "being real."

*O*nce there was a girl in Japan, a daughter of
American missionaries. The girl lived happily until
one day, when she was nine, her parents took her away
from Japan. They took her away to the States, never to
return. For the next two years, she cried herself to sleep at
night, longing for her friends and her dog in Japan, griev-
ing for the staccato syllables of her mother tongue, for the
way the frogs sang in the rice paddies and the pine trees
bent in the typhoons. For a world lost to her forever.

By the time she was sixteen and living with her parents in the Indian city of Varanasi, she'd lost too many
people and places to grieve anymore. Instead she came
to believe in a secret religion all her own, a patchwork of
idiosyncratic notions stitched together with Hindu and

Buddhist ideas borrowed from the people her parents tried to convert. And in her religion, love was an illusion, a trick her heart played on her. She traced the pain she felt at leaving people and places to her love for them, and she traced this love to her mistaken belief that they were real, when in fact nothing lasted. When in fact every world she'd ever known had vanished from her life with the twirl of an airplane propeller.

Already at age four, she had begun to doubt what her senses told her. One day, as she stood on her doorstep waving good-bye to a friend and watching him walk home, something amazing happened. Before her very eyes, he grew smaller until he disappeared into a tiny point on the horizon.

He's not real, she thought.

After that, the world of people and things seemed to her like an optical illusion, a movie on a screen. Sometimes the girl felt an almost unbearable yearning to go into that mysterious point on the horizon, to pierce the screen and see the reality behind it.

At sixteen, in Varanasi, she watched the wandering seekers come and go—naked, mud-smeared men who had no homes, no wives, no possessions, their wild gaze fixed on a distant point—and she knew that one day she too would leave everything behind. For the path to the real lay in forsaking the unreal, in forsaking people, places, and property. To chase the far horizon, to walk through the veil of illusion to the bliss beyond, vanishing in a flash so pure the very thought of it made her rejoice—for this, she was willing to give up every attachment. And so the act of leaving ceased to feel sad for her. Instead, she embraced it as her art form, her holy sacrament. She came to love the whir of airplane propellers, the thrill of hurtling across space and through time, of watching people, cities, and continents grow smaller until they disappeared, because it meant she was getting closer to the real.

The girl knew by heart the story of the Buddha walking out on his sleeping wife and child one night to go find enlightenment. Far from questioning this scenario, she took its rightness for granted, for she had noticed how little thought her own father gave to her and her mother when God called him to a new place. What troubled her about such scenarios was not that the hero's lover always got left in the lurch but that she herself would not be able to leave properly, when it came her time, unless she first acquired a lover. The classical Hindu ideal of the life-cycle confirmed her lack: To earn the status of homeless wanderer, one had to pass through the stages of student, lover, and hermit. While most people got stuck in the first three stages, the girl vowed to herself, at sixteen, that she would advance through them quickly, checking them off one right after the other like Girl Scout badges and wasting no time in becoming a homeless wanderer. She added "getting a lover" to her list of things to do.

Two years passed, and the girl went to college in the States. One night she met a blue-eyed boy from Oregon. Unlike the girl, who had few friends and often withdrew into closets to escape her roommates' chatter and meditate, he laughed easily and was popular with girls. On the night they met, he told of living his whole childhood in the same house. He said he missed his cat and golden retriever, and especially he missed the damp, mulchy smell of the Oregon rainforest. She talked of the places she hadn't been yet and longed to go—Tibet, the Sahara, the Mountains of the Moon.

One morning in February, after the girl and boy had

gone out together two or three times, she emerged from her 8:30 class and saw him standing outside in the snow, waiting for her. He smiled.

"A little gift," he mumbled, somewhat apologetically, as he thrust into her hands a slim blue paperback book with a Buddha-image on the cover.

Later, sitting cross-legged among the shoes on the floor of her dorm-room closet, she opened the book, Hermann Hesse's tale of Siddhartha, a man wandering in India on a spiritual quest. She saw a description of the hero underlined in light pencil. A few people, it said, "are like stars which travel one defined path: no wind reaches them, they have within themselves their guide and path." In the margin the boy had written, "You are also like a star." Farther into the book, he had written, "Siddhartha reminds me of you." Could he have guessed her secret goal? Never had she told it to anyone, never had she dreamed it possible for people to communicate their inner beings to each other, never had she even remotely hoped for such a thing as intimacy, and for all these reasons the aphrodisiac effect of feeling understood took her completely by surprise.

Though she hadn't previously thought about her appearance, now she got her hair cut in a stylish sassoon. She traded her glasses for contact lenses. From an Indian student she borrowed black kohl powder to outline her eyes; from her roommates, miniskirts to replace her frumpy missionary hand-me-downs. She even dieted her 5'9" frame down to a Twiggyish 120 pounds, all in an effort to look alluring to the blue-eyed boy from Oregon.

Soon they became lovers. When they were together, she spoke little, and it pleased her that he respected her silences. She was surprised at his gentle touch, at the explosion of colors his caresses could fire inside her mind, at the pleasures to be given and had by the body. Even more, she was surprised that these pleasures didn't sate her appetite but only intensified it.

Before starting the romance, she hadn't considered how she was going to end it. Now she felt out of her depth. She'd just assumed a popular boy like him couldn't be hurt by someone like her, could always find other girls, and now it occurred to her that her plan might be cruel. Most of all, she worried that a bungled ending might poison her future homeless wanderings with a sour after-taste, leaving her feeling guilt, regret, or envy of others' happiness, dooming her to repeat the same cycle with other lovers, trying again and again until she got the ending right.

One spring evening, the girl and boy slipped into a public garden after closing time to make love beside a lotus pond. Later, as they lay spent on the grass, listening to the crickets, he asked her to marry him.

"If I were going to marry anybody, it would be you," she said. "But I don't need to marry. I've already put in enough time in schools and closets to check off 'student' and 'hermit' from my list, so all I need now is a good romance and I can check off 'lover.'"

"Is that really what you want from life? To check things off a list?"

It occurred to her that something might be missing from her plan, but she pushed the thought aside.

"What do *you* want?" she asked.

"I've never really thought about it. The good life, I guess. Satisfying work, a woman to love, a house in Oregon. Mountains. Ocean. The time and money to enjoy all those things."

"I guess we want different things then."

The boy's face looked sad in the moonlight.

This was not going right. She should do or say something kinder, more graceful, but none of the stories she'd memorized about the Buddha and other famous homeless people covered this particular point.

Befuddled at how to end the romance, the girl simply left things hanging and disappeared, hitchhiking to San Francisco. She paid all her money to a travel agent to get on a flight to India. She pictured herself as a seeker, sleeping in temples; bathing in holy rivers; following dusty paths thronged with pilgrims from Assam, Rajasthan, and Orissa; walking beside sadhus and bear trainers, princes and prostitutes, thinkers and humbugs. Her favorite image was of rising before dawn. She could see herself walking, alone and unafraid, down to the banks of the Ganges to wait for the sun to turn the river blood-red.

Plenty was wrong with that vision, and she knew it. Among other flaws, she remembered from living in India with her parents that she would have to run a gauntlet of flirty men if she took a solitary stroll to the Ganges. Though she chose to airbrush those men out of her fantasy picture, part of her felt afraid to travel by herself. Perhaps that was why she phoned the blue-eyed boy and talked him into going on the trip with her. Or perhaps she wasn't ready to give him up yet. Anyway, he joined her in San Francisco. After the travel agent told them they wouldn't be allowed to room together in India without proof of marriage, they got married. Then, the day before they were to leave, the travel agent took off with their money.

Although the memory of her interrupted trip to India

faded into a back closet of her mind, from time to time she would recall a Hindu myth—the story of Narada, a man who took a walk in the desert with God. When God got thirsty, Narada offered to fetch some water, and God sat down to wait. Narada walked to the nearest village. As soon as he knocked on a door, a young woman opened it, a woman so beautiful that Narada forgot what he'd come for. Her parents, as if they'd been expecting him, immediately offered him their daughter's hand in marriage. Gradually, he was drawn into the family business. Twelve years went by happily as Narada prospered and had many children.

Like Narada, the girl who didn't believe in love, now a woman herself, settled into marriage instead. Quite by accident, she'd married into a tribe of lawyers. Dinners at her in-laws' house in Oregon were loud free-for-alls on politics and world affairs, with daughters challenging their fathers and mothers their sons. Raised by Southern Baptists who valued innocuous table conversation above all else, except perhaps the rapture of "being saved," which was, of course, beyond logical scrutiny, she found this rowdy new world of reason and debate exhilarating. Before long, she entered law school. Meanwhile, her husband, the only one in his family who didn't want to be a lawyer (he was too nice), studied to be a wildlife biologist. They moved into a house near her husband's parents in Oregon.

Whenever the story of Narada flitted through the woman's mind as she pored over a casebook in the law school library, or swam in a cool mountain lake with her husband, she would feel a little shock of memory. It wasn't the nagging feeling that attends procrastination. It was more like one of those silent laughs she sometimes had in her sleep when she realized she was dreaming but she liked the dream and was in no hurry to wake up. From a childhood of being dragged about the world by parents who themselves seemed to move like puppets on strings, going wherever God called them, she'd acquired a certain fatalism. It hadn't occurred to her to question the travel agent's stealing her money any more than she'd questioned his advice that they marry; she simply yielded to her fate, making the best of her new life in Oregon.

Since the day they'd married, she had left one suitcase packed. Sometimes she checked to make sure it was still under their bed, gathering dust in readiness for the day when she would leave. The man noticed her checking it but said nothing, for it was his nature to accept people and animals as they were. He would no more have commented on the woman's peculiar habit of checking her suitcase than reproach a fish for jumping or a cactus for prickling. Instead, he studied her habits, as he would those of a wild animal, to discover what made her look up from her law books and notice him.

They often went backpacking together in the Oregon wilderness, whose protean beauty reminded her of all the places she had lost in her childhood—the rocky seashores of New England, the cone-shaped volcanoes of Japan, the desolation of the high Himalaya. She marveled at her husband's bond with the animals he studied, at his ability to sense where they'd be, what they'd do next, how to get close to them.

Once, on a summer hillside, he picked a wild blackberry and put it in her mouth and she closed her eyes and tasted its sweetness as if she had just been born, a sweetness so real it made her shudder, then open her eyes. For the first time, she looked at the man and did not see a mere fleeting apparition. For the first time, she saw how blue his eyes were, how full and sensuous his lips, how golden the hair on his forearms. Together the man and the woman followed deer in the rainforest and tracked the spoor of coyotes to their desert dens. Together they sat silently in a canoe observing great blue herons stalking their prey, and lay down on a bed of moss to make love with rain splashing on them through the trees like fresh green paint. And the woman began to forget her belief that the world was illusory. When the man showed her birds and butterflies, grasses and glaciers, the colors of the rainbow, she saw them through his eyes, and this made them real to her.

Eventually the woman accepted a lawyer job in San Francisco, and the man quit his job to go with her. Unable to find work as a naturalist in California, he laughed less often now. With the woman always so intent on her legal papers, he felt abandoned in a foreign country. He slept fitfully, dreaming of Oregon, of the shrill whistles of marmots above the timberline, the bugling of elk in the foothills and the yowls of coyotes in the high desert.

Her sleep, too, became troubled. In her dreams her younger selves appeared and spoke to her, but she didn't recognize them as her selves, so deeply was she lost in her present life. One night she saw a Japanese girl with light brown hair, about seven years old, kneeling on a tatami floor, her head bent over a low table, as she penned what appeared to be a letter. Because only the back of the child's head was visible, the woman didn't realize the child's face was the same as hers, though she was able to peer over her shoulder at the letter and read, "My dear auntie, how long will you go on living remotely on your own rear end?" Then the woman's present self appeared in the form of a naked giant, crawling along the ground on all fours. Balanced precariously atop the giant's bare bottom rode a miniature version of the woman's kitchen table, at which she and her husband sat, two tiny homunculi, drinking their morning coffee and reading their newspapers, oblivious to their absurd perch.

Another night, she saw a baby girl in a crib inside a cabin of a ship crossing the Pacific to Japan. Over the crib floated three witches who shrieked, "Birth and dying, birth and dying, birth and dying," and with every shriek they forced the baby to see a terrible vision, a vision in which all the suffering that had happened in the history of the world seemed to be happening in the same moment, and the baby was forced to see all of it at once: King Herod's soldiers putting an infant to the sword; an old man hemorrhaging to death of dengue fever in a thatched hut; a large frog cannibalizing a smaller one; a lion eating a newborn zebra while the zebra's mother was still giving birth to it; a serial killer torturing a young woman; an Ice Age family huddled together in a blizzard, slowly dying of cold and starvation. The baby in the ship's cabin turned red in the face and screamed for the vision to stop, but the witches only shrieked louder, drowning out her cries with their chant.

When at last the shrieks and screams ceased, the woman felt the sun on her shoulders and realized she was standing on a summer hillside with her husband, her eyes closed, her lips parted for him to feed her a wild blackberry, and in a flash she understood that this had been the sweetest moment she would ever have in her life. Her eyes still closed, her lips still parted, she waited to taste the moment again. But before the berry touched her tongue, the three witches began screeching, "Birth and dying, birth and dying, birth and dying," and forced her to watch the unbearable vision over and over again, until at last she screamed herself awake.

One night she came home from work to find a candle-lit dinner, and on her plate a single red rose. It still shocked and pleased her that the man would think her worth taking the time to cook a five-course dinner for. In the family she'd grown up in, loved ones didn't count as much as work, certainly not as much as God's work. Though she adored the man for making her feel she mattered, she'd never been able to fathom how love could be as important as he treated it. Though she loved him dearly, she'd always kept something back, always kept that packed suitcase under their bed. Now the thought crossed her mind that maybe she'd been wrong. Maybe love was the only real thing.

Before he sat down, he smiled and stroked her cheek, and she sighed with contentment, putting aside the troublesome thought. They ate their soup in silence.

Then he leaned across the table towards her, his eyes no longer smiling. "Remember when we first met and I said you were like a star that travels its own path?" he said. "I guess I hoped that by being with you and watching you I could learn to go inside myself and find my path, but it hasn't worked that way, and I seem to be losing my path, not finding it. So now I'm asking you to teach me how you do it. How does a star find its path through the sky?"

She stared at him, saw tiredness and despair in his eyes, and didn't know what to say. She was lost herself.

"I wish I knew," she said.

He winced as if she had hit him.

"All these years, and you're still shutting me out, we're still not really close."

She looked at him across the table, drinking in his face: at thirty-five he remained a beautiful man, with the bluest eyes she'd ever seen. When he looked away in hurt defeat, she noticed a new crease on his face, a little worry-line carved down the center of his forehead, and for the first time, she knew she could not leave him. For the first time, she knew she would love him until she died. It was not his beauty or his kindness that finally bound her to him. It was the aging they had done together.

But when she started to tell him how she felt, he looked uneasy and changed the subject.

That night they made love too fast, too hungrily and desperately, as if it was their last time. The woman fell asleep, and her future self appeared to her as a middle-aged, sari-clad Indian woman with piercing black eyes. In her dream, the woman was sitting next to the Indian on a plane, chatting about being on her way to a job interview in Los Angeles, where she planned to meet her husband and coordinate their career plans. As the woman talked, the Indian fixed her with a quiet stare. The woman shifted her eyes uneasily. The longer the Indian stared, the more manically the woman prattled about husband and career and the higher and falser her voice sounded to her.

Finally, the Indian broke in: "You are not going to Los Angeles. You know that, don't you? You know where this plane is really going."

The woman's eyes met the Indian's, which grew larger and larger until they ran together and became a whirlpool that drew her inside. "Yes," the woman admitted as she plunged into the vortex, "I know."

After the swirling waters released her, she found herself back on the plane facing a movie screen onto which
was projected a map of the world. A red line, like the
ones used by in-flight magazines to indicate air routes,
appeared on the map. From San Francisco, it advanced
slowly across the Pacific Ocean towards Asia.

The woman awoke in her bed in San Francisco,
thirty-five years old, exactly twelve years after her
missed flight to India. But she awoke from more than
a dream. In that moment, she recognized her past and
future selves, waking at last from the stupor of living
in the present. And in that moment, the accretions of
her settled life in America washed away from her. Her
mind went clean, and she remembered what she had
to do.

When she told the man, he wasn't surprised. This
time, though, he would not agree to go with her, saying
he was going home to Oregon. For her part, she couldn't
say when she'd be back—maybe next month, maybe
next year, perhaps even the year after that. As crazy as
it may seem, she wanted him to wait for her in Oregon.
Though she still loved him, perhaps what she loved
about him was less being with him than going home
to him, and less going home than knowing she could,
knowing that at the end of her journey he would be
there to hear how a star finds it path through the sky.

Six months after the dream of the red line and a week
before her scheduled flight to India, the man stood in
front of the fireplace in their apartment, his face white,
his lips pressed together in a tight little line, the crease in
his forehead deepening until it looked like it was hurt-
ing him. He enunciated slowly, as though each word cost
him tremendous effort: "I want a divorce."

She drew her breath in, went stiff with shock, then angrily demanded to know why.

"I'm not happy anymore."

The woman protested, she fumed, she marshaled her defense, she cross-examined, she split hairs. Though she'd never planned to part from him so gracelessly, she couldn't help herself, she was in too much pain. Even sitting in the closet failed to calm her. Eventually, after she exhausted her fury, she saw how useless it was to try to argue a person into being happy with her. She'd known even before the dream of the red line, even before the man's announcement, but wouldn't admit to herself, that she was losing him.

When the plane lifted off the ground, an old, familiar joy of hurtling across space and through time soothed her into a long sleep. She woke up missing the man and sobbing—and stopped, embarrassed, when she noticed other passengers staring at her.

She thought of Narada, the man who had promised to fetch some water for God but instead married a beautiful girl and forgot about his promise. Twelve years after Narada got married, a torrential rain came. Narada's house and all the riches he'd accumulated were swept away. Despite his frantic efforts to save his wife and children, they, too, were torn from him by the raging flood. He fainted from the shock. When he came to, he found himself lying in a desert, weeping. The torrent had subsided to a tiny rivulet that was about to dry up. At the sight of it, Narada suddenly remembered his original errand and stooped to catch some of the water in his hands. "What took you so long with that water?" chided a familiar voice behind him. "I've been waiting almost five minutes!"

Reflecting on the story, the woman saw why she'd had to wait twelve years to begin her journey. Before she could get free from the world of illusion, she'd had to do far more than foolishly tick off a checklist; she'd had to wait until the illusion grew real enough to trap her. And it was not until the moment when love finally became real that her release could begin.

A flight attendant handed her a hot towel roll, and the woman wiped her face. Lifting her window shade, she saw that the sun was rising. Across the farthest cloud bank a fiery red streak lengthened and thickened, expanding to color the whole horizon. A familiar voice inside her said: *You have no reason to hurry back.* Her mouth went dry, and the hairs on the back of her neck quivered, as the sweet thrill of freedom coursed through her.

Judy Copeland teaches creative non-fiction and composition at Richard Stockton College of New Jersey.

Aunty Mame Learns a Lesson

What do you do when your best attempts at being loveable fail?

*A*s our tour bus passed the Circus Maximus, our guide suggested that to see the arena as it might have looked in ancient Roman times, we could watch the movie *Ben Hur.*

My twelve-year-old niece turned to me with a shy smile and said, in a tiny voice: "We watched that movie in school."

I nearly leapt from my seat and kissed the tour guide. A day and a half into our trip to Italy, this was the first complete sentence Miss Thing had volunteered. As it happened, it would be about the last.

Was it her age, just a hair's breadth from teenaged?

Was she just a very quiet young lady? (I don't think I could have remained silent for a full day, much less a week, at her age.) Was it severe culture shock? Or did she merely loathe me?

I embarked on this trip with Auntie Mame ambitions. My husband and I are childless, but not immune to the delights of time spent with the next generation. I wanted to reach out to the future, so I borrowed a child. My generous gesture was selfish but, I like to think, in a good way.

I planned to show Miss Thing a different kind of life than she saw at home and introduce her to the wide world, the thrills of travel, independence, and girl-power. I wanted to give her a glimpse of limitless possibilities.

Because we lived in different cities, Miss Thing and I saw each other only once a year, but always got along well. She was quiet, but inevitably loosened up with me. I figured we'd need just a few hours for the awkwardness of unfamiliarity to drop away. I imagined us giggling on tour buses, snapping pictures of each other among the antiquities, sharing sinful desserts, ogling soulful-eyed Italian boys.

Miss Thing lives in suburban northern California, in one of those shiny new developments that seem to appear from nowhere, swallowing up entire hills and fields while you're away for the weekend. She attends Catholic school, plays soccer, goes to a local swimming pool, watches TV reality shows, spends a week each summer in church camp, takes family vacations to see her cousins on the East Coast. This would be her first trip abroad. We would spend most of our time in Rome with a side trip to Sorrento and Pompeii, which was her idea and a place I'd longed to see since I was a difficult twelve-year-old myself. Sullen young ladies like the idea of entire towns buried in molten lava.

My intentions were honest, but all my most sincere attempts at being loveable were met with polite dispassion. Miss Thing, to my dismay that on one occasion drove me to tears, had nothing to say to me.

I brought a scrapbook, colored pencils, and glue sticks so we could record our memories each evening. I gave her the window seat *every time*. I tried to buy her t-shirts and jewelry and ice creams. I asked questions which received the most minimal responses—either "O.K.," "That's O.K." (translation, "no thank you), or "I don't know," sometimes represented only by a shrug. I chattered determinedly, sometimes depressed but never defeated by Miss Thing's obstinate silence. Heaven knows how irritating I might have been. Miss Thing wasn't saying. We called her parents frequently—I thought it would help quell homesickness. She whispered into the phone while I discreetly retired to another room (usually the bathroom) in case she wanted the freedom to vent about terrible Aunty Mame.

Was it the chaos of Rome that rendered Miss Thing silent? Certainly nothing in her tidy world could have prepared her for the assault of Rome's streets in midsummer. The Trevi Fountain, steps from our hotel, was hectic at all hours. Each night after dinner, we bought gelato and ate it sitting on the fountain steps in front of the Pantheon while the carnival of life surged around us. One night we watched a junkie tenderly feed water to a sickly little bird before carrying it gently away in cupped hands. I had a hard time shaking the image. "I wonder what happened to the baby bird," I mused to Miss Thing the next afternoon. She blinked.

If Miss Thing scorned my obvious, foolish vanity each time I was mistaken for a local, she didn't so much as let an eye roll. If her feet hurt from treading Rome's baking pavement in flip-flops, she never complained. (I advised sensible shoes in my packing list, but as I recall, my mother and I never agreed on shoes, either.)

Pompeii was hotter than I could ever imagine, and thrilling as I always had. Miss Thing snapped copious photos. "My favorite part was the houses," I said later, over dinner, with a satisfied sigh.

"   " replied Miss Thing, thoughtfully.

We visited the Blue Grotto on a busy Sunday, waiting for ages outside the cave entrance before it was our turn to climb into a rowboat and duck into the cave, where our oarsman bellowed "*O Solo Mio*" as he rowed us once around. "That was a lot of waiting for a five minute ride," I complained on the speedboat ride back to the marina.

"Mmm" said Miss Thing, in what I like to think was hearty agreement.

I sought ways to make Miss Thing feel more at home. Our hotel in Sorrento had a lovely, large swimming pool and we spent hours there. Miss Thing took a break from pizza and *spaghetti pomodoro* by ordering what was listed as an "American-style hamburger" in the hotel restaurant menu, but seemed disheartened by a suspicious bun-free patty that was placed in front of her, garnished with a sliver of ham. "Maybe they think the ham makes it a hamburger," I volunteered.

"   " said Miss Thing, skeptically.

In Rome, to escape the midday heat, Miss Thing and I frequently retired to our room to indulge in an activity that seemed to soothe her: watching TV. We had one English-language channel, SkyNews from the BBC, but opted instead for Italian and French TV once we discovered a language nearly as universal as love: game shows. On game shows, hosts are universally smarmy, formats are familiar, pop culture references are shared ("Michelle Pfeiffer" is the same in any language) and we could almost, nearly, just about, play along. Sometimes I heard Miss Thing whisper a guess at the answers.

For a particularly homey feeling, we watched the Italian version of *The Bachelor*.

"He looks gay," I said of the handsome bachelor.

"Maybe that's the twist at the end," Miss Thing said, in a tantalizing glimpse of the humor she withheld.

Though she lolled comfortably through our TV hours, Miss Thing remained, for the most part, silent.

Miss Thing did her job of sightseeing dutifully and without complaint. She was entranced by St. Peter's, I could tell by the way she burned through her film. She sprinted purposefully ahead of me through the Vatican Museum toward the distant Sistine Chapel. She listened intently to her recorded tour of the Colosseum. She even broke down and bought herself souvenirs—a silver ring, a dainty blouse, some fashionably dangly earrings—near the end of our trip, but not until I told her that the money she spent would not be mine, but money her father supplied for this very purpose.

I was cheered on our next-to-last night when, instead of her usual gelato in a cup, she ordered a cone instead. A cone seemed more festive. Perhaps, I thought, as we sat in our regular spot by the fountain, she was loosening up.

"No matter how many times I see the Pantheon, it still thrills me," I said, licking a drip of chocolate-orange gelato from my wrist.

"   " said Miss Thing, cryptically.

I finally blurted out the situation to Miss Thing's parents when we were nearly ready to return home. They were dismayed and as puzzled as I.

But then, back home, looking at my pictures from the trip, I was stunned to find Miss Thing smiling happily in all the posed photos I took of her—in front of the Pieta, over her spaghetti one night in Rome, in the spa in Pompeii. It was a smile I never saw in our interactions, didn't notice through the viewfinder. Her father tells me she started chattering about the trip the moment she got home.

I'm not sure what to make of this. I am Aunty Mame deflated and sobered but not discouraged. After all, I did give Miss Thing her first trip to Europe. And she gave me my first trip to the dark side of adolescence from an adult's perspective.

When I told my mother about the trip, a strange expression crossed her face. "You did the same thing to me when we you were fifteen and I took you to London," she said.

"Oh," I replied.

Sophia Dembling is the author of The Making of Dr. Phil *and* The Yankee Chick's Survival Guide to Texas. *She lives in Dallas.*

ℬ ℬ ℬ

In the Hamam

A Turkish bath offers a traveler a glimpse behind the
veiled lives of Muslim women.

During a visit to Istanbul I became enchanted by
the sensual enjoyment of life evident in Byzantine
and Turkish art and culture. The intricate work in tile,
mosaic, and wood, and the subtly hypnotic geometric
designs of the richly dyed carpets and carved plaster
moldings evoke a conception of life and beauty mysterious and mathematical in its complexity. Though I
expected to be and was disturbed by the way most of
the women in the city seemed so covered up and hidden
away, by how they stayed behind a latticed enclosure in
the back of the mosques when they went to pray, if they
went to pray, so as not to distract the male worshippers, I
came to understand an entirely different attitude toward
pleasure and being—beneath the more apparent aspects

of life in a country where the predominant religion is
Islam.

During my stay, I went twice to the beautiful
Cemberlitas Bath, or *hamam*, and experienced something
I've never known before. Commissioned by the wife of
Sultan Selim II, mother of Murat III, the bath was built
in 1584, based on a plan by the great Turkish architect,
Mimar Sinan. Each side of the double bath—one for
men, one for women—consists of three separate spaces.
After arranging for your bath, as well as a massage, if
you like, in the entrance hall, where you can also have a
glass of fresh orange juice later, you enter into the long,
carpeted dressing room, where lockers line the walls;
here you leave your clothes and are given a towel. You
proceed to an inner room that acts as a buffer between
the huge inner hot room and the dressing room. Here
are more towels stacked on shelves, toilets, benches
for resting. The inner room of the bath is constructed
completely of marble: the enormous dome, with star-
shaped or round cutouts that allow light to enter; the
walls, floor, and several open washing cubicles set with
fountains of warm and cool water. The big circular slab
of marble in the center is heated from beneath. All of the
marble surfaces are warm, exuding heat, but the circular
slab where you lay your towel and stretch out is hot.

We women lay out on the circle dreaming and luxuriating like great cats. We were all nude, of every conceivable size, shape, color, age, and nationality, including
several Turkish women. The heavy, wet heat, almost suf-
focating, seeped into me, causing in seconds the sweat to
pour profusely down my body. Women's voices echoed
off the marble walls and caught like wisps of mist in
the heavy air—the voices of women speaking in many

different languages, women sighing, laughing, chatting. For half an hour or more I lay there, every fiber of my being relaxing, melting in the heat, my soul relaxing, floating in the dense, humid atmosphere, my mind emptying, voices echoing in my blood, it seemed. I lay with my eyes closed, or I watched the suds being worked into the flesh of a woman lying on the edge of the circular slab by one of the Turkish women who worked there. Finally, one of these women motioned to me to come and lie down before her. I stretched out on my wet, hot towel, first face down, while she scrubbed my body hard with a rough sponge. She scrubbed me as if she were scrubbing a carpet—up and down, up and down. She held up my legs and scrubbed those, one by one. Then she tapped me to turn over and repeated the process on the front of my body. She tapped me again and motioned for me to sit up. She did my arms as I sat happily and lazily before her, gazing at the skin of her upper breasts and the lovely skin stretched over her belly.

These women wore bikini underpants and bras. Most of them were what in the West would be called fat, but looking at them, admiring them, I thought, they are not fat. They had large breasts and had let their stomachs fall forward after childbirth—round and beautiful. I am sure this is considered beautiful in Turkey. I found myself wanting to rub the stomach of the woman who worked on me and make a wish, or lay my head on her breast and fall asleep, for I felt like a child being lovingly yet firmly washed by her mother. She threw buckets of warm water over me to wash off the dead skin, which hung in pieces from my arms and legs. Then she motioned me to lie down again and began the massage with warm, soapy water. She worked up each vertebra and down again, pulled my toes, kneaded me. They use fine cotton material folded and sewn together on one side, so that when they dip it into the soapy water and hold it up over you, the material opens up in the middle and they wring and shake the bubbles out over your prone or supine body. I was in a trance of physical delight, given over and without a care. When I sat up she massaged my arms and shoulders and neck, pulling the muscles up, then smoothing them down, as if she were pulling and relaxing taffy. She then led me by the hand so I would not slip in my own soapy runoff on the smooth marble to one of the wall fountains, where I sat on a marble bench while she washed my hair. Again she threw buckets of warm water over my head and body until all the soap was washed away. Sometimes she sang snatches of Turkish song.

When she left me I sat there and rested awhile. Then I walked back to the center of the room and lay down on the marble slab until I was ready to return to the middle room, where I discarded my soaking towel and took a fresh one to dry myself and wrap up in. When I came out into the locker area and looked in the mirror, I saw I was beet red in the face from the heat, but all the pores of my body were open and clean. I felt every impurity had been sweated out and washed away.

I've never had an experience like this, naked among other women, no one at all self-conscious (as I would normally have been); we were women enjoying the fleshly camaraderie of other women, all women, just because we were women. This was our beauty: that we were women, and our beauty resided not in youth or shapeliness but in the female body itself. I understood, as in a revelation, that the body is beautiful in and of itself, whatever its age, size, shape. All the bodies I had been among were beautiful. My body was beautiful. I felt this very strongly for the first time in my life. There was a perfume of women, an atmosphere of women beautiful in their bodies. When I went to the dressing room to retrieve my clothes from the locker, we women smiled at one another, as if we had shared a sweet intimacy, which we had, and we looked at each other from the corners of our eyes as if we had a secret. I smiled at the Turkish woman who had so thoroughly washed and massaged me. She had come out to cool off and rest, and I touched her on the shoulder and looked in her eyes. Warm. She smiled back and looked into my eyes.

My time at the bath was a liberating and enriching experience, a stupendous opportunity to shake off that peculiarly Western sense of shame in the body, and the accompanying neurosis about what one has to look like, should look like, what beauty is, how ugly aging is, how one is no longer considered appealing after forty-five or so—which is all unnatural, wrong. I felt I'd been given an unexpected gift—that I'd slipped behind one of the veils and seen something previously invisible to me. We live too often on the surface of things in the West, and most of all in youth-driven America. Too much is surface-defined and evaluated, including beauty, talent, Eros. Though we may fight against this, the pressure is almost overwhelming to read, judge, and register things on the surface and according to superficial values, and you see and feel yourself being judged by others according to those values. You have to escape in your own way and battle or ignore what belittles life—and seek out what illuminates and enlarges it.

My sojourn in Istanbul, an intense experience lived through the eye and the body, opened me to other, deeper conceptions of beauty, naturalness, and grace, and to the wisdom of possibilities of communion and understanding that reside in these soul-bodies that we are.

Sharon Balentine has published poems over the last thirty years in several literary magazines, such as Aileron, Borderlands: Texas Poetry Review, Stone Drum, Poesia y Calle, *and* West Wind Review, *as well as two chapbooks of poetry (*Isis *and* Spellbound*). A poem published in* Skylark *was nominated for the Pushcart Prize, and she is included in the anthology of poetry,* Terra Firma. *Several prose pieces have appeared in* Travelers' Tales *anthologies, including* Women in the Wild *and* A Woman's Path. *Her short stories have appeared in* The Missouri Review, The Tulane Review, Pangolin Papers, *and* StoryQuarterly, *among others.*

GISELE RAINER

ɬɬ ɬɬ ɬɬ

Passage Out of Madagascar

Her exit would prove shaky indeed.

"Carry these insects over the bridge, and I promise you a ride into Tana. It is the best offer you will get." Jean-Baptiste crouched down to wrap my fingers around the plastic grip on the trunk in the dirt between us. He removed his wire-rimmed glasses and turned his face into the khaki covering his shoulder, wiping the sweat out of his eyes. He replaced his glasses and caught me admiring him. One corner of his mouth turned up. His green eyes crinkling with his smile.

"What?" he asked, now grinning fully.

"What?" I answered, eyebrows raised. I felt the heat rising in my cheeks. I managed to blink and look away.

He shook his head, still grinning, shuffled me around, and then bungeed his other trunk on top of my pack and sleeping bag. He took my right hand and raised it to the side. "Use this hand to balance and to grab with if you go down. Aim for the wooden ties. Try to avoid the empty spaces in between." He started to heave one of his suitcases to his head.

"Wait! What if the drawers slide open? I don't want these bugs running up my arm and down my neck out there in the middle. And how do you know I won't get a better offer? One that doesn't, say, involve hauling trunks of insects while tight-rope walking across a 100-foot gorge on what's left of a mostly-collapsed railroad bridge?"

"First," he opened one of the tidy little drawers in the trunk, revealing two arachnid cadavers spiked to Styrofoam, "they no longer run." He shoved the little drawer back into place. "Second, this is Madagascar. I do not know how the first twenty-eight days of your holiday on this island have evolved, but the next two may be tricky. Believe it or not, Gisele, you are not necessarily in control of this situation. Come on. Before the rest of this bridge collapses."

I leaned toward the cliff and peered over. Smashed bridge timbers lay splayed across the rocks like Pick-up-Stix. "Are you sure it's safe?"

"Were you sure you would be safe when you crossed half the world to come to Madagascar?" He bent down to lift one of his suitcases. Sandy curls, not quite as gray as those visible just above the last button of his open collar, fell across his forehead.

"Wait! Tell me again: how will we get to Tana?"

He sighed. "My headquarters in Tana is sending a car and driver to collect me, but the car will not be able to cross the bridge for the same reason that your train could not cross it. As you have seen," he raised one arm toward the gorge, "the bridge is no longer passable." He paused, his sea-glass eyes watching for my reaction. "Look, I've known you for half an hour. I did not find you. You found me. You spotted me at the station and asked if I could help you get back to Tana so that you would be sure to be on your plane to Seychelles day after tomorrow. I am offering you a way back."

"All right," I whispered.

He must have realized, suddenly, how frightened I was. He reached out and brushed a finger down my cheek. "Concentrate very hard on where you place your feet. After each step, look forward to the next tie. Do not look through. Stay to the left, but not too near the edge. There is no longer a rail. We will travel very slowly." He heaved both suitcases to his head, then swiveled back to me. "Do you know a song you want to sing? If you sing, your mind will be too occupied to be frightened. Let's go." He wobbled around, regained his balance, and started across. I hooked my right index finger through his back belt loop and followed, placing each step in the spot where his had just been.

"You are my SUNshine, my only SUNshine." It started low, under my breath. On every other beat we managed one more tie. "You make me HAPpy, when skies are GRAY." The river tumbled over rocks and broken timbers 100 feet below. I didn't want to see it. I focused on Jean-Baptiste. I sang louder. "You'll never KNOW, dear, how much I LOVE you..." By the time we were mid-span, I was shouting out the words between sobs.

What was left of the bridge trembled and creaked with each of our strides. The gaps between the ties shimmered in and out of focus. Only Jean-Baptiste stood out in hyper-clarity. Sweat beaded in my eyebrows and on my upper lip, ran between my back and my t-shirt, and threatened my grip on the plastic trunk handle.

Then scent of earth and foliage began to overtake old tar and petroleum. Shrubs and trees on the far side came into focus. Weeping, gasping, singing, laughing, we collapsed in the red dirt on the other bank. Thunder erupted from the locals who had gathered back on the Moramanga side to witness the two foreigners' strange progress. Jean-Baptiste lifted my hand into the air like a referee with a winning boxer after a fight. The crowd sent up another cheer.

We managed three or four kilometers on foot, but the bugs and Jean-Baptiste's Samsonites were unwieldy and slowed us down. We walked the pot-holed road for an hour, then sat in the grass for two, then walked some more, hoping for a distant whir or an approaching red dust cloud. Neither materialized.

We traded stories of our hometowns—Nice and San Francisco. We lunched on half a package of chocolate biscuits. We took turns napping and reading. We played charades on the riverbank.

"Do you play gin?" I ventured. We lay back in the grass, our heads on my pack.

"I'd rather drink it." He twisted a strand of my hair around his finger.

"Don't you get homesick and lonely studying bugs in the forests of Madagascar for months on end?"

"Probably no more lonely than you get traveling around the world on your own for months on end."

By five o'clock, Madagascar's winter sunlight had thinned to dusk, and we realized that the car would not come. We had walked ourselves out of reach of any habitation. The temperature had dropped into the forties. In layers, over my shorts and t-shirt, I put on everything left in my pack: my leggings and another t-shirt, my jeans and sweatshirt, two more pairs of socks. Jean-Baptiste stood by, watching me evolve into the Michelin man.

"Aren't you going to get anything out of those suitcases of yours?" I asked him.

"They carry notebooks, not clothes. I am afraid I am entirely in your hands." He grinned.

We chose a rising spot of earth at the base of a ramy tree to spread my tarp and our rain jackets. We unlaced our boots and tucked my sleeping bag up under our chins. Clouds slid over the moon in the midnight blue. Bright eyes flickered in and out of the rustling darkness.

"Can't sleep?" Jean-Baptiste whispered.

"Not really."

He reached out and pulled me up against him. "Don't worry. There are no poisonous snakes in Madagascar."

"Nonpoisonous ones can also deliver an unpleasant bite."

"Good night, Gisele."

We finished the rest of the chocolate biscuits with a bottle of water for breakfast. Lanky Indri-Indris flew through the canopy above us, crying their infant-like cries. A sudden yellow stream of lemur pee arced its way out of the branches and sprayed the ground next to me. We scrambled, laughing, out of range, back into the road's clearing.

We walked until we came to a small cluster of buildings. A hand-lettered sign on the central building advertised a café. Three or four brick homes with pitched tin roofs rose up around the fringes. We introduced ourselves to the owners.

"So you are Jean-Baptiste, the visiting French scientist. Your colleague, Roger, stopped by yesterday. He asked if you had been here. Apparently, the director of the international aid organization for which you work recently made a comment that was badly received by our president. Shortly after you radioed for a car, your director was expelled from Madagascar and your organization's offices in Tana were indefinitely closed. No car was sent, but Roger said to say that he would be in the next settlement visiting his daughter, if you still needed a ride."

Jean-Baptiste took my face in his hands and planted a firm kiss on my mouth. "You see, I am keeping my promise to you." My legs trembled like the Moramanga bridge.

We set out to find Roger. "I am not surprised," Jean-Baptiste confided to me. "The government's relationship with the foreign aid organizations at work here is tepid at best. Neither group feels it is sufficiently appreciated by the other. It was inevitable. *Tant pis*. I needed a vacation anyway. How long will you be in Seychelles?"

Jean-Baptiste recognized Roger's Land Rover in front of a house not half an hour from the café. Guitar and accordion music accompanied raucous singing flooding from its windows to the road. The brick walls of the tidy common room scarcely contained the extended family that had gathered there. Roger shouted a welcome over the clamor, then shoved cups of something sweet and strong in our hands. The music developed into a *sega*. Jean-Baptiste and I locked hips and swayed our way through the crowd until we swam in each other's sweat.

Hours later, we climbed, wet and unsteady, into the Land Rover for the last stretch back to Tana. There were twelve of us, plus gear. I squeezed in on Jean-Baptiste's lap. His hands drifted to the skin under my t-shirt and along my thighs as he and Roger argued politics. I leaned my arms and forehead against the back of the seat in front of me and tried to focus on the discussion, but my mind kept slipping down to Jean Baptiste's hands. Ultimately I gave up trying, and let my mind go where it wanted. By the time we rolled in to Tana town I could hardly breathe.

"You can drop us at the Select, Roger." Jean-Baptiste brushed the hair back from my face. "It's not the best hotel in town, but the rooms are clean, and it's safe. Is it O.K. with you?"

"Any place. Really. Wherever."

We tumbled out.

"No man should be made to suffer so sweetly for so long." He smiled, adjusting his khakis, smoothing them out at the fly. "Let's check in first, then have dinner, and then I have something I want to show you."

I followed him on buttery legs through the security door and up a flight of stairs to the registration desk.

"Monsieur Jean-Baptiste!" The clerk reached for Jean-Baptiste's hand, taking me in at a glance.

"I need a room, Michel," he smiled over at me. "And one for my friend."

His words hit me like a knock-out blow. As I came to, both men were watching me, waiting for me to respond to something.

I shook my head. "Sorry?"

"Michel says they have only one room left. Do you mind if I take it? I stay here whenever I come into headquarters from the field station. My employer has a contract here. The Hotel de France is just down the street. It's a much nicer place. I'll walk you."

"No, no. I don't mind. No need to walk me." The linoleum floor came at me in waves as I tried to maneuver myself and my pack back over to the stairs.

"Really, Gisele. You must not walk alone. It is almost dark. Michel, can you find someone to accompany her? Gisele, I will meet you in the dining room of your hotel in half an hour."

I staggered the block and a half to the Hotel de France behind the young boy Michel had rounded up as my security guard, asking myself how I could have so badly misread the situation. Was I really that lonely? Had I been away from things so very long? By the time I reached the registration desk, I had convinced myself that Jean-Baptiste was just being discreet.

I asked for the best room they had. It was a corner room on the second floor, with a double bed. I ran the hottest water I could manage into the tub, added shampoo for bubbles, and sank back against the porcelain.

The phone woke me. Nothing looked familiar. Then it streamed back in: Moramanga, the bridge crossing, the night on the road, Jean-Baptiste's hands, the scene at the Select. The water was still warm, but not hot. The bubbles had evaporated. The phone rang again. I leaped out of the tub, grabbed the robe from the hook on the door and ran for the phone.

"Jean-Baptiste?"

"You're late. I'm downstairs."

"Come up."

"I'll be in the dining room." He hung up.

I pulled on my jeans and a t-shirt and found him

downstairs. He stood up, took my hands in his and kissed me on each cheek. "Is your room comfortable?"

"Come see for yourself." I smiled and tugged him toward the stairs.

He stared hard at me.

"Jean-Baptiste, what…"

He pressed his finger against my lips and shook his head. "Let's eat. I have something I want to show you after. I don't want it to get too late."

We tucked into our zebu steaks and *pommes frites* with embarrassing appetite, and got tipsy off a bottle of house red. It was nearly ten o'clock when we slipped out through the iron gate and into the back seat of the Land Rover.

I leaned my head on his shoulder. "Where…" I traced the outline of his cheekbone and jaw with my fingertip, "…are you taking me?"

He caught my wrist and placed my hand back in my lap. "Don't. Please. Be patient."

Roger sped through Tana's labyrinth. He ignored the stop signs. "Too risky," he'd say, as he blew through, blaring his horn. He pulled to the curb somewhere. "Don't let go of my hand," Jean-Baptiste whispered to me as he drew me out of the car. "Stay alert, look around you, and if you see anything that frightens you, scream as loudly as you can." He held a knife in his other hand.

We jogged down a blackened alley then up some back stairs to a third-floor landing. The air pulsed with the stench of open sewers and old garbage. He knocked at a rotting door. A flurry of Malgache exploded out of the alley.

"Come on, come on. Open up," he whispered. He shifted his weight from one foot to the other. He looked back over our shoulders, then brushed his lips over my hair. "Do not be afraid. They will open in a moment."

A rustling came from somewhere inside, then some sliding sounds, scraping of furniture, maybe, across wood floors, then more shuffling and the light clinking of keys on a ring. A woman's voice floated out on a whisper: "*Qui est là? C'est toi, Jean-Baptiste? C'est toi?*"

"*Oui, oui. C'est moi, Adele.*"

A key turned in the lock and we slid in through the brief, narrow opening.

A smooth-skinned Merina woman in her mid-forties embraced first Jean-Baptiste, then me. She took my hand in both of hers and stroked it, her eyes searching Jean-Baptiste's. "Whom have you brought us, Jean-Baptiste?"

"Adele, this is Gisele. She is an American. Her father is French. We've spent the last two days together, stranded along the Moramanga-Tana road after the bridge collapse, and," he paused to pass the backs of his fingers over my cheek, "I was glad to have a companion." He dropped his arm and shifted his eyes to hers. "I want her to meet Sophie and Maxim." Adele gave him a soft smile.

"You will find yourself in trouble again, my dear Jean-Baptiste, if you do not take care."

Adele led us two or three steps through the cramped kitchen, which looked as if it had at one time been just a back porch, then up a step and through a door, into a room so dark, that at first nothing made sense. Then slowly, like a negative developing in solution, things began taking shape. To my left, by the window, where Adele was motioning me to sit down, were two slingback chairs with a small table in front of them. To my right was a bureau with women's hairbrushes, a men's shaving kit, and a stub of a candle burning on top. Against the far wall, but only a few feet away, was a broad, low platform with something on it.

"I will make some tea," Adele whispered.

Jean-Baptiste stood at the dresser, picking up this and that, and then putting whatever it was back down again.

"Jean-Baptiste, who are Sophie and Maxim? Why are we here?"

A small sound came from the platform against the wall, which suddenly materialized as a large bed. The something on top of it stirred, and the sound became a cry. Jean-Baptiste strode over to the bed and drew the blankets away to reveal a lovely oval face framed in a cascade of black hair, and then another, very tiny, head, topped with a diminutive stocking cap. Jean-Baptiste scooped up the baby in one arm and whisked him over to me.

"My new son, Maxim. Will you hold him?" He pressed the child into my arms, then went back to Sophie and stroked her shiny mane. "She's had a hard time. No milk yet, and Maxim is hungry. They've been feeding him by hand, but he's not well. Can you tell?"

"No, I can't. But I don't know much about babies." I carried him back to his mother.

Adele, Sophie, Jean-Baptiste, and I shared a pot of tea heated over a butane camp stove, Sophie in the big bed with Maxim, Jean-Baptiste reclining on his elbows beside her, and Adele and I in the sling-back chairs under the window. I stayed as long as I thought I could bear it.

"Thank you so much, but I have to get some sleep. My plane leaves at seven."

Jean-Baptiste stood up. "I'll take you back." He bent over and kissed the top of Sophie's head. "See you tomorrow."

He held my hand fast as we jogged down the stairs and back through the alley. Roger was waiting for us. I stared out my window as the car careered through the maze of Tana's streets. Jean-Baptiste sat silent next to me. Roger whistled in front.

"Go home, Roger. I'll get myself back to the Select," Jean-Baptiste reassured Roger as we pulled up to my hotel.

The clerk buzzed us in through the security gate.

"Can I come up?"

"No visitors after ten…" the clerk mumbled as we disappeared up the stairs.

Jean-Baptiste closed the door behind us and gathered me to him. "I am sorry."

"No, I'm sorry. I'm so embarrassed. I am so supremely self-absorbed. It never occurred to me…I just assumed that you wanted…"

"But, as you can see, it is not possible." He kissed the tears coursing down my cheeks. "Oh, Gisele. It is not so tragic. Tomorrow night you will be in Seychelles enjoying a glass of South African wine at some enchanting restaurant overlooking the Indian Ocean, and all this will seem absurd."

I dropped my forehead to his chest. "I'm so tired."

"Come on, then. Get in bed. I'll stay until you fall asleep."

The phone rang at 5:30.

"Your car is here, mademoiselle."

"My car?"

"Your driver is waiting for you."

I threw on my clothes and my pack and stumbled down the stairs.

Roger was there in the lobby.

"Monsieur Jean-Baptiste asked me to be certain that you made your flight this morning." He studied my face in the rear view mirror. "Monsieur Jean-Baptiste takes care of his people."

"Yes, I suppose he does."

Gisele Rainer lives with her husband, Albert, in San Francisco, where she practices securities law to support her travel habit.

KARI J. BODNARCHUK

☙ ☙ ☙

Awash in the Jungle

Two hikers get more adventure than
they bargained for in Malaysia.

*I*t was monsoon season in Malaysia. Perhaps not the
best time to be contemplating a hike through the
jungle. But the region had been experiencing only short
late-day showers, so we weren't very concerned. To me,
this was a great opportunity for adventure. If Geri had
had even a slight hint of the danger that lay ahead, she
never would have followed me into the jungle.

I first met Geri at a Javanese guesthouse, the week
after I was nearly attacked by four Indonesian hoodlums
posing as travel agents. I told her about the incident
and when we realized we were heading in the same
direction—west through Java and then north through
Singapore and Malaysia—we decided to stick together
for safety.

We were the most mismatched of travel companions. Geri's an accountant from Ireland, who's up by 7 A.M. every day, goes to sleep by 10 P.M., and follows a steady routine in between. I'm a writer from New England, whose brain won't function before 10 A.M. and works best after 10 P.M., and I thrive on constant change. Geri is one of eight kids; I'm an only child. She hates the water; I love to scuba dive. She also prefers a slow, easy pace, while I thrive on pushing myself to the limit.

Despite our differences, Geri and I shared an interest in exploring, and we soon discovered that traveling in a pair opened up all sorts of doors: we felt more confident staying in strangers' homes, hitchhiking through Malaysia, and trekking on our own through a jungle. Three weeks after meeting, we decided to do a nine-day hike through a Malaysian rainforest to climb the region's tallest mountain, Gunung Tahan. It was an eighty-five-mile trip, described by our guidebook as "the trek for the really adventurous," with elephants, tigers, and spitting cobras. Adventurous we were; experienced we were not. Geri had spent time walking hills near her home in Ireland, but she'd never camped or done any long-distance hikes. I'd camped dozens of times and covered quite a few trail miles, but my backcountry treks hadn't taken me far from paved roads. And all I'd ever encountered were cows, garter snakes, and a feral turkey.

The Malaysian government requires hikers to hire local guides to reach the mountain, due to the poorly marked route and tricky river crossings. But guides cost $250 per person, not including entrance fees and food, and Geri and I didn't want to blow our budgets. We figured we could make it on our own for $40, tops. It was off-season, meaning we might be the only hikers along the trail. We talked to a few locals in Kuala Tahan, a village at the start of the trek, who told us we'd find our own way, no problem. That was all I needed to hear.

We didn't want the rangers to know we weren't taking the mandatory guides, so we slipped past the park headquarters office one morning and made our way into the woods. We walked along a moderately level trail that proved easy enough to follow, despite the absence of blazes (trail markers) and other hikers. Taman Negara is the world's oldest and, in sections, densest rainforest. As we walked farther, large sections of the trail became covered in brush—not a good sign, I would realize later, but we pushed on.

We had full camping gear and food for ten days, plus the only map we could find, a locally produced, hand-drawn, not-to-scale "artistic rendering," which was photocopied and given to backpackers like us—for free—by the manager of our guesthouse. It measured six-by-nine inches and contained sketches of hikers who appeared as tall as the mountains, and exotic-looking birds and butterflies three to four times larger than the hikers. The most distinct element on this map was a dark, thick line that cut straight up the middle of the picture: a mountain-fed, green-hued river called Sungai Tahan, measuring about seventy-five-feet wide.

Our plan was to spend the first two days of the trip wending our way through the thick forest, then another two days walking alongside, crossing over, and, where possible, fording the river. After that, it was anybody's guess—our map simply depicted a black line (the river), a triangle (the mountain) and an extraordinarily tall hiker leaping up the left side of the triangle in a single bound.

Geri and I took our time hiking that first day, stopping often to look at the unusual vegetation. One bush radiated fifteen-foot stems topped with leaves the size of doorways. Massive fig trees stood so wide it would take twelve people with outstretched arms to fit around each one. Others had twenty-foot-high buttresses that resembled fins on a rocket ship.

The first night, we pitched our tent in the middle of a steep, slanting trail, unable to find a clearly marked campsite. We used bags and bug nets to try to create level sleeping surfaces, but my makeshift bedding soon shifted underneath me and I fell asleep in a ditch, sandwiched between two rocks, a root running up my spine.

The next day, we completed a grueling hike across twenty-seven hilltops on a ridge called Bukit Malang, or "Unlucky Hill." We were still having trouble deciphering our map, and it grew dark again before we found the next campsite. We pitched our tent beside the trail, on top of moss-covered branches, and I lay in bed listening to a chorus of jungle sounds—cicadas buzzing, birds squawking, and strange, unidentifiable chewing noises. I wished we were closer to the river. There is something very eerie about being deep in the woods, in an unfamiliar forest, with big animals and a bad map. I barely slept that night, especially after hearing two dead trees tumble over nearby.

The sights along the way made up for some of the discomfort. We trekked through brilliant, sunlit forests with aqua-colored palm trees, bamboo stands, and long, prickly vines that look like whips covered in thorns. We didn't see any elephants, tigers, or spitting cobras—just as well, since we didn't have a defense plan figured out anyway—but we did spot a three-horned frog, a brown snake, and a wild boar.

The end of day three took us through dense jungle and along a hillside where the narrow, steep path was slippery from wet roots and yellow clay soil. Leeches were plentiful, so we had to do regular "leech checks" as we walked to see if they had planted their suckers into our legs. As the path wound down along the river's edge, walking grew more challenging. Leaves, fallen trees, and big branches littered the trail, but it never occurred to us why there was so much forest debris along the embankment. Geri and I fought our way through the brush until we could eventually walk along a section of dry, rocky riverbed. When we stopped for water around four o'clock, I watched Geri slump onto a rock and fade.

"This is the closest I've come to hell," she declared, once she'd mustered the energy to talk.

Geri sat hunched over on the rock, with her shoulders resting on her knees and a stream of sweat trailing down her face. I had boundless energy that day and felt like I could walk at least another five miles, but I thought of Geri and said, "You know, this is a good place to stop. Let's get some rest. I'm sure we'll feel better tomorrow."

I brought Geri the stove, a pot, and four packages of curry noodle soup, and she stirred dinner while I pitched the tent. We were now thirty miles upstream on the banks of the Sungai Tahan, which was about seventy-five-feet wide here and flanked by thick jungle bush. It was a calm, idyllic setting, though, and appeared to be the perfect place to camp. With a steep, brushy slope on one side of us and ten feet of rocky riverbed on the other, there was just one spot to put the tent—in a manmade clearing at the foot of the hill, about thirty feet from the water's edge.

A late-day shower hit as dinner was served, so we ate in the tent, leaving the dirty dishes outside for morning (in retrospect, not a good idea, but luckily they didn't attract any animals). Geri collapsed from exhaustion while I fumbled with my journal, trying to record the day's events before light disappeared. Our "long-lasting" flashlight batteries had died the first night in the jungle, so we were forced to bed at sundown, 7 P.M. Geri can fall asleep before the stars are fully awake. I can't go to bed before midnight, regardless of how tired I am, which is why I took two sleeping pills around seven o'clock and then drifted right off to sleep. It seemed only minutes later when I heard a distant voice.

"Hey! Wake up!" Blah, blah. Swish. I fused these sounds into my dream.

Shhhh..."Kari!"...Shhhhh. Was I dreaming of a waterfall?

"Look!" Blah, blah. Was I dreaming of someone beckoning me to come see frothy water plunging over an embankment?

Cashoosh. Or maybe a flushing toilet?

"Get up! Get up! It's coming in here!" Geri now yelled into my ear, trying to snap me awake.

"What?" I asked, still punchy from the sleeping pills.

"I said, it's coming in here! The river," Geri insisted.

"Oh, Ger. That's not the river," I said, as water gushed through the bug-net door and slapped against my sleeping bag. We're too far away from the river, I thought to myself. It can't be the river.

I lay in a dreamy haze, refusing to believe what was happening, but then, swooshhhh—another wave hit and my survival instinct kicked in. "My god, it's the river," I suddenly realized. I threw on my rain pants and jacket and scrambled to the door.

"C'mon. C'mon," I muttered, jerking and tugging at the rusty zipper. "C'mon. It won't open!" I yelled. Geri rustled around for a knife to slash our way out, but the zipper finally came unstuck. I yanked open the door and we lunged outside, like birds spooked from their nest. The river, once calm and soothing, was now a thundering torrent, carrying prickly vines, palm trees, and logs as big as telephone poles toward us.

"Quick, Ger. Get the boots! We have to find the boots," I shouted over the rumbling floodwater.

Several short, scraggly bushes kept the debris from hitting us while we scrambled to find the smelly boots and dirty dishes we'd left outside under the rain flap for the night. Faint moonlight filtered through the trees, but our eyes hadn't adjusted enough to see. Frantically, we combed the water with our hands.

"I found one!" yelled Geri, chucking a boot onto the hill.

"Great! Just three more," I called back, still searching.

But within thirty seconds, the water rose from our ankles to our knees, and the current made it nearly impossible to stand. We had to escape. I threw on my backpack, ripped the tent out of the ground and ran— tent pegs, dishes and boots still floating somewhere behind us.

Barefoot and hunched over, we clawed our way up the steep, muddy slope behind our campsite. The igloo-shaped rental tent I dragged behind me was still set up, and I could hear poles snapping as I forced it between trees. When I looked back, Geri was about fifteen feet away, grasping for branches to pull herself up and struggling to see without her glasses.

"Whatever you do, don't fall," I yelled. She didn't know how to swim. And, truthfully, I didn't want to have to save her. With my luck, we'd both get swept away.

After Geri made it up the hill, we sat in the mud, staring down at the angry river.

"Good Lord!" she said. "Do you think we'll ever make it back?"

"Not a chance," I said. "We've trekked thirty miles into a jungle without a guide, we never registered or bought permits to enter the park, no one knows we're here and the path is long gone." I didn't know yet that our photocopied map was also completely soaked and illegible.

I fought to swallow the lump welling in my throat—a combination of tears, vomit, and desperation—and hugged my knees so they'd stop shaking. Geri didn't reply. We sat in silence for a while, until I eventually gathered my courage and said, "We'll make it, but it won't be easy—especially without boots."

Along with our camp stove, dishes, and tent pegs, three boots had washed away. We passed the one surviving boot back and forth, taking turns feeling and smelling it. It was definitely mine, we agreed. Then we curled up on top of the collapsed tent and wrapped ourselves in emergency blankets. The sky was now perfectly clear, moonlight dancing across the whitewater below and water dripping from the trees overhead, making a crackling sound as it hit our aluminum blankets. Chilled and exhausted, I hoped the sleeping pills were still in my system. Something, sleeping pills or shock, finally knocked me out, and I slept seven solid hours on a wet tent with my feet in the mud.

The next morning, the sun shone brightly in the clear blue sky, and the river, although brown with sediment, had partially receded. We slid down the mucky, chewed-up slope to survey the damage and do a full inventory of our gear. Amazingly, I found my metal cooking pot about ten feet from where our tent had stood. It was sitting upright, between the exposed roots of a tree, half filled with sand and topped off with water. Without that pot, we'd have had to chew on dry rice and dehydrated soup for three days. The stove was gone, but we had fuel tablets and could easily make our own cooking platform.

As it turned out, the surviving boot wasn't mine. My $190 Garmonts were somewhere downriver. "That's that, so get over it," I told myself. But I watched with envy as Geri laced up her left boot, then put a thick, red sock on her other foot. Unlike Geri, who'd bought new clothes for the hike (this being her first big trekking adventure), I was wearing stuff I'd had for months. None of it was pretty, and most of it was just barely functional. I glanced down at my threadbare socks and then twisted them around until their holes peered up at me. We slathered our feet with salt to keep the leeches at bay, and then, after one more fruitless search for my boots, began our three-day, thirty-mile jungle trek back to safety—in four socks and one boot. I was truly dreading the idea of hiking through a leech-ridden jungle wearing just socks.

Although the river had receded somewhat, we were no longer able to cut across the riverbed as we had the day before in order to avoid the densely overgrown patches of trail along the embankment. Instead, we had to clamber over downed trees and piles of debris deposited at bends in the river by the flood (so that's how they got there). It took a while to climb over these four-foot-high mounds of tangled brush or scramble through thick vegetation to skirt them, yet we always managed to get back on track.

The path eventually led away from the river, along narrow, slippery ledges that hadn't seemed as treacherous with boots. One ledge was only wide enough for our feet; we had to shuffle along its slick surface with our backpacks protruding over the edge. I lost my footing just as I cleared this section and fell sideways down a steep slope, saved from dropping any farther by a thin tree.

We continued on our way, slipping, clutching branches, concentrating hard, and stepping gingerly through the forest. We eventually arrived at a campsite, which, judging by its corrugated surface and the washed-up trees, appeared to have flooded the night before as well. Geri repaired the tent poles and set up our oddly shaped "dome" on the highest spot of land we could find—about thirty feet above the river—just before the sun disappeared and the thunder began. We planned our escape routes and slept fully clothed on the hard ground inside the tent, just as a precaution. No rain fell that night.

The path now led us deeper into the woods, where the trail was covered in roots and sharp stones. Dragging one's feet when tired is not an option when walking barefoot, especially on steep terrain; the rocks and thorny vines underfoot brought tears to my eyes, and I stubbed my toes dozens of times. Just an hour into the hike, a huge splinter lodged itself into the soft cushion of my left heel. It was in too deep to dig out along the trail, so I spent the next four hours walking on the toes of that foot.

Geri's hurdle that day was getting over the twenty-seven hilltops again. She almost made it, but then collapsed on top of number twenty-six and lay motionless for half an hour. When she finally sat up, she vented her frustrations. She had taken a break from accounting work and set out to travel, she said, hoping to have a few adventures along the way. Now, she said in tears, she didn't think she could handle it.

"Ger, I can assure you this is not a typical adventure," I told her.

We spent the rest of that day in a worn-out stupor, sliding around the muddy track and tripping over fallen trees. Despite having the security of the one boot, Geri spent a good portion of the final hill on all fours. Finally, we made our way into the next campsite—another dirt clearing next to a small stream—where we would spend our last night.

I dug the splinter out of my foot and then realized I had gotten my period—two weeks early and totally unprepared—probably from the shock of the whole flash flood experience.

Just as it was my turn to eat (we had only one spoon between us), it started to rain, so we dashed into the leaky tent and watched a puddle form in the middle of the floor. The downpour lasted only about an hour before the moon and stars came out, shining brightly on that calm night. And then, about an hour after the rain, we heard it: a distant rumbling sound that grew louder and louder as the floodwater came rushing toward us from upstream. The ground seemed to shake from the force of the water. Geri and I began grabbing our back-packs, scattered clothes, and her one boot, and headed for the tent door, just as the water roared past us, about twenty feet away. The flood drove up the stream's water level within seconds. Under the moonlight, we could see whitewater bubbling over the top of the embankment, but much to our great relief, it never reached the tent. I can't even imagine how we would have handled spending another night on a muddy hillside, with our belongings floating downriver.

The last day, with feet as swollen as sausages and numb to any pain, we hiked through a level, muddy forest where the leeches seemed more prevalent and aggressive. As we covered the last few miles, we collected more cuts, scrapes, bruises, and bloodsuckers, up and down both legs—good conversation pieces, we agreed. Yet our spirits remained high, knowing that with every (painful) step we were getting closer to the end of the jungle trail. Eventually, we made it back to park headquarters, filthy and temporarily scarred, but otherwise just fine. We took off our socks to avoid drawing attention to ourselves as we passed by the park headquarters office (why would anyone hike in socks, after all!), and then walked up to the village store, where we bought rubber flip-flops to tide us over. Later, two kind local policemen would give us each a pair of dusty and abandoned hiking boots from their lost-and-found box—ideal for our future hikes and adventures.

Recently, Geri and I have started talking about doing this hike again—on a shoestring budget, with the proper walking permits, two pairs of boots each...and maybe water wings.

🖙 🖙 🖙

Kari J. Bodnarchuk is a Maine-based freelance writer who spends her spare time hiking in the New England wilderness—but never without an emergency blanket, a barometer, and a spare pair of shoes. She earned a gold award in the 2004 Lowell Thomas Travel Journalism Competition for a story on Rwanda and is author of Rwanda: Country Torn Apart *and* Kurdistan: Region Under Siege. *She writes for* Outside, Hooked on the Outdoors, Islands *and* The Boston Globe, *and has contributed to* LIFE: The Greatest Adventures of All Time, *and several anthologies, including* The Best Women's Travel Writing 2005 *and* Her Fork in the Road: Women Celebrate Food and Travel.

Bandit Territory

An American ex-Buddhist nun attempts to pass for Malay on a train trip through Thailand.

I am on a train in southern Thailand headed north up the Malay Peninsula. The train, windows shut tight against the black night air, rattles from side to side. Outside, thick vegetation crowds a landscape so different from the mountains of the north where I have spent two years. If I squint hard, I can make out rubber trees, dark tendrils reaching to the ground, bright red flowers like flecks of blood on a shadowy body, shuttered houses on stilts. Each stop seems ominously static, like the set of *Swiss Family Robinson* might look once movie production has shut down.

Southern Thais say two things to me. The first is phrased as query, after a sharp glance at my sarong and local sandals: "You. Malay?"

"No, American," I usually admit, reluctantly owning up to all that it implies. Unless I'm negotiating for budget accommodations, in which case I give myself leeway to claim my father's nationality: "Nigerian."

"You could be Malay," they insist, eager to explain that there is an indigenous group on the peninsula with Negroid features. Light brown skin and curly hair—just like mine! With my smooth Thai, they assure me, I could almost "pass."

These earnest ethnic Chinese and Thai and Lao encouraging me—a Nigerian Nordic-American girl—to pass for Malay, make me smile. The idea of passing has long intrigued me, my child's fancy piqued by accounts of light-skinned blacks who left home and became white, trading all ties to self and family for freedom, something I could understand, or wealth, something I could not. The only biracial member of my family, I devoured tales of tragic mulattas who married white men then waited in horror to see how dark the children would turn out.

For me, with my brown skin and dark curls and round nose, passing in its most commonly used sense—for white—was out of the question. As if to underscore the point, I'd been born to a Nordic-American mother whose family of tall blondes embodied American ideals more than most Americans. While it didn't bother me not to look like them, it was frustrating not even being able to pass for what I actually was. I was fascinated by those mixed-race children with golden skin and wild sheaves of hair like straw. Delicate, exotic birds, they clung to their white mothers in public, as if their blue and green and hazel eyes that passed through and over me, refusing to see the world staring at them, were indeed transparent.

Unlike them, I looked like every other brown girl, my split heritage hidden from the naked eye.

I worried. How, then, would my tribespeople, the other Nigerian-Nordic-Americans, recognize and come to claim me?

What I wanted most to be recognized as was Nigerian, a foreign identity I imagined might account for my perpetual feelings of misplacement. In college, I studied other African students—their dark skin firm as tree trunks, their bodies so strong they nearly burst out of their flimsy European clothes—and gave up. There was no imitating the deliberate roll of the girls' hips, the way the boys threw back their heads and laughed, white teeth flashing. They were too confident to have come from any country I knew. And so I passed for African-American, a dynamic which carrying no privilege, was not even considered passing. I was just another insecure brown girl on the unwelcome shores of America.

The second thing locals on the Malay Peninsula say is: "Be careful. Armed bandits."

Southern Thailand is notorious for gun-toting robbers and smugglers who roam in bold bands, sometimes posing as shaven, saffron-clad monks, oftentimes murdering their victims. The Bangkok papers teem with sensational reports of gangs attacking long-distance buses then slinking into jungle lairs or melting over the border to Malaysia. It is whispered that some villages are virtually owned by bandit leaders, who conscript young men into service like the drug warlords of the north. Popular books and movies, on the other hand, claim bandits find easy followings, due to Robin Hood-like tendencies to steal from the landed and give to the poor.

So far I've been lucky. A woman—and *farang* (foreigner)

at that—traveling solo with her wealth in a single bag is a laughably easy mark. When queried about the existence and location of my Protective Male, I reply that I am a serious student on *thudong* (pilgrimage) and have only recently stopped being a Buddhist nun. No men for me!

"*Buad maechi?*" the Thai exclaim in disbelief, and I nod, yes, I did indeed ordain. My close cap of curls, just now recovering from the razor, supports this wild claim. All interest in my recalcitrant Protective Male now lost to the desire to make merit for their karma, they confide which guesthouses are not in league with bandits, which towns to avoid. And except for once hearing gunshots during dinner near the Malaysian border and having to shutter the kerosene lamps and lie with faces pressed to the floorboards for the rest of the evening, nothing untoward has happened.

Staring out the train window at the murky, abandoned streets, I decide that good karma and luck may not be enough this time. It occurs to me that the Thai's two discussion points are somehow enmeshed to my advantage, that I can best *be careful* of armed robbers by *passing* as Malay. Many of the bandits are rumored to be ethnic Malays, members of the Muslim separatist movement fighting against Thai Buddhist government. The less foreign I am, I try to reassure myself, the greater the likelihood that I will be passed over when choices are made to rape, rob, and kill.

I stand up and stagger through the rocking train, keeping my movements muted and tight, resolving to be less forthcoming in my conversation. In the north, no matter how Thai I acted, I was always too big, too brown, my body movements too unrestrained. There was never any possibility of melting into the scenery. Now, if viewed at a distance, my very brownness might save me.

In the dining car, three men in the snowy shirtsleeves and dress slacks of Thai businessmen blow my cover. First they send the waiter to my table to ask if I speak English; then they insist on buying me dinner. They look to be in their mid-twenties, which means thirty-something, and are on a slow, steady path to drunkenness, having chosen pricey Singha beer rather than cheap Mekong whiskey. Everything about them, from their pinkening faces and expansive gestures, to their courtly invitations of "Please to join us," seems more intent on impressing each other than me.

I accept.

Their questions, phrased in excellent English, are the usual suspects: *Where do you come from? How do you like Thailand? Where is your husband? Can you eat Thai food?*

I reply in English, with a few Thai words dropped in, pretending to speak far less than I actually do. This is Plan B: if unable to pass as Malay, always make sure your opponent underestimates you.

They crow with delight to hear my simple Thai, and when I cover my rice with tiny green heaps of chilies, there is much giggling and nudging. "Look, look," they tell each other, squirming with delight. "The *farang* eats Thai chilies!"

I begin to doubt the likelihood of them being hustlers. Still, I shake my head when they ask if I drink Singha and keep to tiny, chilled bottles of orange Fanta.

They order another round and tick off a list of beautiful beach islands near the Gulf, places like Phuket, Haad Yai, Koh Samui, the so-called James Bond Island, all of which will later be immortalized in big budget movies, blonde starlets spilling onto the sand like oil slicks.

I explain that I'm not on vacation. I'm on a pilgrimage in search of famous nuns.

In my pocket is my most valuable possession, next to my passport: a list of nuns and temples. Next to each woman or *wat* (temple), my teacher has scribbled the name of the province in which she or it is located or, if I'm lucky, the town. Nothing more.

Imagining myself a black female Paul Theroux, I will traverse Southeast Asia from Malaysia all the way up to Burma, throwing myself off the train wherever I hear of someone or someplace I should see. The words "I've heard of some nuns living near..." are enough to start me fumbling for my bag, heading for the exit.

"Let me see," the youngest and best-dressed business-man insists, holding out his hand. It occurs to me that this might be his promotion celebration or that he could be the CEO's son who has just landed his first big deal. He stud-ies the list, his eyes tiny slits of slate in a lobster-red face. I feel drunk just looking at him.

"Wait a minute," he says, his whiskey-softened shoul-ders tightening in alarm. He jabs a manicured finger at the very next stop on my list. "You can't go there! Petchaburi is owned by bandits!"

The train jolts around a corner, throwing my heart against my rib cage. I am scheduled to disembark in Petchaburi tonight. The town is crucial to my pilgrimage; one of the only centers for nuns is rumored to be nearby.

I shrug, feigning indifference. "*Mai pen rai,*" I say, invoking Thailand's most commonly used phrase. *Never mind. It's O.K. No problem.*

"No, no," he insists, his eyes sharpening with increasing sobriety. "The train gets in at three in the morning. They know who arrives, where they stay!"

He whips around to his friends and blurts a flurry of southern dialect. Though most of the words are familiar,

I assume a blank expression, heart still racing.

"What should she do?" one of the men asks. *"Mai dii leuy." It's not good.*

"She shouldn't go alone," he replies. "They kidnap visitors and plantation workers to extort money."

"Why doesn't she get off at your stop?" the third suggests.

"Yes," my would-be savior agrees, turning his palms to face upward, a gesture I think might be safe to interpret as sincere. "My town is larger and more secure. I can make sure she gets to a guesthouse. In the morning I can come with my car to drive her to *samnak maechi." The nun center.*

"Dii lao," the second man counsels. *Good enough.*

It is indeed a good plan. I decide to accept. I know that to ask a Thai for help, even directions, is to embark on an extended relationship in which his responsibility will not end until I have achieved my goal or safely reached my destination.

The first businessman, face red above his pristine white linen shirt, turns back to me and proposes his solution, speaking careful, clear English. "You should not get off at Petchaburi, which is the next stop," he cautions. "You should get off at Ratchaburi, the following stop, where I live." He explains why.

I look skeptical for a few minutes before making a show of allowing myself to be convinced.

The bill is then settled, a ritual involving a drunken race to unzip their clutch wallets of Italian leather, plus shouted claims and counter-claims of being the eldest and thus responsible for paying. Each tosses red and tan bills onto an increasing mound on the table.

I thank all three, placing my hands together in a steeple

and bringing them to my forehead in a traditional *wai*. This delights them immensely, though their drunken attempts to return the gesture look more Three Stooges-like than Thai. Afterward, I head back towards second-class, while they exit out the front of the dining car, to first-class, fresh bottles of Singha clinking in their hands.

"See you in a few hours," the first businessman says. "Remember not to get off at Petchaburi—wait for Ratchaburi!" We agree to meet on the platform.

Back at my seat, I find that a family, a tiny mother with three children, has joined me. Trying to keep my head respectfully below the mother's, I duck into my window seat, diagonally across from hers. Once seated, I nod and smile. The broad planes of her face twitch a moment, as if processing the information that she has inadvertently installed her family next to something strange, be it Malay or *farang*, then smooth into determined pleasantness. The two younger children freeze in mid-gesture, saucer-eyed and speechless.

The eldest child, a boy of about ten, has ended up in the seat next to mine. Spine rigid as a dancer's, he perches at the absolute edge; one more inch forward, and he would be levitating in air. He makes a fluttering gesture with his hand, an unspoken plea. His mother snaps a single syllable in southern dialect, its meaning unmistakable: *Stay!*

Keeping his head perfectly still, the boy monitors me out of the corners of his eyes, pupils rotating in their sockets as if he were performing *khon*, a Thai masked dance based on the Ramayana. He is Hanuman, the Monkey General, terrifying the demon army with his jerky movements and wildly spinning eyeballs.

Grinning to myself, I fall into that half-waking state of train travel. My limbs loosen and follow the jarring rhythm. Outside an epic battle rages, blue-faced demons pitted against Lord Rama and the monkey soldiers, little Hanuman poker-straight at my side.

When the conductor comes through the car, calling Petchaburi, my original destination, I consider jumping up and dashing for the exit. *Why have you allowed your plan to be modified?* I reprimand myself. *What if the businessman, now drunk, has forgotten our agreement? Or what if he was just talking? What if there are no armed robbers?*

I press my nose to the cold glass and peer out. The platform looks empty, though it's too dark to be sure. *What does a bandit-owned town look like?* I wonder. I imagine clusters of men with machine guns on every corner. Will they be dressed in dark blue farmers' shirts with red headbands and sashes like the opium smugglers of the north? Or in snug polyester pants with flared legs and mirrored sunglasses, like the blood vendetta gangsters in Bollywood movies? I imagine a banner strung across the train station: *Welcome to Bandit Territory!* spelled out in six-inch letters.

I decide to get off the train. Stick to my original plan. Rely on myself. I lean forward to grab the knapsack under my seat.

Just then one of the children beside me nods off, his head dropping face-first into the crook of my elbow. He is warm as a furnace, his soft cheeks like sun-ripened peaches against my skin.

Startled, I bolt upright and jerk my arm away. The stubble of his shaven head scrapes along the tender flesh of my inner arm. He squirms into fetal position, his small, round head falling into my lap like a gift.

Across the aisle, his family dozes, piled atop one another, the younger children's mouths half-open like tiny, budding flowers. I rest my hand lightly on the shoulder of the sleeping boy. The train hurtles through bandit territory.

An hour later we reach Ratchaburi, my new destination. Reluctantly, I lift the boy from my lap. His eyes flutter open for a split second, momentarily wild, and then close, the lids settling into smiling gold crescents. I drape him over both seats, and then grab my knapsack and sprint to the end of the car.

The conductor watches as I disembark and scour the length of the train in both directions. *"Khon oen?"* he asks. *Someone else?*

I nod.

A minute later he jerks his chin at me—"Malay?"

I nod.

We wait some more. The station is locked and dark. No banner, which is good. Except for a *samloh* driver asleep in the back of his three-wheeled rickshaw, the platform is empty.

Finally, the train conductor shrugs. "Sure this is the right stop?"

I wonder if I got them mixed up and was supposed to have gotten off at Petchaburi, the first stop. "Did a man get off at the last stop?" I ask.

He shakes his head, the gold braid on his cap glinting in the light from the train doorway. "No one likes to get off at these stops at night."

This is why he has kept the train waiting.

I stare open-mouthed, just now beginning to comprehend the size of his concern, of my stupidity. I know nothing about this town, other than it is an hour north of my original destination, closer to Bangkok, and therefore supposedly larger and safer. For all I know, this is the heart of bandit territory, and the businessman gets a commission on all *farang* women he lures here.

The train begins to snort and strain, like an animal in restraint, and the conductor hops onto the metal step. "*Glap maa?*" he offers. *Do you want to get back on?*

I shake my head. In the *wat* they taught us to confront the very things that terrify us. Or perhaps I am simply paralyzed with indecision.

With a great squeal, the train pulls away. "Good luck," the conductor calls. "Be careful!"

I hoist my knapsack to my shoulder and turn to find the *samloh* driver sitting up regarding me.

"*Samloh?*" he inquires.

I nod briskly and scramble into the back. "Take me to the Chinese hotel," I bark. "I'm late."

As the driver begins to pilot the *samloh* through the abandoned streets in that slow, standing pedal that resembles slow motion running, I pray that the stereotype about *samloh* drivers being drug pushers, pimps, or bandit informants is greatly exaggerated. I also pray that there *is* a Chinese hotel.

Though the town doesn't seem as large as promised, the center resembles any other Thai town at night—dark and shuttered, with metal grates pulled down over shop entrances, crushed glass atop stucco gates, and decorative grilles covering the windows of upstairs apartments. These are standard security measures, as common as the high sidewalks to protect against flooding, so I tell myself there is no reason to read them as ominous.

I think about Maechi Roongdüan, the head nun at my *wat*. It was she who inspired me to make this pilgrimage. When she was in her late twenties, not much older than I, she spent three months walking from one end of Thailand to the other with only an umbrella, a mosquito net, an alms bowl, and the robes on her back. She reached the Malay Peninsula during rubber season, which meant that the villagers worked at night stripping trees by candlelight and slept during the day, when alms rounds happen. As a result, she went for days without food and had to meditate to overcome hunger pangs. Often, alone in empty fields, the stench of rubber heavy in the dark air, she came out of meditation to find cobras with their heads in her lap.

"Perhaps drawn by my body heat," she'd marveled to me, and I had instead marveled at her and her fierce determination to love all creatures, no matter the cost.

To my amazement, the *samloh* driver deposits me at what is indeed a Chinese hotel, a modest gray stone building in the center of town. I pay him, tipping just enough to suggest gratitude but not wealth, before thrusting my hand through the iron gate and ringing the bell.

The ubiquitous old Chinese watchman in white undershirt, drawstring pajama bottoms and slippers shuffles across the courtyard with a lantern and heavy ring of keys. He shows me to a room, clean and Spartan, and points out the shower room. We exchange not a single word.

Once inside the stone shower walls, I ladle cool water from a giant jar over my body, shaking a bit in the chill air, allowing myself a few tears of relief under the camouflage of water. For a short time in this tiny, gray space, I am me. Not moving. Not negotiating. Not passing into any particular shape.

I have just returned to my room when the watchman knocks on the door and announces that someone has come for me.

My heart thuds. This is it. The *samloh* driver has sold me out!

"No visitors," I cry, eyeing the flimsy bolt. "It's too late, and I'm a respectable girl."

"No, no, it's me," a familiar voice protests, and I crack the door to find the businessman from the train standing in the hallway. He is red as ever, his boyish face sheepish. "May I come in?"

"Only for a minute," I say, "I must sleep."

He enters the room and plops heavily on the bed.

Alarmed, I leave the door open wide and stand between it and him. "What happened to you?"

"I fell asleep," he says, rubbing his puffy eyes, "and missed our stop. I had to get off at the next town and find a taxi to bring me back to Ratchaburi. It was difficult at this hour. Then I had to get to this hotel."

"How did you know where I was?"

He chuckles. "How many *farang* disembark in the middle of the night? I went to the train station and asked the *samloh* driver. He brought me here."

I join his laughter, though it occurs to me that my initial assumption was correct and the driver did indeed sell me out, albeit to this bumbling businessman instead of a bandit king.

"How did you know about this place?" he asks.

It is my turn to chuckle. "I didn't! I knew this wasn't a tourist town, so if there were a hotel, it would be a 'traveler's hotel' for traders. I just guessed that ethnic Chinese would run it. I said, 'Take me to the Chinese hotel' and it worked."

He roars. "That's very clever. You're quite resourceful!" He shakes his head. "Here I was supposed to protect you, but you did fine without me."

I duck my head modestly.

When he expresses some interest in more drink, I tell

him it's time to go. He stands up, shoulders slumping in exhaustion, his fine linen wilting like a warm carnation, and says he'll be back with his car at eleven to take me to the nun center.

"I will make it up to you," he vows. "Eleven it is!"

At half-past noon the following afternoon I consider my options. Who knows how far the nun center is and how long it will take me to find it? I need to budget time to travel back to Petchaburi, time to find the center, time to meet the nuns and see the place, time to return here to Ratchaburi. I want to be back on the train this evening and get the hell out of bandit territory before dark.

The Chinese hotel owner confirms that there is indeed an evening train and tells me where the marketplace is. He's never heard of a nun center in this town or the next, however.

"If a man comes," I tell him, "please explain that I had to go but will be back for the evening train."

The walk through town skirts new territory. I am used to two extremes, either tourist metropolises like Chiang Mai and Bangkok that teem with expatriates and English-language signs or small, traditional villages, where everyone turns out on the dirt path to greet the *farang*. I have never before negotiated a mid-sized city filled with ethnic Chinese, Thai, Lao, Indian and Malay. I feel like an extra who didn't get the script.

At the market I wait beneath the sign for *tuk-tuk* going to Petchaburi. Several Nissan pickups pass by, the narrow, padded benches in back already crowded with passengers. Finally a newer Nissan pulls up and parks. The driver gets out and heads into the market. A pretty young woman remains behind in the passenger's seat.

I approach and lean in though the open window. "Are you going to Petchaburi?" I ask. "I'm looking for this center—" I proffer the piece of paper. "I think it's on the road between here and Petchaburi, somewhere in the country."

She squints at the paper, frowning. "I'm not sure," she says, "I'll have to ask him."

The driver returns with a giant burlap bag of rice draped over his shoulder. He staggers to the back and tosses it in, then joins us, slapping his palms together. He has the same face as the girl and looks a bit older, in his early-twenties. "*Arai na?*" he asks us. *What is it?*

"Can we take her to this place?" the girl asks. "It's a *wat*."

He gives me a quick once-over. "A temple?"

"Well, a nun center, really," I explain.

The three of us study my teacher's list of names and provinces. I know what they must be thinking. Thai *wat* are cursed with long, flowery names that no one uses. In common parlance, they are known by descriptive nick-names: Marble Temple, Temple of Golden Caves, Temple of the Emerald Buddha, Temple of the Reclining Buddha, Temple of the Ceylonese Buddha. If you don't know its nickname or address, a *wat* is nearly impossible to find.

"Get in." The driver motions for the girl to slide over.

"Oh no," I protest, "I can get in the back."

"No, no," both insist, and so I squeeze into the front. We start off immediately, without waiting to load more passengers.

Worried that I've allowed my fat *farang* itinerary to supercede everyone else's, I glance back to check on the others through the small window in the cab. The pickup bed is empty, save for the bag of rice. There are no vinyl benches, no intricate grillwork on the canopy, no passengers.

This is not a *tuk-tuk*.

I whip around to regard my companions. The young man drives hunched over, conferring softly with the girl.

Then it dawns on me. They are brother and sister come to market to do shopping, not pick up fares. I have just commandeered the private car of some family out doing errands.

"*Khaw thôod!*" I cry. *Excuse me!* "I thought you were a *tuk-tuk*! I am so ashamed! Please," I beg, fumbling for the door handle, "you don't have to take me."

"No, no," they assure me. "*Mai pen rai!*" *Never mind. No problem.*

For the next hour I cringe against the door of the cab, trying to make myself as small as possible, as if the size of my gall could somehow shrink with my body, while my shy hosts motor around town, silently intent on their task, asking none of the usual, eager questions.

At each bend in the muddy, rutted roads, the brother disembarks and asks for directions from befuddled monks and laypeople. At each wrong temple, we are directed to another, equally wrong.

Finally an old woman sends us to the long-distance bus park, where a driver in a silky disco shirt and wraparound sunglasses assures us that yes, he passes by the road to the nun center.

As they hand me over, my hosts apologize for abandoning me before my destination has been reached. They would like to take me to the center themselves, the sister explains, a crease appearing between her perfect brows, but their mother expected them home an hour ago. Can I possibly forgive them?

They lean forward, twin faces rosy with sudden boldness and affection, looking for all the world as if we have spent a lovely afternoon together.

"Are you Malay?" the brother blurs out, finally daring to ask something of me, of this interaction.

"No, American," I say, for once happy to be so, eager to give them a story for their mother that's a fair exchange for their generosity. "I used to be a nun in the north, and now I'm on pilgrimage. You've helped so much."

Their eyes widen, and we all grin. I entered their truck under misapprehension and they invited me under a misapprehension of their own, and all this time we've been sitting side by side, mistaking each other for someone easier to imagine. Passing.

"Good bye!" the sister calls out the window. "Good luck!" her brother adds. Both wave. "We'll miss you."

When I return to the Chinese hotel that evening, after the bus ride into the countryside and the three-kilometer hike down a dirt road, after my tour of the nun center and my afternoon spent talking with the head nun, after a catching a ride back to Ratchaburi with some local farmers, I find the businessman from the train waiting in the lobby.

He looks forlorn yet dapper in fresh linen and glossy leather sandals.

"I overslept again," he wails, standing at my approach. "It took me forever to get home last night—the *samloh* driver didn't wait outside—so I was completely exhausted." He blushes and hangs his head. "I got here at one."

I make a flowery apology for not waiting and explain that everything worked out. Ten kilometers outside of town, the long-distance bus had stopped alongside a lonely stretch of rice paddies, hectares and hectares of emerald and gold fields broken only by the occasional, morose-looking water buffalo. The afternoon sun beat down, hotter than I was used to in the north.

"Here?" I'd asked the driver. "This is the nun center?"

He'd shrugged, eyes camouflaged behind the sunglasses gripping his face, and pointed to a dirt path bisecting the road. "There are nuns down there," he'd said. "I hear."

Fair enough. I'd thanked him. "*Khob khun kha.*"

The bus lumbered away, and I'd started down the path, trying not to think about how I'd get back to town. After all, I'd made it the entire length of Southeast Asia with no plan.

After reporting on the success of my visit to the businessman, I collect my bag from the old Chinese watchman, who startles me with a flash of betel-stained teeth, and ask the businessman to do me the great favor of seeing me to the train.

Perking up a bit, he ushers me to a sparkling cream Mercedes. As he holds open the passenger door, he shakes his head. "You're a woman alone," he marvels, "a poor student, a *farang.* Imagine!" He pauses, as if pondering this triple source of my supposed isolation before concluding, "but you don't need any help."

And though it isn't quite true, I smile modestly, once again accepting the compliment, momentarily relishing what it is to be Malay.

Faith Adiele, a graduate of Harvard College and the Iowa Writers' Workshop, is assistant professor of English at the University of Pittsburgh. She is the author of Meeting Faith: The Forest Journals of a Black Buddhist Nun. *She lives in Pittsburgh, Pennsylvania.*

ॐ ॐ ॐ

Transcending Language

"When the student is ready, the teacher appears."

would never claim to be fluent in French. That's why I said, "I'm sorry, I don't speak French," when the nun spoke to me in the church in Annecy. When I go to church in France, I always daydream during the readings and the sermon. I consider it a time for private prayer. I don't expect to understand what is being said, and I don't try.

This changed for me recently, suddenly, dramatically.

My husband Richard died a year ago. He loved France, and so do I. We traveled in France once or twice a year for almost twenty years. I want to keep going there, even though it is sad to go without him. This past spring, I traveled with my friend Janet who had never been to France and speaks no French. By necessity, I

179

became both tour guide and translator. My language skills were challenged.

One afternoon in the town of Annecy in the French Alps, we had a low moment. We were tired. We sat in a public garden by the lake, and Janet said, "I hate not being able to speak," and I said, "I miss Richard so much I can't bear it." Janet went back to the room to take a nap, and I went for a walk.

Annecy is set on an Alpine lake surrounded by wave after wave of spectacular snow-capped mountains. A river and a series of canals thread their way through the old town. The water is clean and cold, a light clear aqua blue. As in Venice, the medieval buildings have water gates right on the canals, entrances made to be accessed by boat. The buildings look like Swiss chalets, part stone, part timber, and every balcony is crowded with flowers. Along the footpath by the river, the view includes everything: mountains, water, flowers, medieval buildings. Peaceful.

It was a Sunday, and I hadn't been to church that morning because we had just arrived in town. So that afternoon I walked through the open door of St. Maurice, an old stone church with a canal running right under it. There was no one in the church but the organist, who was practicing, filling the huge space with music. I headed for the votive candles flickering in front of a statue of Mary. I lit a candle, knelt in a front pew, and closed my eyes. And started to cry and cry, tears dripping onto my hands. I was empty and sad. For a short while, I lost track of my surroundings.

When I came back to the time and place, and opened my eyes, I was in the midst of a crowd of German tourists, who were chattering away, pointing to the statues and paintings. I was disoriented, but I felt better. I went back to the hotel room and collected Janet to show her the river walk.

The mood of the day improved from there. After tea and the walk, I left Janet reading in the park while I went back to the church for the six o'clock Mass. I expected a small congregation and a brief spoken service, but when I arrived, early, and slid into a pew for a few minutes of quiet and prayer, there was an atmosphere of preparation and excitement in the church. A small band of local teenagers was rehearsing the service music: keyboard, guitars, trumpet, saxophone, and two or three vocalists. Singing in French, of course. Two or three priests were moving in and out giving instructions to various participants in the service, and the pews in the enormous church were filling up.

To my surprise, a nun carrying a stack of collection baskets walked right over to me, and asked me to take the collection, indicating a section of the church that would be my territory. I tried to refuse, thinking that I didn't really belong there, I was just a visitor, and besides I was seeking rest and quiet and relief, not action. So I shook my head no, and said in perfectly good French, "I'm sorry, I don't speak French."

She did not take no for an answer. "You don't need to speak," she said, and repeated the instructions, telling me what section of the church to cover and where to bring the basket when I was done. Then she handed me the basket and stated firmly, "You understand."

It was true. I understood exactly what she had asked me to do, and I was going to have to do it.

The service began. I hadn't even bothered to pick up a bulletin at the door, thinking I would just sit and let the familiar liturgy wash over me, go up for Communion at the appropriate time, and go back to meet Janet for supper. But this was not a passive service. The church was full of life and activity, packed with people of all ages. Five young people, perhaps twelve or thirteen years old, were being baptized, and they and their families were all participating in the service. I had to be alert; I had a part in the service, too.

The most amazing thing was what happened with the language. First, I found myself singing along with the responses. In French. Without a leaflet. O.K., I had heard the rehearsal, and I can pick up a tune. That was fun. Then one of the mothers stood up to read the Old Testament lesson. It was about Moses. Partway through, I realized that I shouldn't know what it was about. It was in French, and I wasn't translating in my head. The language was going directly to my heart, bypassing the translation step. This had never happened to me before. I listened to the Gospel. I followed the sermon. I understood.

When the congregation stood up for the renewal of the baptismal vows, I joined right in with the responses, easily, naturally, without thought or preparation. Do you believe in God the Father? Jesus Christ? The Holy Spirit?

"Oui, je le crois." Yes, I believe. And I receive peace, and grace, and language, without translation.

There is an expression: When the student is ready, the teacher appears. That nun was my teacher. I didn't know I was ready, but I was.

When the time came, I stood up with several others, and passed the collection basket. And brought it to the back of the church, and handed it to my nun, and said, "I understand."

Susan Butterworth is a freelance writer and adjunct professor of English Composition at Salem State College. She has published literary biography and reference articles in addition to travel essays. She has traveled extensively in Europe for the last twenty years and is currently working on a novella set in Sicily.

BONNIE SMETTS

Turquoise Dreams

A sailing fairy tale.

Once upon a time, a girl was born with the ocean in her eyes. While other little girls floated off to sleep on the black velvet of night, this little girl drifted away on swells of shimmering turquoise.

When she grew up, she became an artist and tried to make sea pictures of her own, but they never matched what she saw when she closed her eyes. And with eyes open, she was never safe: Idyllic coves jumped off magazine covers in waiting rooms and boiling arctic waves flew off the pages of fellow commuters' books. Tahiti. Palau. Anguilla. Sometimes words were even more dangerous than images. She was never free from her thirst for turquoise.

She took a job designing a sailing magazine in an office overlooking a marina. She averted her eyes, careful not to gaze too long at the pictures while she worked. In the end, the ads were her downfall. A sloop lay at anchor on a glassy jade bay above the incantation, "Bareboat Adventure."

She had to ask, "What does this mean?" pointing to the headline.

"You rent a sailboat without a skipper, bare. Big boats in the best water around the world," her boss explained.

Oceans, seas, bights, and crossings, all she needed was a crew. Her grumpy husband knew how to sail—it was the only reason she kept him. Her father had sailed the seas as a young man and still knew how to chart a course by the stars. Her mother would come along, and her girlfriends—they always followed her on adventures—all she had to do was ask.

She asked. A month later her crew assembled on the dock at Marsh Harbor.

The low-lying scrub islands of the Bahamas barely held their heads above water. But the water—it was what she'd waited for since birth.

But the girl-with-the-ocean-in-her-eyes could not yet succumb. She was responsible for the girlfriends, and the parents, and fifty feet of luxury yacht. Before she left home, she'd arranged for a captain the first few days of the voyage—just to be sure. She had imagined a tanned, round fellow with a gray beard and a blue cap.

No.

When the crew stepped aboard the *Lucky 7*, they were introduced to Adonis: Michael was twenty-something, sun-scorched with corkscrew-curly hair falling around a golden face. When he uttered his first British-tinged Bahamian words, the water-girl knew they were in trouble.

The voyage started innocently enough. Michael showed everyone the boat, explained the rigging, and talked about navigating by the stars.

Then he turned his attention to the girlfriends. He showed them how to crank the winches, raise the main sail, and drop anchor. He stood behind them and wrapped his golden arms around their waists as he demonstrated. He flirted with everyone, even the mother.

When his work was done, he draped himself leopard-like on the stern, letting his now-trained crew sail the boat. He had come from generations of boat builders and these waters were his home. When he felt the softest kiss of the keel on the sand, he leapt to the wheel, gunned the engine, and freed the boat from the bottom before the grumpy husband could say, "I think we're..."

The girl-with-the-ocean-inside was annoyed by the commotion. She had stretched herself over the side of the boat and was raking the turquoise water with her fingers and tracing the outlines of starfish glued across the sandy white bottom. Sandy.

"*You slept with Michael?*" the once-upon-a-time girl gasped when the girlfriend Sandy told her. Then she remembered.

"I'm sleeping on deck," the girlfriend Sandy had said the second night. The damp air had hung inky and close, and Michael who had grown up on the sea had slept on deck, too. But the ocean-girl never guessed the two would dare to hook up while the second girlfriend, the grumpy husband, and the parents slept below.

Wow. When she planned the voyage, she never imagined the girlfriends might cut into the magic.

The ocean-girl saved the picture she took that morning: the girlfriend Sandy stood on deck in her red-and-white striped dress with Hope Town lighthouse similarly clad behind her. They had just dropped off Michael. He disappeared down the dock taking with him the spell he had cast on them all.

"Sandy is immature," whispered the mother, taking a turn at spell wrecking.

The girlfriend Sandy hated the mother back. The night before, the mother had passed the salad dressing without screwing the top back on. When the girlfriend Sandy shook the bottle, she drenched herself in dressing, and laundry was not possible onboard ship.

Not to be overshadowed, the grumpy husband was grumping.

But nothing could cloud the ocean-girl's dream. She took over as captain, steering away from Hope Town, driving the boat up and down pillows of waves, pushing her chariot on toward Treasure Cay.

That afternoon they anchored off a reef rumored to hold a shipwreck. The girl-with-the-ocean-in-her-eyes, the grumpy husband, and the girlfriends climbed into the dinghy and steered toward the sunken treasure but a terrific wind whipped the water into an aqua frappuccino, obscuring the view below.

They pounded back through the foam toward the boat. The parents were nowhere in sight. The night before, while the crew danced in the sand to a steel drum band below palms scratching the sky, the parents had disappeared. When the crew returned to the boat, the mother was sitting outside in her underwear, the father below. "It's so hot tonight," the mother had volunteered.

Had they done it again? The ocean-girl hated her role as boatparent, keeping track of who was naked and who was not.

But every day, she sailed and snorkeled and swam. At dusk, she dove off the boat and moved through the water with manta rays until the jade underworld faded to black.

The final day at sea, the *Lucky Seven* anchored in Vixen Bay. The three girlfriends set out to explore the water, leaving the grumpy husband, now lobster-boy, to hide from the sun. At the bottom of the deep channel, angelfish, eels, and snapper were bigger than they'd ever seen and the brain coral were the size of armchairs.

The girl-with-the-sea-in-her-eyes floated. If she held her head just so, sun flickered off swells in the top half of her facemask, while schools of grouper swam in aqua below.

When the sun finally sank low, she guided the sun-burned grumpy husband out to the channel hoping to find the fish again. As they reached the center he tugged on her flippers, "I don't think we should be out here." He saw how deep it was. She was about to suggest that he was an unadventurous wimp when she saw the barracuda—five feet long with a mouthful of picket-fence teeth. Instinctively the lobster-boy and the ocean-girl folded themselves in half and put their kicking legs—and the extra length of their fins—out in front between them and the fish. They circled backwards as the barracuda circumnavigated them.

Scared—she'd never been scared in the water—the ocean-girl put the grumpy husband between her and the fish. Why not? They continued paddling backwards toward shore, rotating to keep the fish in view. The fish followed them to water shallow enough to stand. They touched sand and flapped madly toward safety like two wet clowns, too frightened to stop and release their long fins.

Lucky 7's crew heard their screams. The almost-misfortune lightened the mood for a moment but the boat had become too small for the parents, the girlfriends, and the grumpy husband.

They spent their final night in a hotel. But not before the girlfriend Sandy had to pack and unpack and fold and refold everything in her gigantic bag one more time, the other girlfriend had to make everyone search for her contact lens one more time, and the grumpy husband had to feel ignored one last time. The once-upon-a-time-girl didn't care.

The view over Long Bay from the hotel's veranda was everything she ever hoped to see. The rum cocktail she sipped was everything she ever wanted to taste. She was exactly where she wanted to be.

The next morning the girl-with-the-ocean-in-her-eyes awoke with a fever. She didn't remember the small plane taking off with the parents. She barely remembered Miami. The grumpy husband had dressed in white polyester like a used-car salesman from Ohio. He breezed through Customs while the girlfriends were delayed, the agents going through every corner of their bags. Finally on the plane, the husband whispered to the girlfriends, "They thought you were my mules." The girl-with-the-ocean-in-her-eyes soothed the girlfriends' anger but she never soothed her own.

Time passed. The girlfriends drifted away, the parents sadly went to their places in heaven, and the ocean girl traveled alone.

"Fishermen setting out at dawn…ancient fort overlooking the sea…a cliff facing the vast turquoise ocean."

She tried to look away, but the billboard was there, right next to them on the freeway. She didn't say a word. Her cheerful new husband drove them home, parked the car, and disappeared into the den to retrieve his passport.

Bonnie Smetts is a San Francisco Bay Area art director and writer who divides her time between a house at the ocean and an apartment dangerously close to an international airport.

FRANCINE PROSE

≋ ≋ ≋

Confessions of a Ritual Tourist

Participating in the rites and ceremonies of other
cultures has its high and low points.

I fell in love with Swami Sandcastle on my second
trip to India in the late 1970s. My husband and I
happened to stop at a small South Indian beachside town,
where, as it turned out, people from the surrounding
area came to toss packets of food into the sea: meals for
the departed, offerings to keep their dead from going
hungry. Every morning, we watched this holy man—tall,
bearded, with flowing orange robes and a strikingly
handsome face—making designs and mounds in the sand
and dispensing food packets to the pilgrims in exchange
for small sums of money. We watched him, and he saw us
watching him. By the end of a few days, we had what I

guess you could call a relationship. In fact, we had a huge crush on him, and, in a way, I think he knew it.

We were thrilled when eventually he beckoned to us and, using the little English he knew, made it clear that he would allow us to take him to a nearby tea house. We bought tea for everyone in the tea house, all of whom seemed to know him and to be giving us odd looks as we ourselves drank cup after cup of the hot (well, actually, rather tepid) milky liquid.

The next morning, we awoke with the fiercest cases of dysentery we'd ever had in all our travels. At our hotel, the receptionist told us that no one in the town—in fact, no one except pilgrims from distant villages who didn't know any better—went to the tea house, which was famous locally for its filthiness and for the variety of diseases you could catch there.

It was among the low points of my life as a ritual tourist, by which I mean a traveler drawn to the rites and ceremonies of other cultures—the more unlike mine, the better. My ritual tourism had always had a sort of freeform, improvisational nature. If I happened to be somewhere that a ceremony was in progress, or living in a place where I knew they celebrated a particular holiday, so much the better. Only rarely have I purposely coordinated my travels to correspond with some local celebration.

But I have known people who have gone on journeys of this sort in a more organized, official way—pilgrims who go long distances to observe pilgrimages, you might say. For many years, I had a neighbor whose vocation involved taking groups of New Age goddess-worshipers on trips to holy sites, tours timed to coincide with important astronomical events and exotic fertility rituals. Together, my neighbor and her traveling companions celebrated the solstice at Machu Picchu, ushered in the equinox amid the red rocks of Sedona, and traveled through the Brazilian jungle to watch their Amazonian sisters perform some sort of secret ceremony involving the ghost of a dead jaguar.

As a novelist, every instinct I had made me want to join them to watch these innocents abroad offering incense to the deities and spitting mouthfuls of potent local homebrew into the roaring bonfires. But every instinct I had as a human warned me away from a situation that I feared I might find uncomfortable, embarrassing, and certainly disingenuous as I conducted my own private, voyeuristic study of the ritual tourists. Hesitant to join these trips, I did what every novelist would do, I wrote a book about it instead.

It probably goes without saying that the things we're drawn to satirize are, in many cases, the things we're most wary of, and suspicious about, in ourselves. So perhaps one reason I had so much fun subjecting the fictional travelers in my novel *Hunters and Gatherers* to a succession of highly comic misadventures was that I knew, in my heart of hearts, I was a ritual tourist. The truth was that often I was the traveler you could spot—if not in the front row, then certainly somewhere in the crowd—as the Holy Week procession passed by in the streets of some Mexican village, the one trekking to the cemetery in Oaxaca to watch people picnic on their loved ones' well-tended graves in honor of the Day of the Dead. I was the one in the last pew at the Church of St. Anne de Beaupre in Quebec, watching the worshipers who arrive on crutches, rattling their bottles of pills, in the hopes of being cured and made whole again through the saint's intercession.

I suppose that my career as a ritual tourist began, like many people's on the shores of the Ganges, in Benares, or Varanasi, where pious Hindus come to die or to burn their dead and scatter their ashes in the holy river. I can still recall how thrilling it was to wake up before dawn to reach the banks of the river in time for the sunrise, to watch the crowds of faithful come to wash in the sacred waters, and to hire a boatman to take me past the burning ghats where the wrapped-up corpses smoldered. The crowds, the color and variety of the scene, the sheer sensory stimulation, was so intense, so utterly transfixing that, on that first visit, a sacred cow pissed all over my foot and I didn't even notice. Everything about the city and the ceremonies I was observing fascinated me so much that I remember wanting to stay there, to spend weeks or months, however long it took for me to begin to understand the mysteries I was seeing.

At the same time, I felt sort of guilty. I understood that this was not some performance, some Indian version of the hula and flamenco shows staged to entertain tourists in Hawai'i and Andalusia. Someone's loved one had died, someone was in mourning, someone believed that total immersion in the waters of the river would speed up the long and painful cycle of suffering and rebirth. So what exactly was I doing there with my little guidebook and my little camera, taking notes on my impressions of an event that was, for the people I was observing, nothing less than a matter of life and death?

Over the years, I heard stories about tourists who'd crossed boundaries of privacy and respect, who'd had their cameras seized and smashed for rudely photographing the wrong secret rite. Not until I received my own lesson about the dangers of ritual tourism, courtesy of Swami Sandcastle, did I realize how culpable I had been.

Still, my attraction to ritual tourism persisted. It flourished when I lived with my family in Tucson, Arizona. There, from time to time, we would drive out to the Mission San Xavier del Bac, the beautiful "white dove of the desert," where pilgrims, mostly Yaqui Indians and Mexicans from across the nearby border, performed the ritual of filing past—and lifting—the heavy wooden statue of Saint Francis that lay on the altar in a side chapel. According to the legend, only the sinless and pure of heart could lift the statue, while sinners couldn't budge it, no matter how hard they tried. I myself was always afraid to try—hesitant to subject myself to this instant and public spiritual diagnosis.

Every year at Easter we would go to south Tucson where the Yaqui community enacted an elaborate Easter ceremony representing the victory of light over darkness and good over evil. And every year I found myself in tears when light and goodness won.

That was where I discovered one remedy for my guilt about the voyeuristic aspects of my ritual tourism, which was to look down upon my fellow ritual tourists. What were these crude interlopers doing, trying to get between me and my enjoyment of a solemn ceremony? Many of these travelers happened to be Germans, loaded with cameras, traveling in large groups, shouting to one another, eagerly muscling their way to the front of the crowd. I glared at them. I sighed and rolled my eyes. I did everything in my power to make it obvious that these were real people performing real ceremonies, that this was not some circus being staged for these onlookers' benefit. I wondered why they had spent so much money and traveled so far to see the rites of others when they could have seen their own culture's ceremonies—say, the local Oktoberfest. Was it the desire to see something in others that looked closer to a purer, more compelling sort of faith? Or was it, as I suspected, a kind of romanticism which made the tourists feel as if the people they were watching were closer to some secret knowledge that had been lost in more industrialized cultures? These reflections interested me, but not enough to stop me from wishing that all the ritual tourists—that is, except me—would give it up and go home.

Then, one year, a strange thing happened.

It was just at the crucial moment in the ceremony. The masked figures representing the soldiers and the Pharisees had twice tried to storm the little structure decorated with streamers and paper flowers that symbolized the church. Each time they were rebuffed—pelted with flowers—by our heroes, the dancers. Finally, the soldiers were defeated. There was a storm of flowers, the masks of the villains came off, and the masks and an effigy of Judas were thrown into a roaring bonfire.

That was the moment at which, every year, I burst into tears. But this time, for some reason, I looked to the side and saw that one of the German tourists, in fact the woman who'd been especially annoying to me all through the ceremony, had likewise erupted in wrenching sobs. Suddenly, I realized that she'd been affected in the same way I had, that she was probably there for the same reason I was. What had brought her to south Tucson was not merely the wish to be entertained, but a desire to watch an affirmation of faith, of ceremony, of belief in community and shared history—and in the power of ritual to represent something admirable and enduring in human nature.

ॐ ॐ ॐ

Francine Prose is the author of fourteen novels, including the National Book Award finalist Blue Angel *and* A Changed Man. *Her work has been published in* The New Yorker, The Atlantic Monthly, Harper's, *and other places. She is also the author of a biography of the painter Caravaggio.*

ℬ ℬ ℬ

The Man Who Came in from the Cold

In the Idaho wilderness, a woman faces the dark.

The day in late September that was to be my last on the mountain was the very day that autumn crossed the thin and lovely line into winter, drawing the shades down over the sun, slamming the door on Indian summer and her empty promises. No more the sublime days, fierce with life and light, a crescendo of spotless blue, a stroke of burnished gold. Gone were the vanilla notes of sun-warmed ponderosa pine, the cinnamon of buck brush, and the breeze that ruffled yellow leaves of aspen with cool, clean fingers.

On that particular day, morning arrived reluctantly and without pretense, stiff and sore from the cold, dense night. Snow came sideways, carried on a westerly wind, obscuring a bloodless rising sun that spoke frankly of the dim days to come. The season on the lookout tower had wrapped up.

The only fire for miles was the one in my wood stove, crackling and hissing, chasing the cold outside, where it belonged. The spring had slowed to a trickle, just a ghost of its summer self. The ground squirrels had retreated to wherever it was they'd stockpiled the dog food they had pilfered piece by piece from Bandit's bowl all summer long. As snow in the high country crept farther down the mountain, so too did the elk in their pursuit of green graze.

I was headed to the lowlands too, but my transition from mountain to valley would take place in just a single day. The Forest Service packer would arrive the next morning with his string of mules to collect my things and deliver them to my pickup truck, waiting patiently next to the Selway River miles below. Bandit and I would walk behind, shuffling through soft pine duff on the trail, milking the last of our summer of solitude.

I'd spent the day clearing the area around the lookout of dead limbs and brush to create a defensible space in the event that wildfire would decide to climb to the top of the mountain. Weary from one day's work that should have been stretched out over the whole season, I propped my feet up in front of the wood stove and settled in to enjoy the fire and the last chapters of my book. Sleet and snow, driven by thirty mph winds rattled the panes of glass that separated me from the raw, ruthless elements.

I poured red wine into a cup from a half-full bottle, no longer to be rationed into thimble-sized portions.

The last days of the season are about abundance and frivolity, when precious goods that have been squirreled away become available for unabashed consumption. In addition to the wine, the luxury list contained three cans of milk, a half-pound of coffee, a package of fig bars, some Belgian chocolate, and salted peanuts. I had popcorn, tea, and time—a little more precious time.

The first sip of wine was all mine, and so were the moments that followed, filled only with the faint howl of the wind accompanying the crackling fire. The second sip was cut short, interrupted mid-swallow by the sound of boots on the wooden steps leading to where I was.

Boots. Person. People? I hadn't received a single unannounced visitor all summer. Being situated in the middle of nowhere, eight miles by trail, then sixty miles of sketchy winding road from anywhere does not make for much spontaneous visitation. I'd daydreamed of the unexpected guest, a hiker that would show up one morning for coffee, but this was different, this was night. Bandit sensed my unease and assumed his duties as the assistant manager, barking his best authoritative bark.

I might have barred the door, crawled into bed with the covers over my head, but one cannot hide in a glass house. Besides, there was something hollow and harmless in the sound of the footsteps: slow and deliberate, each echoing with words like "hungry," "lost," "desperate." Fourteen steps total, I knew each one intimately; time enough to assume my stance, to don a brave face.

I opened the door for the man attached to the stomping boots. Robed in cold, clean air, he stumbled past me, unfazed by the barking dog, hackles up, teeth bared.

Drunk, I thought. Here was the drunk man I'd been warned about, the only wild animal I truly feared in my mountain home.

"Have you seen him?" he demanded from behind a frosty mustache. The man bore the unmistakable trappings of a hunter: a mix of blaze orange and camouflage, a 30-06 slung over his shoulder.

Before I could speak, he banged the butt of the rifle against the floor and shouted, "Jim!" in reply to a question I didn't ask. "Where is he?" His speech was slow, slurred, insistent.

Out of the corner of my eye I found my bear spray.

It lived next to the bed where it would be of more use to me in dealing with late-night intruders than to ward off the shy bears that make their living on this mountain.

I assured him no one was there but me.

He scanned the small room in disbelief and stated,

"Well, he's got to fucking be here," ripping his cap off to reveal a full head of gray hair, "or we've got trouble, period." He sat down on the edge of the bed and began rocking back and forth, frantically raking fingers through his matted, damp hair which, like a fresh-cut stump, looked conspicuous and raw, as if a ponytail had been amputated from the nape of his neck with a dull bread knife minutes before.

He looked up at me with panic on his brow, fear flashing in his pale eyes. "Oh, we've got trouble, I'm telling you. Trouble...yes, we've got trouble," he chuckled nervously. "Oh, Jesus Lord, we've got some serious trouble," he repeated, shaking his head over and over.

When asked to explain the trouble we were in, he just turned his face to me, silent and hopeless. It was soft and boyish, unsuited for gray hair, age, or trouble.

He put his hands to his head and looked back to the floor. After a moment, he looked up again and pleaded, "Listen, we've got serious trouble, and you need to help me out, because I...have got...to go to sleep...goddamnit."

As he stretched onto the bed, visibly shivering, I sheepishly realized my misdiagnosis: the beginning stages of hypothermia had looked an awful lot like intoxication to my fear-clouded judgment.

I kicked into gear as the resident emergency room nurse. I found my commanding voice.

I ordered wet clothes off. Boots off. Into the sleeping bag you go. There were Army blankets, a dry wool cap, warm drinks to be sipped. Bandit resumed assistant managerial duties by crawling into bed next to him, offering his sixty additional pounds of warmth.

The feet seemed to have taken the brunt of the cold. Pale and waxy, his were refrigerated rubber versions of healthy feet. I mentally referenced my wilderness first aid training, but having worked the previous eight years in the canyons and rivers of the southwest, everything that popped up related to heat exhaustion and dehydration. Scanning the bookshelf for a first aid manual, I found that serendipitously, I had a book on avalanche safety, rescues, and frostbite.

Soaking another person's feet is awkward, especially when the person is a naked stranger, wrapped in every sleeping bag and blanket you own. But as I added hot water to the dish tub, gradually increasing the temperature of the cool water to lukewarm, things began to thaw. His name was Randy. He was from Oregon.

It was the story of a hunting party of two that had become a party of one. One man had made it back to camp at the end of a long day following elk sign, hungry but unscathed. The other, the one with no food, sleeping bag, map, compass, or experience did not return. He quickly became the missing man, the one left alone in the hands of the night.

Randy had been back at camp, stoking a fire, shooting his rifle into the darkness to identify his position on the planet, to lead the lost to safety. Still alone at daylight, he had launched a search, an aimless day of wandering, of looking for clues. It led him to my door, the only outpost in this part of the wilderness, where he landed, cold and defeated.

The missing man was Jim, Randy's boss, the owner of a sand and gravel company in Oregon. It had been a life's dream of Jim's to hunt elk in the wilderness of Idaho. He'd fancied himself an outdoorsman. He'd gone Marlin fishing in Mexico, he'd been on a Caribou hunt in Alaska, and now Jim would shoot the biggest bull elk he could find in Idaho, that's what he told Randy.

In lieu of experience, Jim had money. He would hire an outfitter to set up their camp, to pack them in on horseback and leave them to their own devices. Randy had the know-how. He knew his place in the woods. This could be seen in the way he carried himself, in the words he used to describe the landscape, by the knife on his belt. His clothes were wool, his boots, leather. He would save Jim the high price of a guide. He was hunter and woodsman, and above all, he was a hard worker. Randy would see to it that Jim got his elk, that's what he told Jim.

"We aren't really even good friends, you know?"

Randy said, looking at his feet in the dish tub. "I mean, I've never even spoken to his wife, and now I've got to find a way to tell her about all this; I've got to figure out how to tell her he's gone." He looked at me so intensely I felt I should offer to do it for him. Instead I reached out in a feeble gesture of condolence, three fingers on his shoulder, too modest to commit a full hand to the effort.

He sat for a moment, gently pinned by my tentative fingers before he shrugged them off and began rocking back and forth again, moaning quietly. I saw a child occupying a man's body, not knowing what to do with the size and weight of it all.

"We really did have a plan," he said finally. "We really did. I showed him everything on the map, I really did."

With the two-way radios, Randy had the means to communicate with Jim through the night and into the day, but the effort was hampered by the fact that the two did not speak the same language. Jim had no map, no compass, no internal bearings. Instead of cardinal directions, Jim would refer to things that were on his right, his left, ahead of him, behind him. He referred to geographic landmarks like, "the rock that looks like a beached whale, a great big fir tree, a steep, burned slope." The information he gave was in reference to the placement of his body on the earth, rendering it all useless, and eventually, communication broke off on Jim's end.

I told Randy that Jim might have been out of range, or maybe just out of batteries.

"Or both," Randy said, shaking his head, "Probably both. The guy doesn't have even a single fucking match."

It was long into dark when I made the call. I left Randy with his feet in the dish tub and went out to the helipad where I could find privacy and hopefully, a signal on the satellite phone.

There was no chance of getting a helicopter on the search until daylight, the dispatcher at the sheriff's department in a town so many miles away told me, but the search party could come in tonight on ATVs.

When they named the said four wheeled machines "all-terrain vehicles," they were not taking into consideration the terrain of the Selway-Bitterroot Wilderness. The trail to the lookout gains nearly a vertical mile of elevation over the course of eight miles and is no more that two feet wide in places. Steep drop-offs, switchbacks, and other features make it dangerous for a string of pack mules, impossible for four wheels. Outside of its location on a map, it was clear that the party on the other end knew little of this piece of wilderness, the place where the roads disappear.

Horses, humans, and helicopters: I told her those were her only choices. They were the only means by which to access this country. I was told to stand by, that they would call me back.

Snow sifted down from the darkness, a soft, glittery dust over the white that remained from the day. I looked north to the mountain where my nearest neighbor lives. Sometimes through binoculars at night I swear I can see his lantern, but maybe the light I see is just the idea that someone is there. The top of his mountain is only 1,200 feet lower than me, but it is another world. Different plants grow there, different trees; summer comes earlier, winter later. It was hard to believe it could still be autumn only a few miles away, that hope could be that close.

The electronic ring of the satellite phone brought me back to the bitter wind and falling snow on top of Spot Mountain.

"We'll have a helicopter up at first light."

Inside, Randy's feet looked like they belonged to a living human being, and complaints of a prickling sensation told me blood was returning to the vessels. In my best hopeful voice I told him about the call I had made and the plans for the early morning search and rescue effort. As promising as it sounded though, we both knew that what separated us from daylight was another frigid night.

We tried to call Jim on the two-way radio, to give him the good news to get him through the night, but there was no response. Nothing.

I took the kettle off the stove and made us two cups of tea.

"There was just one little ridge between us," he said, shaking his head in his hands. "I can't believe he got so turned around. You just go up, up, up...You just keep walking up and out of those drainages, you know?"

I did. The Selway-Bitterroot Wilderness is a deep dark place of secrets. In the parts that haven't been burned by wildfire, its crowded timber is disorienting. It's rare to find a vista, a clear ridge from which to get your bearings. From the inside looking out, it all looks like trees, but up will eventually lead you to daylight.

He paced the thirteen-foot length of the lookout, back and forth, pausing periodically to look at a map on the back of the door. "Christ, these drainages we were in all lead back up to the trail," he shouted, thumping the map with the back of his hand. Randy grabbed at his neck for the phantom ponytail, then slowly slid his hand forward to rub the stubble on his jaw. "You have to just keep walking up."

He absently picked up his cup of tea, peering in through the steam, searching for the reflection of someone he might recognize as himself. He set it back down again without taking a sip and picked up my Raggedy Ann doll, a thirty-year-old relic from my childhood. Though I cringed, chagrined to have been caught with a doll, he was oblivious. He held the doll up and shook her slightly. He told her too, that all Jim would've had to do was to keep going up, keep moving on.

Dinner was a smorgasbord of lentils, dried apricots, and peanuts, a box of macaroni and cheese, canned tuna, some freeze-dried peas. For desert there were fig bars, more tea, and the Belgian chocolate I'd been hoarding.

"I'll tell you what, I tried," he said looking over my shoulder and out into the night. "I told him every single thing he'd need to be prepared. He trusted me," he said to the fork poised in front of his lips. "And now I've failed him."

He set the fork down, pushed the plate aside, and lay back down on the bed, drawing his knees to his chest.

"Jesus Christ..." he moaned rocking back and forth, "I've failed him, and now I've got to live with it."

As I cleaned up after dinner, shoving dirty plates under the wood stove, I thought about the times when I'd been driving a car and became irrationally terrified that for some reason, someone would dart out into the road out of nowhere and I would strike and kill him. I'd imagined the police report, the witnesses, the devastated family—how the victim's reckless behavior would result in me living the rest of my life with his blood on my hands.

I put a kettle on for dishwater, and Randy shifted gears, talking about his life in Oregon. He told me he had a piece of property, three acres of land which he had single-handedly eradicated of the dreaded spotted knapweed by pulling it out by hand over a two-year period.

"I would get out there and just pull it, every single day," he said. "You need to get the whole root. Sometimes they're this long," he demonstrated three feet with his hands, "Like a goddamn tree root."

I noticed he was missing half of the ring finger on his right hand, usually the sign of someone who has worked harder than most, or someone who was careless.

Looking at the contents of Randy's backpack, fastidiously lined out to dry in front of the woodstove, it was clear he was not a careless man.

We both fell quiet again, two strangers in a fire tower lit by lantern light. Watching snow fall outside, I thought of the man without matches, preparing for another twelve hours of darkness. I looked over to Randy, stretched out on the bed and lied, "I've got a good feeling about this..."

The ensuing silence was significant, a gaping space in which something important was either going to be said or someone was going to fall asleep.

"I don't believe in miracles," he muttered finally from the bed, and rolled over. It was a comforting sound though, the slippery shuffling of a nylon sleeping bag. It spoke of a man, well fed and warm, turning in for the night.

Sleep came fast to him, the snoring heavy. I gathered

his clothes from the damp pile on the floor, tenderly hanging them on the line above the woodstove. A strange man's socks, so cold and wet.

My own bed and blankets occupied, I curled up next to the wood stove on my yoga mat, listening to white bark pine popping in the heat. Though warm and comfortable, I found it impossible to sleep. It wasn't for the tea's caffeine, the hard floor, or the lack of blankets. It wasn't for the air of awkward intimacy brought on by a stranger snoring in my bed. It wasn't for the brightness of starlight reflecting blue off the snow. It was for the absence of the second pair of boots clomping up the steps, and the presence of the burden Randy shouldered. But most of all it was for the stillness that I could not sleep, the blanket of new-fallen snow muting the world to a silence so palpable it rang in the ears. It was something I had to witness; it was the loudest sound I'd heard in weeks.

I bundled up and quietly slipped outside, down the stairs and to the helipad. Pin pricks of light seared through the inky blackness, stars so crisp they were felt in the chest as ice cracking, heard in the ears as glass shattering. It was clear; it was cold. It was winter.

"Jim," I spoke into Randy's two-way radio the way a competent rescue worker would on television, "My name is Karla. I'm a fire lookout," I said, pouring out a can of white gas onto the brush pile. "I live up here in the lookout tower and you're going to be O.K.," tossing a lit match into the center of the pile, "Just walk towards the fire," I said of the explosion of flames. But there was no response: No cheering, no click, no static.

And again, it was quiet. The only sound on the mountain was the roar of fire consuming brush. Standing next to the five-foot blaze was gratifying; it gave me a sense of purpose. I was doing something, I thought, though I didn't know exactly what, or who I was doing it for. For Jim, the lost and desperate man? For Randy in my bed, snoring loudly as to drown out the scolding voices in his head? And maybe, I thought, I was doing it for myself. I was writing myself into the script.

The hours that followed were occupied by stoking fires. Outside, there were other things to burn: an old hitch rail, the boards of a former outhouse, cardboard and paper trash. Inside, I added logs to the fire, bringing the temperature of the room to a roast. Tiptoeing to the stove with an armload of firewood I heard Randy shift in the bed he was sharing with Bandit, mumbling the thoughts of the dreaming.

Over the cast iron creak of the wood stove door I distinctly heard the words, "Honestly, it can all be explained with science."

Back outside, speaking into the radio, I told Jim about life on top of a mountain. As I tended to the brush fire, I told him about the magical water at the spring, about the huckleberries, the mountain lion tracks, the bear that rolled rocks over on the trail looking for grubs to eat. I told him about the sky with its moods and my uninterrupted view of it. I told him about my friend on the neighboring mountain and how one hot, still day earlier in the summer we had gotten involved in a lengthy conversation of mirror flashes back and forth across the fifteen miles of air. I described what the middle of a lightning storm looks like, the veins of the clouds backlit for a split second, an x-ray glimpse at the bones of the sky. I told Jim about water dogs, the white wisps of ground fog, often mistaken for smoke, rising from wet ground as gossamer and into the air like individual souls being called off to heaven. I needed him to know that there was something about the wilderness bigger than his fear.

Though I kept talking, kept stoking the fire, hope got lost somewhere in those desperate hours before daylight, disappearing into the end of the thermometer with the mercury, to the unknown place that marks the infinity of degrees below freezing. Inside the warm lookout though, Randy's disturbed snoring became the even breathing of an ordinary, innocent man's sleep.

Morning came, crystal blue and shocking, and not unlike a slap in the face. Out on the helipad, looking out across miles of white, I reluctantly told the dispatcher that our victim had been missing now for thirty-six hours. She wanted to know what the temperature had been. I cushioned my answer by a few degrees, rationalizing that an embellishment of the truth would somehow increase Jim's chances for survival.

She told me they would do what they could, this woman so many miles away at a desk, looking at a map of where I was.

Inside, over steaming mugs of coffee, Randy's face told the story of the imminent trip back to Oregon. It was the face of a man returning home, empty-handed.

Sitting near a heart contemplating such weight, I felt guilty for the lightness. I felt guilty for the truth that I had the ability to wander into my own trivial thoughts, to wonder what I would eat when I returned to town that evening.

"There's no way he made it last night," he said with conviction. He too had seen the thermometer that morning, the bowl of dog water out on the catwalk frozen solid.

Speechless, I looked up at the ceiling then out to the blue sky, but found no answers there either.

The day was otherwise still on. There was a helicopter on the way. There was a man riding up a quiet trail on a creaky leather saddle leading a string of mules, naïve to the goings on just a few miles away. He would expect me to be waiting, my things packed, ready to load onto his mules for the trip down the mountain.

As I chipped ice off the steps with a rusty ax, Randy stood with his coffee in a nervous way that gave me the impression he had never watched another person work before. He told me more about the sand and gravel business in Oregon, how he got started in it, his goals for the future. He told me he didn't really believe in luck, that the only thing that ever brought him what he wanted was hard work.

I told him I thought that luck was what kicked in when you had worked hard enough.

Slurping the last of his coffee he said, "I just want to go home." He swirled the grounds in the bottom of his cup around and tossed them over the railing with a flick of the wrist. They landed below, a spray of black against the otherwise undisturbed white of new snow.

I walked back inside to grab the coffee pot from the stove, that's what I could do—keep clothes dry, fires hot, cups filled. As I did, the two-way radio, the one my words had disappeared into all night, crackled to life. Static, and a man's voice. "Randy," it said unmistakably, then, "Randy," again. That was it.

Shots fired from the rifle of the lost man were so close I felt them in my teeth. A piece of orange flagging on a knoll less than a mile away gave Jim's location. This would be a live rescue, I assured the dispatcher, not a recovery effort.

Randy was gone in no time, headed down the mountain to where Jim was, wearing warm, dry clothes, pockets stuffed with peanuts and fig bars. Every trace of him was packed up and on his back, save for the coffee cup perched on the railing of the catwalk, the impression of a sleeping man left on the unmade bed, some coffee grounds in the snow. We'd shared a tearful embrace punctuated with sincere thank-yous and vows to keep in touch. As he walked away though, I knew it would be the last I'd see of him.

We would not get together to talk about what had happened; though in our own words, in our own lives, we would keep each other alive by telling our own renditions of the same story in the voice of the character we had played.

What we had shared belonged only to that space and time. Back in the other world we would not know one another, but in the wilderness, stripped clean of our societal markings, we recognized one another as friend, as ally.

It was a scene in wide angle: the distant sound of a helicopter rotor, an insect in the distance, then a bird entering the frame. The shot tightened as the bird became a machine, flying so low over the lookout I could read its tail number. As it flew on, the blizzard of snow it churned-up in its wake died down, settling back into a silent blanket, covering up any mistakes, any evidence. It flew to the spot where orange flagging, visible with the

naked eye, marked the place where a man stood waiting
for a ride out of his nightmare.

What happened from there was not unlike the end
of a movie where the war is won, the dog comes home.
And at the end of our movie, everyone lived, miracu-
lously, keeping all of their limbs, even their toes.

I thought about the ride, and how sometimes with a
happy ending in sight, even the most harrowing experience is over too soon. The space between raw terror and
comfort becomes a small crack where once was a chasm.
A helicopter flight, a horseback ride, an eight-mile walk
to the rest of the world is never long enough to process
what actually happened in the space of two nights, three
months: a lifetime in the wilderness. Too soon the introduction of people who were not there, of people who
haven't visited the outskirts of their lives. On the other side
of the buffering spine of the Bitterroot Range, people were
waking up to alarm clocks, driving to work with mugs of
coffee sloshing between their legs. Over there were people
who would never know the heart of a wild place.

A sinister gang of stratocumulus, thick-bottomed
and heavy, approached from the southwest, coming in
so low it appeared they would shear off the top of the
lookout. Judging from the distance it had already traveled through the pale winter sky, it was clear the sun
would slow its trip to the western horizon for no one.
The packer would arrive soon and there were duffle
bags to be packed, floors to be swept, and shutters to be
put up until next season. And as quickly as it had begun,
the adventure was over.

In the end, it was just another day on top of a perfectly
good mountain, and there was work left to be done.

❧ ❧ ❧

Karla Theilen spent years in the Grand Canyon at the working end of a shovel before migrating north to watch for forest fires and roam the hills in the presence of animals much larger than herself. This piece also appears in A Mile in Her Boots: Women Who Work in the Wild.

❧ ❧ ❧

Flying with the Honguitos

A traveler in Mexico partakes of
an ancient and sacred ritual.

In her cement kitchen painted a mildewing peach, Feliza sets down a plate arranged with three rolled-up ham slices, white bread, and mayonnaise—the bland, mushy American dinner she has gone out of her way to buy for me. "Here you are, *maestra*." She insists on calling me teacher rather than Laura, even though I am twenty-four years old and feel like a disoriented little girl.

"*Gracias*." I make a point of dumping loads of chile on the ham rolls.

"Oh! You eat our food!" Feliza says, pleased, and heats up some spicy *mole* and tortillas. Then she directs the conversation back to the *honguitos*—the mushrooms known around the world as psychedelic, hallucinogenic, entheogenic, or just plain magic.

This has been the main topic for the past hour, since I arrived in the indigenous Mazatec town of Huautla de Jiménez, Mexico. When Feliza's younger brother, Santy, picked me up from the bus station, he gave me a sweaty handshake and listed the famous people who have come for the *honguitos*. ("Even the Bay-aht-less came, *maestra!*" "The Bay-aht-less?" "You know, Yon Lennon!") My series of bus rides here lasted all day, starting at dawn in the parched, rolling hills of the more southern Mixtec region of Oaxaca, where I teach English, and ending on a steep road winding up into dusky white mist.

The ancient "mushroom cults" of Mesoamerica first began to fascinate me a few years earlier as an anthropology student. The Aztecs revered the mushrooms as *teonanácatl*—flesh of the gods—and ingested them in royal, sacred rituals. The Spaniards, however, called the mushrooms flesh of the devil and used torture and murder to try to eradicate their use. I hadn't realized how close I was to the living mushroom tradition until my student Victor—Feliza's son—invited me to visit his hometown.

I've read somewhere that every person has one fundamental question running through the fabric of her life. If so, my question is this: how can I move back and forth between the mundane world and another, hidden realm, knowing both the surface and depths of life? This is what I hope to learn with the mushrooms, with a shaman.

Feliza scoops the chocolate *mole* on my plate and shakes her head. "How sad you won't be able to take the *honguitos, maestra*."

Yes, I am disappointed. Santy told me earlier in the car that the mushrooms only grow during the summer rainy season. And it's February now.

Feliza seems so maternal and conservative in her flowered polyester skirt suit and permed hair that I can't resist asking if she's taken the *honguitos* herself. Like her, I tack "*ito*" onto the end of "*hongo*" to show affection for the mushrooms.

"Yes," she says. "With my mother."

"Your mother?" I'm stunned.

"She cures with the *honguitos*. She began at age twelve. That's when she had her calling to heal. The *honguitos* taught her how."

"Can I meet her?"

"Yes, tomorrow evening, *maestra*. She gives our house a *limpia* every year, to clean out any evil air. She will also give *limpias* to our family, including you, if you'd like."

The next evening, the grandmother arrives in a whirl of red fabric, a flash of gold from her painted teeth and dangling earrings. Epifania is her name. Epiphany. She looks at me curiously, smiling, her eyes penetrating, seeing me, knowing me, knowing that words are little things pasted here and there over top of what is real. It doesn't matter that we don't speak the same language.

Feliza explains to her in Mazatec that I am Victor's teacher. She nods and smiles, touching my hand gently. She smells of wood smoke and incense and forests.

We look at each other often throughout the evening, across the kitchen table. Periodically she asks a question in Mazatec about me, which her daughter translates. She is the only one who doesn't talk to me all the time about the mushrooms. Instead, she asks questions. "Why are you here? Your mother let you come here alone? What plants grow where you live?" With thick hands, muscular from a lifetime of hard work, she touches my hair and smiles, her eyes wide with wonder. "It looks like corn silk, doesn't it? What color will it turn when you get old?"

In bed that night, as I'm drifting to sleep, I have the sensation that Doña Epifania is lying next to me in my bed. Her presence is tremendous; it defies the rules of space. She is the shaman I have waited for.

At dawn the next morning, the whole family sits in the kitchen in a thick haze of incense smoke. Wrapped in her red shawl, Doña Epifania chants hypnotically. Feliza whispers to me that she is thanking God, the saints, and the Lord of the Mountain—*chicon tocoxo* in Mazatec. Doña Epifania moves the clay dish of smoldering copal—crystallized tree resin—around our bodies, one by one, bathing us in sweet, piney smoke, cleaning our spirits. From an ancient tin box she picks out sacred corn kernels to scatter and divine our state of health and fortune.

The ceremony lasts for hours. As sunlight floods the room, Doña Epifania looks like a being from another world with her halo of copal smoke, her face glowing with beads of sweat, sometimes serene and focused, sometimes amused. We all assemble banana leaf packages of feathers, cacao beans, eggs, *piziate* (a blend of tobacco and mineral lime), and bark paper as offerings.

After breakfast, Santy and Victor and I take their giant seventies sedan to drop off the offerings for the Lord of the Mountain. The car bumps along curvy dirt roads over green hillsides, swerving around chickens and dogs. "Jesus walked across this landscape," Santy says. He has the same smooth, brown skin and strong cheekbones as Victor, only with extra padding around his belly. "Where his drops of blood landed on the earth, the *honguitos* sprang up. *Niños santos*, we call them." Saint Children.

We pass a cluster of shacks, one of which belonged to the shaman María Sabina. I've seen her on posters in American head shops, an elderly woman in braids and an embroidered *huipil*, smoking a cigarette. She was made famous by Gordon Wasson, a banker-turned-amateur-mycologist who described taking mushrooms with her in "Seeking the Magic Mushrooms," published in *Life* magazine in 1957. The article opened the floodgates for waves of hippies to journey to Huautla, marking the start of the psychedelic era.

"Some of the foreigners respected our way of taking the mushrooms and some didn't," Santy says. "You should take them only in the darkness of night or you could go crazy. And keep a *dieta*—no sex, no alcohol—for days afterwards." Things got out of hand, Santy continues, with some hippies stumbling along the streets in daylight while tripping, having sex indiscreetly in the cornfields.

We hike up the Mountain of Adoration that towers over Huautla. An ocean of mist stretches out through the valleys, and mountain peaks poke through like islands. At the summit, in the full sun, stand three large crosses and a plaque of the Virgin of Guadalupe in brilliant shades of rose, gold, and blue. We walk down a small path to a stone nook, damp and cool and secret-looking, drenched in shadows between rocks and earth and tree roots. There's a stone slab at altar level covered with burning candles and pools of melted wax.

We leave our offering and climb back to the summit, where Santy extends his arms and leans into the wind. "My mother flies," he says. "And she's never been in an airplane. Sometimes she flies to California to visit my brother. Gently, like a bird." He forms a sphere with thick, calloused hands. "See, the earth is tiny when you travel with the *honguitos*."

All the way down the mountain he talks. "Taking the *honguitos* is like school. The first time you take them you are in nursery school, then in primary school, then secondary school, and then high school. Each time, you learn more."

He tells me about the first time he took the *honguitos*. After a soccer injury, he suffered from severe back pain. The doctor said he could be cured only with risky and costly surgery. One night, his mother gave him the *honguitos*, which talked to him and showed him how to cure his back.

I turn to Victor, who has remained quiet. "Aren't you curious to try the mushrooms?"

"No, they're medicine." He shrugs. "I don't need them now. Anyway, I'd be scared. They're really strong."

I leave Huautla and return to my teaching position in Oaxacao. Over the next year and a half, I delve into transcripts of María Sabina's mushroom ceremonies, pure poetry about oceans and stars and hummingbirds.

…I am a sap woman, a dew woman [the mushroom]
says
    I am a fresh woman, a woman of clarity, says
    I am a woman of light, a woman of the day, says
    I am a woman who looks into the insides of things…

I read and re-read the beautiful essay, "The Mushrooms of Language" by Henry Munn, who has lived in Huautla for fifty years. He writes that the mushrooms allow words to flow spontaneously out of the shaman's mouth, "as if existence were uttering itself through him." He quotes a shamaness, who says, at the end of the night, "We are going to return without mishap, along a fresh path, a good path, a path of good air, in a path through a cornfield..." She shows the way there and back.

During rainy season, I head for Huautla with Manuel, my boyfriend at the time, a brilliant Central American nearly twice my age. We get along terribly, yet never seem to be able to break up. We arrive Saturday afternoon, exhausted and hungry, in the tense aftermath of a fight. My secret reason for wanting to take the mushrooms is to make sense of this relationship with Manuel. Mazatecs don't draw a distinct line between disease and misfortune; maybe my distress can be treated with the *honguitos.*

In her house, Feliza gives us sad news: Doña Epifania has been sick, and although she's recovering, we can't take the mushrooms with her. Francisco offers to take us instead to a shaman of supposed international fame, a man I will call Gregorio.

I hesitate. The thought of taking the mushrooms with an unknown man makes my stomach feel jumpy. What if the mushrooms trigger a panic attack?

Manuel decides not to take them. I wonder if I should. Over the past year, our relationship has chipped away at my self-confidence, distorted my vision. What I need is clarity.

Woman of clarity, little fresh flower woman, woman of sap, woman of dew. We are going to search and question... untie and disentangle... let us go searching for the path...

I decide to take the mushrooms.

Victor's father, Francisco, drives Manuel and me up the mountain outside of town to a cluster of shacks where chickens peck at weeds. An elderly woman leads us to a hut with a dirt floor, four chairs, an ancient TV, and pictures of María Sabina plastered all over the walls. After a long wait, Gregorio staggers in, barefoot and wearing a stained undershirt. He's in his thirties, with a beautiful sculpted face and bloodshot eyes.

He turns on the TV, slumps in a wooden chair, rubs his eyes, and after several minutes turns to us and asks hoarsely, "What can I do for you?"

As Francisco speaks to him in Mazatec (some things are more easily discussed in their native tongue), he sits up straighter, more awake now. Francisco translates what I need to bring to the ceremony: candles, white flowers, the herbs *ruda* and *hierba María*, copal incense, and 300 pesos (about $30).

Gregorio turns to me. "*No tenga miedo, güera.* Don't be scared, white girl. And don't eat anything for the rest of the day."

"Nothing?" I already feel light-headed. "I've hardly eaten all day."

"*Bueno,* a small taco should be okay. And some water. But no black food. You might vomit, so you want an empty stomach. Don't be scared. When you vomit, all the bad things come out. Don't be scared, *güera.*"

I'm not scared until the third time he tells me not to be. My mouth turns dry. Looking for reassurance, I glance at Manuel. He remains quiet, expressionless, wary of situations out of his control.

Gregorio grows animated, telling us stories of rich and famous clients. He shows us photo albums packed with pictures and newspaper clips about him and María

Sabina. Still, I think back to my first meeting with
Doña Epifania, and how a single brilliant glance from
her impressed me more than all Gregorio's stories and
pictures do now.

"Don't be scared," are Francisco's last words as he
drops us off at Gregorio's place at sunset.

Gregorio is chopping firewood when Manuel and I
approach him. His eyes seem less bloodshot, his clothes
less disheveled. He leads us into a newly built shack,
with a wooden floor, two beds, a chair, an altar, and a
kitchen with no running water.

He backs out of the room. *"Ahorita vengo,"* he says. He
puts his forefinger and thumb an inch apart, the Mexican
gesture which theoretically means, "Just a second."

Around the room hang velvet-framed pictures of
María Sabina, barefoot in her *huipil* embroidered with
birds and flowers, two braids interwoven with ribbons
hanging down her back. On the wooden altar are five
pairs of mushrooms on a banana leaf, candles, a vase,
the flowers and herbs, a clay copal burner, and several
framed pictures of saints and Virgins.

It grows dark outside. Thunder rumbles, at first
faintly, then loudly, with flashes of lightning. Rain drums
the roof, and Manuel and I wonder where Gregorio is.

After an hour, Gregorio rushes in the door, wet with
sweat or rain. "I have other clients in another cabin," he
says. His voice is apologetic bordering on deceptive. His
gaze flickers around. "They traveled a long way. I can't
turn them back."

This is disappointing. Feliza told us earlier that the
shaman should be with you for the entire night, not
dividing his energy with others.

"*Ahorita vengo.*" He slips outside again.

Manuel and I examine the mushrooms. There are ten, eight with small, rounded caps, two with wide, flat caps, all spotted with clumps of dirt and mold. A while later, Gregorio hurries inside, dripping, shivering, rubbing his hands together. Breathless, he picks off the larger pieces of dirt and mold. He grabs the vase from the altar, dashes outside, and returns with the vase full of fresh water for the flowers and *ruda* and *hierba María*. I think of a busboy under pressure, clearing and setting tables in a slammed restaurant.

Now, still breathing hard, he faces the altar and chants in Mazatec, his arms moving in broad rhythmic strokes of crosses and circles. He burns the copal and moves the smoke over our bodies, chanting. He smoothes *piziate* on my inner elbows to protect me. Then he hands me the banana leaf with the mushrooms.

I take tiny bites, chewing thoroughly with my front teeth before swallowing, as Feliza instructed. Every once in a while, I get a gritty dirt clump in my mouth and spit it surreptitiously onto the leaf—probably disrespectful but Gregorio doesn't seem to notice. As I chew, he slouches in a wooden chair and brags that he is the best shaman in Huautla. "A relative of mine cures with the *hongos*, too. But she has a bad temper. She accuses me of stealing clients, but the clients feel more comfortable with me."

I can feel Manuel shooting me a sarcastic look. I finish the *honguitos* after twenty minutes of snail-paced chewing. They leave an acidic taste on the sides and back of my tongue. I wait to slip into another mode of consciousness, what Munn describes in his essay as kaleidoscopes of color, the dawn in the middle of night, the brilliance of stars, echoes of the creation of the world. Very subtly, I start to feel the effects. I notice the wind rattling the panes and blowing the curtains, and the patterns in the wooden walls, as though I've had a puff on a joint.

Gregorio gives the little *"ahorita vengo"* sign with his thumb and forefinger as he ducks out the door.

I ask Manuel to turn off the bare light bulb. The only light now comes from the two candles on the altar. I close my eyes. Patterns emerge—to my embarrassment, hundreds of yellow smiley faces, geometrically arranged, pure psychedelic clichés. Rainbows and hearts appear next, images straight from my third grade sticker collection. Then Pac-Man-style graphics—Atari quality, the pre-Nintendo days of my childhood.

I'm laughing when Gregorio barrels into the room.

"What do you feel?" he asks nervously.

"Ummm...I feel different, a little..." I try to sound positive.

He realizes I'm not feeling much. There is a comic desperation in his desire to compensate. He chants some more, using broad, rhythmic gestures.

I try hard to appreciate his efforts.

It works. His gestures and words and sing-song voice fit together perfectly. His arms and hands leave streaks like comets. I am mesmerized. Ah, so this is why he makes those gestures! This is why he chants!

He takes the flowers and *ruda* and *hierba María* from the vase and gives me a *limpia*. The *ruda* smells strong and pungent, piercing and clarifying. The flowers are wet and their petals cling to my forehead and neck and face like hundreds of soft, cool fingers. Water drips from my eyebrows and chin and runs in little streams down my cheeks. Ah! So this is why they use dripping wet flowers—because they turn me into a mountain, alive with springs.

At the same time though, even in this altered state I am aware of being an outsider, a representative of my generation, a child of the eighties, drilled in materialism, thoroughly and inescapably American.

After the *limpia,* Gregorio squeezes my head hard between his two hands, chanting, his voice full of effort, as though he's pouring forth an enormous amount of energy. Once he finishes, he falls into a wooden chair, spent. I feel compassion for him. He seems a victim himself, somehow, of the commercialized venture that mushrooms have become in Huautla—far from the wise, trustworthy shaman he desperately tries to portray. He leaves, bowing and whispering good night as he backs out of the room.

I try to talk to Manuel but he looks annoyed.

"I just want to sleep," he says.

I study his face. He is an old man with dark circles and grayish, wrinkled skin. His black beard is flecked with silver, his hairline receding. He likes the idea of a young lover, but he has no patience for me. He has already come to his conclusions about the world.

I kiss him on the forehead and go outside. The night is clear now, the sky studded with stars, and the valley below with tiny lights. The moon is just shy of full. The corn plants wave their leaves with a consciousness of their own. I wish I had come outside earlier, into this expanse of sky that is like the ocean, the stars like scattered shells. I reach my arms toward them, these treasures that are still too far away. I am an old woman, looking back at this moment, this moment in the nursery school of the spirit. A woman who looks into the insides of things. A woman of clarity, a shooting star woman. And I know that someday when I do fly, Doña Epifania will be there, her smile wide, her expression beckoning me. Together, we will fly to pluck the stars, then back and forth and back again.

Colorado-based Laura Resau is an anthropologist, teacher, and writer for youth and adults. Her essays and stories have appeared in magazines including Brain Child, Pilgrimage, Matter, *and* Cicada, *as well as a Lonely Planet humor anthology. Her encounters with healers in Oaxaca inspired her novel,* What the Moon Saw. *Visit her website at www.lauraresau.com.*

DEBORAH FRYER

Every Body Needs Milk

Could a child's fantasy to race on a Minneapolis
lake bring her family back together?

*T*his is a tale of two sisters, two canoe paddles and 300
gallons of milk. The year: 1971. My age: seven. Hair:
piano-colored. Eyes: grape. Teeth: seventeen. Album of
the Year: Simon & Garfunkel's *Bridge over Troubled Water*.
Most earth-shattering event: the launch of Apollo XIII. It
interrupted my piano recital and riveted the grown-ups
to a black-and-white television set that snowed despite
the rabbit ears on top. The reception was pretty much
like driving through a blizzard. As the adults watched,
the static grew louder. A rocket blasted off. Everyone
cheered. I didn't see what the big deal was, so I admired
my reflection in my black patent leather shoes instead and
practiced the Clementi sonatina I was going to play in
my head. The green shag carpeting curled up around my

oval feet like grass, which reminded me that life was, in general, pretty groovy. Favorite food: chocolate chip cookies. Favorite drink: milk.

In Minnesota, where I grew up, we drank milk three meals a day, and then some. We had our own personal milkman named Bill who wore a blue hat even in the summer, and delivered us three gallons of milk and a pound of butter every week and milk chocolate bars at Christmastime. At night I'd fall asleep with a warm milkstache on my upper lip and count cows instead of sheep. Milk was in.

That year, the Beatles separated and soon thereafter, so did my parents. My father moved out to a bachelor pad with a whirlpool and a vibrating hip-and-thigh-toning machine in the exercise room. My sister and I visited him once a week. We'd listen to Simon and Garfunkel's *Greatest Hits* over and over on the record player. We'd eat peanuts salted in the shell. When my father was done, he'd make funny smacking sounds with his lips. That meant he was ready for a cigarette. His lighter tinkled like a handful of pennies. He'd light a Winston-Salem, and then look out the window vacantly, blowing smoke towards the moon. *Hello darkness, my old friend, I've come to talk with you again.*

He always served us the same thing for dinner: buttered pumpernickel toast, scrambled eggs, and milk. He chewed with his mouth open, which reminded me of my dog, which made me miss being at home in my own house, where I was somebody. In my father's bachelor pad, I felt as beige as the walls. "Drink your milk," he'd say in a monotone. "Why?" I'd ask, because I was seven, because I was testing him, because I just wanted him to talk to me about anything. "Because I said so," he answered, pouring himself another glass of scotch and retiring to his easy chair. *And no one dare disturb the sound of silence.*

My sister cleared the table and loaded the dishwasher—all except for my glass of milk. I read the milk carton with as much concentration as my father was directing towards his newspaper. *Pff pff* went his lips, *jingle jingle* went his lighter, and then a blue cloud of smoke collected over his head like a genie, waiting to grant a wish. My sister got her Nancy Drew book and settled on the couch in the living room with my dad. I stayed at the Formica table and swiveled in the vinyl avocado chair. "Stop swiveling," order a detached voice from behind a screen of newsprint.

I focused hard on the milk carton in order to push my sadness back into my body. It was like trying to get toothpaste back in the tube. A cud-chewing, polka-dotted cow with a wagging tail smiled at me from the side of the milk carton. There was another cartoon on the other side, of a beaming blond boy, bobbing on a raft. Even the sun was smiling in his world. Upon closer inspection I noticed that the happy little boy's boat was made entirely of milk cartons. EVERY BODY NEEDS MILK! proclaimed a parade of dancing letters that looked like they were part of a chorus line. I reluctantly took a tiny sip of milk. "It's warm now," I said to myself. I didn't think anyone was listening. "Drink it anyway," my father said, getting that angry edge in his voice. I wished I were that little boy without a care in the world, drifting on a gentle lake, in the warm sun. *And a rock feels no pain. And an island never cries.*

While my father read about the war in Vietnam, I pretended to find equal fascination with what I was reading. I glanced back at the genie over my father's oblivious head, squeezed the tears back into my eyes, and made a wish. And then, my mind magically began to swirl…and the path to love and recognition appeared right in front of my nose in Technicolor like the yellow brick road. The milk that moments before had seemed so odious and been a source of contention and disgust became my new elixir of love. The milk carton said this: "There are many different ways to build a milk carton boat! Tape milk cartons end-to-end, making long snakes with which to form a canoe. You can build catamaran hulls, outriggers, sail boats, giant gerbil-wheels! You are limited only by your imagination, and perhaps your experience in construction." I could already feel the sun on my face and the water tickling my bare feet. I could hear the ducklings and mallards quacking at me to come play with them. My spirits rose like sunshine at dawn. "MILK CARTON BOAT RACE. LAKE CALHOUN. JULY 25TH!" I would build a boat and sail away and win a lot of money and everyone would be so proud of me, including my father. I felt this in my bones, which would be super strong from all the milk I would have to con-sume. My father interrupted my super galactic fantasy. "Drink your milk or I'll get the hairbrush." I gulped it down without issue. "I get dibs on this carton when it's empty," I said. My father finally looked up. "Why?" His eyes met mine. I had scored one little victory already. "Because I am going to build a boat out of milk cartons," I announced.

For the next six months I drank even more milk than usual and I enlisted my sister's help. We drowned our lumpy Cream of Wheat in oceans of milk, creating archipelagoes in our cereal bowls. We made pudding every night, vanilla, chocolate, butterscotch; it didn't

matter, as long as we used up a quart. We baked cheesecakes and soufflés, plied our friends with milkshakes and
malteds after school, took baths in milk, washed our hair
in milk, even shampooed Delilah, the miniature poodle,
in 2 percent. By the time summer started, my sister and
I had gone through 300 gallons of milk. The garage was
piled high with empty, expectant cartons, waiting to be
transformed and reincarnated into a boat that would be
the envy of the whole Twin Cities. My picture would be
above the fold of the *Minneapolis Tribune*. I would get
a call from President Nixon congratulating me. I practiced my acceptance speech and vamped for the press in
the bathroom mirror. "It looks like it's going to be wild,"
wrote one newspaper reporter. "Teams around the city
have already started building their boats. Milk sales are
skyrocketing. This is an event not to be missed." I didn't
feel so alone any more. I was part of something bigger
now, something exciting and newsworthy. I drank up.
The more milk I consumed, the more it consumed me.
The milk revolution was going to change my world.
*Your time has come to shine. All your dreams are on their
way.*

In 1971, *Ms. Magazine* was launched. My mother
burned her bra, took up pottery, and started practicing
yoga. My father grew his sideburns longer, moved back
into the house, and complained my mother was brain-
washing us with women's lib and brown rice. He coun-
tered her measures by bringing a TV into the house,
drinking Dr. Pepper with dinner, and taking us out to
Dairy Queen for dessert. They argued about Nixon and
the Vietnam War, smoking in the house, and whose
turn it was to walk the dog. The only thing they agreed
upon any more was that my sister and I still had to drink

milk at every meal. We were caught in the middle, with a garageful of stinky milk cartons and a houseful of increasingly sour parents.

That summer *I'm Okay, You're Okay* made it to the bestseller list as my mother and father drifted farther and farther apart. They stopped speaking to one another except when absolutely necessary. Their anger seethed like a lake whipped into froth by an impending storm. I became the bridge between their hostile shores. My milk carton boat would bring the family back together again. My dream for recognition became more urgent than a full bladder in a traffic jam. I would drink my milk obediently and gaze enviously at the happy blond boy on his boat. He would seem to look right back into my eyes. *I'm on your side when times get rough.* I knew I would have to navigate my own course. And I had just the plan to keep us all from capsizing.

My father met me in the garage with plywood, chicken wire, and a staple gun. My mother came armed with twenty rolls of waterproof duct tape. My sister and I folded over the tops of the cartons and my mother taped the spout ends flush to create the building blocks for my boat. My father laid the cartons end to end like dominoes to form beams, and then encased the beams in chicken wire to form pontoons, and then stapled the pontoons to the plywood board. Together we assembled that milk carton boat on a sunny Saturday afternoon and it almost felt like we were a normal family again. Little did I know that this harmonious folding and taping and stapling and hammering was merely the calm before the storm. When the last nail was pounded in, I was proud of my raft. I was proud of my family. I wanted them to be proud of me. I couldn't wait to try out my boat.

Sunday, July 25, race day. The morning came warm and clear. I tied on my yellow flowered halter-top and squirmed into cutoff shorts. I examined the scab on my knee and wriggled my toes into pink flip-flops. I was ready to go! It was only 7:00 A.M. "Have some cereal. You'll need the energy today." My mother poured the milk on my Cheerios in a clockwise direction. I smiled at the boy on the raft one last time and he grinned back at me ear to ear. *If you need a friend I'm sailing right behind.*

8:00 A.M. My sister and I had our first fight over who got to sit in the front seat. She won because she was bigger. I got mad. We arrived at the lake. I was still mad. 8:30 A.M. The other contestants eagerly dragged their crafts to the shore. People had constructed boats that looked like school buses and toilets and gophers and Viking ships, boats with rows of oars and paddlewheels and triangular prows. My heart sank. Our square little pontoon raft that we had worked so hard on seemed so small in comparison, so insignificant and puny. Racers were beginning to line up behind the orange buoys. Twelve hundred milk-swilling competitors dressed in tie-dyed t-shirts and crocheted bikinis waded into Lake Calhoun. I was awestruck and suddenly afraid. The applause began like gentle rain at first and then grew louder and more enthusiastic. "Girls, get over here and help me carry your boat to the water," ordered my father, his lips clenched around a burning cigarette. My sister and I both grabbed the same side.

"I got here first."

"No you didn't." She pushed me.

"Did so." I clung harder.

"Did not." She pulled my hair. I spit at her.

"God damn it, girls!" my father snarled. I started to cry. I ran to the other side. The sand felt good between my toes. I didn't want to miss the start of the race. I caught the blond boy's kind, waxy eyes peering at me through the chicken wire. *When you're weary, feeling small, when tears are in your eyes, I will dry them all.* We ran to the shore. We slid our raft into the water. It floated. It was a miracle. *Your time has come to shine. All your dreams are on their way.*

My father stood on the beach, puffing in silence. I watched the smoke curl around his hair. I could not see his eyes through his sunglasses. My mother pushed us up to the starting line and handed us our paddles. The whistle blew. There was splashing and shrieking and cheering. The milk carton boats were off. Racers quickly passed the orange buoys. The lake water sparkled and danced as hundreds of milk carton boats churned the water into diamonds. People were paddling, sailing, kayaking, pedaling, paddlewheeling, even kicking their milk carton contraptions across the lake. Everyone, that is, except for me and my sister, because we had both started paddling on the right side of the raft."

"Paddle on the other side!" yelled my sister.

"But I got on this side first," I paddled harder. The boat veered to the left.

"No you didn't, I got here first."

"You're ruining it," I cried.

"No you are," she snapped.

"Meanie."

"Baby."

"Shut up."

"You shut up."

My mother waded out to where we were spinning in circles, straightened out the raft and pushed us back towards the middle of the lake. I switched sides, pretending to accidentally splash my sister in the face. She sprayed me back and switched to the left also.

"I'm going to paddle on this side. Stay on the other side," she said bossily.

"But I just was on the other side and you told me to switch."

"I changed my mind." We argued. She pinched me. I cried. She gave me the silent treatment. I glared at her. All the other boats were halfway across the lake and turning around to come back, and we still had not even crossed the starting line. *When darkness comes and pain is all around, like a bridge over troubled water, I will lay me down.* I paddled as hard as I could, but our boat just spiraled like a broken record. I looked back at the shore for help. My father was gone. My mother stood knee-deep in the water, waving, encouraging us on, but unwilling to intervene. By the time my sister and I forgave each other and figured out how to paddle together as a team and go forward, the race was over.

Needless to say, we didn't win the milk carton boat race. We didn't even come close. We couldn't paddle my parents back together, no matter how hard we tried. Instead, my sister and I unwittingly turned their marital drama into our own version of a pathetic water ballet. Perched on two separate pontoons, we went around in circles because we couldn't agree on anything. Try as we might, we were stuck and furious with each other, and the more mad we got, the more we whipped the water into whitecaps with our useless paddling, and the farther we floated from our goal. Even if we had been able to paddle perfectly in sync, and had won the blue ribbon that day, our parents' story would still have ended the only way that it could have. I suppose it was no accident that we as a family had built a boat with two independent flotations instead of a single hull. A few months later, my parents got divorced, and the milk carton boat went into the trash.

The Minneapolis Aquatennial Milk Carton Boat Races were started in 1971 because the advertising agency Campbell Mithun, Inc. had wanted to increase sales for the Milk Foundation of the Twin Cities. "Publicity Stunt Snowballs Into Wild Event," raged the headline in the *Pioneer Press*, on July 25, 1971. Reporter Linda Kohl quipped of the boat race: "It could be the most spectacular nautical event since the sinking of the Titanic, and at the very least may someday be hailed as one of the great advertising coups of the decade."

Thirty-four years later, the milk carton boat race is still taking place every summer on Lake Calhoun in Minneapolis, Minnesota. I have recently been toying with the idea of testing my mettle again. My sister and I have become best friends. We both have strong bones and share an abiding love of the water. I know we could easily take turns paddling on opposite sides of the boat now. Maybe we could even be contenders. We still love Simon and Garfunkel. But there is just one problem: we have both developed an allergy to milk.

Deborah Fryer is a filmmaker and freelance writer who has won numerous awards for her documentaries and creative nonfiction essays, including first place in the Moondance International Film Festival Short Story Contest in 2004 and 2005. She is the founder of a video production company (www.lilafilms.com) in Boulder, Colorado.

REBECCA LAWTON

The Tongue

Two women endure a harrowing boat trip
down an Oregon river.

*I*t's time I told the truth about that day on the
Rogue River. I've embroidered the tale, changed
names and details, and made myself the hero—most
likely in hopes of remedying the many mistakes I made.
It's true that after the accident, all I wanted to do was
stay home and chop wood. As if I could cut away what
I'd done. After all my other chores, I'd go outside and
hack and saw until dark, bit by bit splitting all the oak
rounds in the shed. As I worked I kept seeing the river,
how wild it was the day we ran it, rising hard in the
eddies. Trees sliding by, big and torn up, rocks and mud
still in their roots. The whole flight of steps from the
boat dock folded like a ladder toward the lodge, pulled
and tucked away.

One night after about a week of all my wood chopping, when I was tired but still swinging hard, pushing, sending chips flying, I missed the stump and just grazed my left boot. That scared the piss out of me, so I had to quit for a while. I sat outside watching the wind shake boughs in my big cedar tree. Wondered how much longer I'd have to spend at the woodpile before I'd ever want to get on the river again.

Driving to the boat ramp with Michelle the morning of our river run is still fresh in my mind. She was the girlfriend of a friend, and she wanted a lift down the river to the lodge at Half Moon Bar. For some reason she trusted me to be the one to take her. We planned to row to Half Moon, in a driftboat I'd borrowed from my boyfriend Harvey—to this day I'm amazed that he lent it to me. He'd just bought it, and it was a beauty: mint green, with black trim and sideboards. It had new ash oars and brass alloy locks. A perfect boat for chasing down salmon and steelhead for sport fishing, Harvey's chosen profession.

Harvey drove us to put-in, and we saw the madrones in the headlights, wet from the weeklong rains.

Michelle asked, "What's that shimmering?"

Harvey leaned close to the windshield and looked up. "You mean the madrone leaves?"

"Yes! That's it—all silver in the lights."

Michelle's eyes glowed like the undersides of the leaves. Her face looked pale and bright, a headlight of its own.

"They're beautiful," she said. "Magical." She turned the bright light of her face toward me. "I see why you spend so much time out here. It's gorgeous!"

When we arrived at the Grave Creek boat ramp, the river looked even higher than the phone report had said. Although the rain had stopped, the feeder creeks and sidestreams downstream of the depth gauge in town must still have been pumping in runoff. The three of us stood at river's edge, in our slickers and woolies and milking boots, and watched the muddy water.

"Shit," Harv said. He liked to swear. "It's god damn bigger today than I thought. Are you guys sure about this?"

"No," I replied.

"Why not?" asked Michelle. "Is it too high?"

"I don't know," I said.

Something seemed strange, even besides high water, and Michelle put her finger on it. "There's no one here. Do you think we'll have the river to ourselves?"

"No, we're just early," I said. "Don't you think someone's bound to launch later, Harv?"

"Maybe so."

"Oh, I hope they don't," Michelle said. "I love it here, all wild and empty."

She was so excited about it. And I did expect other boaters to launch that day, clouds or no clouds, because in that country, you never get out if you don't run in bad weather. Besides, we'd promised to meet friends at Half Moon that evening. So I decided to go ahead and run.

We backed the trailer down to the water, though we didn't have to back very far, since the river covered half the ramp. Then we lined the boat into an eddy, loaded a bit of gear for overnighting at the lodge. Finally I kicked off from shore and took the oars, and we whipped into the current like a leaf in the wind. Michelle sat up front, braced on the gunnels with her mittened fingers. We yelled good-bye to Harv, our hands too busy to wave. Our voices no doubt lost out there.

The river surged down the middle in big sets of rollers. High water covered most of the rocks. From time to time, Michelle looked back at me, smiling and big-eyed. Sometimes surprise side waves hit the boat in the belly or caught the sharp rails at the bottom, a feeling I've never liked much considering how easily those driftboats flip. I struggled like a madwoman to control the boat. But Michelle didn't seem to know it was scary—she just laughed.

"Is it always this exciting?" she asked.

"No, not always."

"But it is today. The river's alive!"

About two miles down from Grave Creek, the rain started again. Soon Michelle noticed all the tributaries pumping in dark water from the side canyons. "What's different about the creeks?" she asked. "They're not muddy like the river. They look like tea. Or coffee."

Dark, leaf-stained water poured from gullies and swirled into the foamy water out in the current. With the ground already soaked up the way it was, little canyons normally choked with gooseberry and fir flushed and spilled that darker water. Some of them might not have run that high in years, dark and churning, streaming from places we couldn't see.

The huge falls at Rainie had washed out, just an easy channel of small swirling waves. That was no sweat, although it spooked me to glide over a ledge of rock, normally so tall above the river, buried far below tons of water. At Horseshoe Bend, the water had risen as far up the bank as people say it gets when the gauge reads 20 feet, more than twice as high as had been reported that morning. And in Mule Creek Canyon the water reached clear to the top of the gorge. But I had no way of knowing how high the river was by then—it was higher than I'd ever seen, and higher by far than anyone runs solo. I didn't say anything to Michelle, so of course she got me for being quiet.

"Everything okay, captain?" she asked.

I didn't answer. I was listening. "Shh."

Michelle turned to me, surprised. Then the question left her face, because she heard something, too. Something like a train coming from a long distance, or a thundering jet. Or every last bear out in the woods growling. But it wasn't any of those things. I knew what it was—rapids. Big rapids. Above a certain size they lose their friendlier white noise and start roaring. Maybe they become all water and no air, and the rumble fills the sky and shakes your ears and heart. I knew that the sound meant that downstream, not quite around another bend, was some big whitewater. Blossom Bar in flood.

The startling thing to Michelle was there was nothing to see. Blossom bellowed below us, but just the lip of it showed. High water had filled the rock garden down in the belly of the rapids and covered the marker boulders, so from up top we could only see a curved edge of muddy water rolling ahead. Deceptively smooth, the tongue led into the rapids and then tumbled rocket fast into whitewater.

The only thing to do was pull to shore. I rowed so hard to get over, I almost overshot a little rock cove I was aiming for in the right bank. We got into the cove, though, and I pulled close to a cliff where we moored the boat. My hands shook as I tied up the bowline, while

Michelle waited. Then we kind of crept downstream to scout the rapid.

"Good God," I said when I saw it.

Blossom looked huge and ugly. The usual house-sized boulders were under water, and they made nasty reversals that kicked up froth and spit like I'd never seen before, and haven't seen since, on that river. The standard run, where you swing wide to the left and cut back hard right, was not the usual highway through. Not nearly so. Rowing the normal route would mean pulling through some ungodly rowdy water and around two deadly sucking holes.

Michelle watched me as I watched the rapids. Finally, she asked, "Why's this so much nastier than everything else?"

"Blossom's got the biggest rocks on the river, for some reason."

She asked the million-dollar question. "Can we do it?"

"Well, I've run stuff this bad before," I said. But I never had in a driftboat, and I never had when there wasn't another boat waiting downstream to bail me out. Which for some reason I didn't tell her.

She kept looking at me, just waiting, I guess.

"We could walk from here," I said. "It's only two miles to the lodge." But we were on the wrong side of the river—we'd have to line the boat back upstream about a half mile before rowing across. The thought of the two of us lining there, with all the fast current and slippery rock, scared me. "Or we could hike out to the road." Ten miles on the river path. We could make it, but well after dark.

"What should we do?" asked Michelle. Her face was bunched up and worried, and I wanted her to stop looking that way. I thought of the driftboat, so pretty, bucking at its mooring upstream. Overnight like that, it might bash up. What would Harv say to that? At least if we made it through the rapids and got to the lodge, there had to be a quieter eddy above Four Mile Canyon.

From the corner of my eye, I could see Michelle's anxious face. "I think I can make it through," I said. "It's just two good pulls."

At that, her face lit up like a full moon after a storm. She tightened the straps on her lifejacket. "Then let's go."

I peeled off my heavy clothes, a habit I'd picked up on trips running big water. But I decided to keep on my rubber boots. Michelle chose not to strip down—she was cold enough already, she said. She just sat on her haunches on shore, one hand holding the bowline, waiting for the signal. I stepped into the driftboat. From my seat at the oars, I listened to Blossom and strained to see my entry. I had to make it across the river, to the tongue of water that led to the safest path through the rapids' spray, shock waves, and foam.

"O.K., Michelle!"

She coiled the rope, and we pushed into the current. I rowed left with everything I had, reaching far ahead of me, finishing each stroke with my legs. Michelle watched downstream, sitting as still as you please. I made the quickest, strongest strokes possible, arching all the way up as I pulled, recovering quickly. Even so we only reached mid-river by the time we'd floated to the top of the rapids. The current was just too fast for me—something I hadn't felt before, not even earlier that day.

As we swept closer to the falls, Michelle got a good look at what lay ahead. She turned and screamed, "Pull, pull!"

The tongue I'd been aiming for was still far to the left. We'd only made it as far as the big pyramid rock, at that water level just a tip of granite in a huge mound of brown water. At the last minute I punted and ran a chute between the pyramid and the gorilla-faced rock. We dropped over a little falls, where the boat made a sickening, scraping sound over something below us. Still, we landed straight. But it was a hard fall that popped the oars from their locks.

"Shit." I slammed the oars back in place.

Michelle still held the gunnels. "We're O.K.! Pull! Pull!"

I pivoted to the best angle I could and rowed, but the upstream rail of the boat caught in a surge that spun us. We washed out of control toward the Volkswagen rock, just a monster midstream hole at that water level. The driftboat turned nose first into the hole and stopped, but just for an instant before shuddering, snaking up, and twisting over on top of us.

I've always thought that life's like the river, but anybody can see that. There are backwaters and shallows, bridges and dams. There are smooth parts and rough parts. There's the tongue, the smooth "V" pointing to entry for boats, usually followed by rough, bucked-up water in a rapids. The tongue, for all its glassy tranquility, accelerating toward chaos. With all its metaphors of probing, licking, and truth-telling. Once you're on the tongue, you're committed. There are no brakes—you have to ride it out.

In Blossom that day, riding it out meant feeling a wooden boat crash down on my back in the middle of a river in flood. Being sucked straight down by the water tugging on my boots—staying down so long and tumbling around so much I doubted I'd see daylight again. And swallowing enough water to make myself heave, with no one waiting to pick us up.

Michelle's swim was bad, worse than mine, maybe because she'd kept on her heavy wool clothes. When my boots finally sucked off and I shot to the surface for air, though, she looked fine. Seeing her facing the waves as they came and turning her head to the side to breathe, I felt inspired to do the same. To put aside the panic that had gripped me underwater. But she was a hundred yards downstream, and something told me I had to close the distance. Make sure we both got out of the water. By the time I got within twenty yards of her, things had changed. She was stuck in some whirlpools along an eddy fence, wheeling around like a spinner cast out for trout. Floating low, she barely churned the surface with her arms, looking too weak and lost to find shore. Her nose red, her hair hanging in her eyes.

I caught the eddy. "Swim, Michelle! This way!"

As I reached for her, she looked around but not far enough to see me. A current shot her back out into the river.

God, I thought, I can't catch her. There's no way I'm strong enough to go back out there.

Then I saw it—one of Harv's oars sliding by, fast and sleek, out in the river. It looked so streamlined going by us that I knew what to do. Took a deep breath. Pushed back out into the mainstream and swam low and hard, telling myself to go like the oar. Far ahead, Michelle's head showed up past dozens of curlers, and I strained and shoved and broke through each wave, never taking the long ride over the tops, but slicing straight through them, a ten-foot, solid-ash oar.

When I closed in again on Michelle, she was swirling on another eddy fence. This time she floated even lower than before, swallowing water, and got caught in the swift current headed upstream.

"Michelle! No, stop!" I swam for her, afraid she'd wash out the top of the eddy into the river again.

But, no, I caught her. With my right hand, I grabbed for her lifejacket, pulling her back from the whirlpools on the eddy fence. With my left hand, I reached wildly for shore, catching hold of something thin and tough hanging in the water from the muddy bank. It didn't feel like much, but I held to it as if it were a gold-plated lifeline. As I pulled on it harder, I saw what it was—a tree root, hanging down from the bank and washing along in the water.

I pulled us over and dragged Michelle up the steep bank. We tumbled onto a little patch of slicked-down grass, gasping and coughing. When I looked up, I saw Harv's boat in the water, just across the river. All I could do was stare. The driftboat looked like a big fish come to surface, slowly turning in the current. I had to sit and watch the boat roll out of sight when I wanted so much to run along after it, to do something, anything. But I sat next to Michelle, holding her hand, and didn't move.

"Thanks," she said. "You saved me."

"The hell I did, Michelle. I about killed you."

"No, you saved my life, so let me thank you."

"O.K."

"Thank you."

We stayed the next two nights in the Paradise Lodge, just across the river from Half Moon Bar. Willis, Paradise's winter caretaker, had been reading by the fire when I knocked at the door. Still wearing my lifejacket, searching for any shelter, I was amazed to have stumbled onto another lodge. Michelle followed behind, staggering on the path. Willis's jaw dropped when he answered the door. He said later that with my skin so pale and eyes so frightened, I'd looked like a phantom.

Willis took us in, fed us, gave us dry clothes. For all his hospitality, though, I still felt I'd never be warm again or that I'd stop shaking deep inside. We played cards and word games, passing the time as the storm still raged outside, and I felt racked by tremors. Tried to hide them. Excused myself to go to the outhouse, hide behind the lodge trying to throw something up, only to return to the fire and tremble some more.

The first night at Paradise, I called Harv on the lodge radiophone.

"We flipped in Blossom," I told him.

"Shit!"

"I lost the boat." Silence. "The last I saw, it was headed for Four Mile Canyon."

"Damn!"

"I'm sorry."

"Hell, don't worry. I mean, shit—"

The radiophone operator interrupted. "Excuse me, sir, this is a citizen radio system. You'll have to watch your language."

"Sorry. Shoot, don't worry about the boat. I'm just glad you guys are all right."

"I guess I shouldn't have run Blossom."

"Maybe not. But hell, you made it out."

Harv never did get mad about the boat. Even when we recovered it, bashed and bruised, a week later. Someone had pulled it up on a gravel bar, visible from

a road across the river. On our way home from Half
Moon, we spotted the boat. Sitting out of the water,
green and wet in the foggy morning, looking like a ghost
come out of the mists. Still, we trusted our eyes, that it
was really there. We drove around to get it, loaded it
up on the jetboat trailer we were hauling, and returned
home. Both shaken and triumphant.

I never saw Michelle again after that fall. One of the
factual things I've written about our trip was that she
died not long thereafter. I'm forgetting now just how
much time she had, but she was taken by cancer. And
although I've told it otherwise, I wasn't there in the end.
Whatever choices she made about treatment, how she
fought or didn't, what things went through her mind—
none of these are subjects I can discuss with authority.

Michelle and I never talked much about the accident,
although I wanted to. Those few nights at Paradise
Lodge, she'd said that she believed she was going to
drown after we flipped. She thought few people would
miss her. So she felt okay about giving up—in fact, she
admitted that by the time I'd pulled her out of the water,
she'd surrendered. Still I was always fishing for something more—maybe validation for running Blossom
that day, even though I knew it had been harebrained.
After recovering Harv's boat from the gravel bar, I
hazarded a question. Asked Michelle, "Do you regret
running it?"

She thought about it. "It might have been the right
choice for you," she said. "But from now on, I'm making
my own decisions."

Her words have stayed with me. They especially
dogged me in the weeks that followed the accident. As

I went over my own bad choices again and again, the frightening tape of the river played in my head—the water too high, the speed of the current at Blossom, the helpless sensation of not making the tongue—all of it. The weeks passed, and I chopped wood, taking care not to miss the stump again. Splitting green rounds, dry rounds, junk wood—anything—talking to myself. Going over and over the truth.

Rebecca Lawton, a former Colorado River guide and author of Reading Water: Lessons from the River, *has boated and swum plenty of whitewater. She lives and writes in northern California.*

JILL LOWE

ॐ ॐ ॐ

Goodbye, Brenda!

She dreamed of traveling to India. What did she care if
her traveling companion was difficult?

I chose India for all the wrong reasons. I knew almost
nothing about it, but I had heard it was not too
expensive.

London lay shivering. The gleam from a single street
lamp shone through the frozen mist of the January evening on to the floor of my room. It fell in a mute pool
of light on to an empty suitcase and, beside it, a jumble
of clothes, books, boxes, and bottles. I shivered, not
from cold—the radiators were on, and orange and blue
flames leapt and danced from the fire in the grate—but
from fear, fear of the unknown, of a flight to Madras
and a three-month stay in India. I asked myself for the
hundredth time, "Why am I doing this?" But I knew the
answer. I was fifty-two, and I needed a change.

"Madras'll be easier than Delhi. Leave the north for later." Rosy, a travel agent who specialised in India, smiled across her desk. Comfortably round, with pink cheeks and frizzy hair, she was very British. "You'll find the south less shocking." She hesitated. "Well, you know what I mean...the poverty, the smells and, well, you know."

Rosy arranged a hotel for the first two nights, and recommended some guidebooks.

Terrified by the thought of going to India alone, I answered an advertisement in *The Times*. By return post, "Traveling Partners" sent me two telephone numbers. The first belonged to a Scotsman who wanted a companion for a weekend in the Outer Hebrides. I tried the other.

"Tea next week would be quite convenient," said a high-pitched female voice.

In the dark lobby of a hotel in Henley-on-Thames, a figure rose from the depths of a brown leather sofa. The highlights in her short, cropped hair looked like nicotine stains. Her designer sweater was stretched tight across her small breasts and down over her long-waisted body to meet short legs in black stretch trousers.

"I'm Brenda," she said. "I need a coffee—I've been waiting for you for hours." She looked at her watch and yawned. I was five minutes late. Leaning across the varnished tabletop, she scrutinized me from behind enormous red-framed spectacles.

"I want to go to Africa to see the tigers. I like cats. I've got two at home—Siamese, actually. They're gorgeous." She beckoned to the waitress. "I'd like a pot of coffee for two, myself. You order what you like."

I did.

While Brenda drank she told me about herself, pausing only to take delicate sips from her willow-pattern cup. After a disastrous marriage in Brazil, she had come back to England to look after her ailing mother, who eventually died of senile dementia. She was left with a house in Bournemouth, which she now ran as a prestigious B&B.

She stopped to drink and draw breath.

"I was thinking of going to India," I said quickly, before she had a chance to start again.

"Well, I hope you realize what you're doing," she said. "Traveling in a third-world country, you won't be comfortable. I've had experience; I know."

By the time we parted I had persuaded her, with promises of wildlife parks full of tigers, to spend three weeks with me in south India. What did I care if our ideas of holidays were worlds apart, our personalities completely incompatible? I had my traveling companion. For my first three weeks in India, I would not be alone—and that's what mattered to me most.

Soon after meeting Brenda, I went to the Indian Tourist Office. The director read my letter of introduction from a mutual friend.

"I'd like to stay with an Indian family as a paying guest," I said. The director summoned a colleague and a pretty Indian woman in a smart gray suit came in, filling the room with a hot, sweet scent. The director introduced her as Nirmala Singh, and asked her if she could help me.

"You want to be a paying guest in Delhi?" she said. "But of course you will not pay—my family will be delighted to be your hosts. They live in a lovely modern

house. But I'm sure you'll want to see more of our wonderful country. Why don't you take my agency's beautiful tour, 'The Grandeur of Rajasthan'?"

After twenty years of working as a tour guide, I had
no wish to take a busman's holiday and pay for it. But I
did want to stay with Nirmala's family, and I didn't see
how I could accept one offer without the other.

"It sounds very nice," I said, wondering where and
what Rajasthan was. Nirmala handed me a glossy bro-
chure. I glanced at the prices and felt sick. Grudgingly
I wrote out and handed over a check—for more than I
had meant to spend on my entire Indian journey.

"You'll love it!" Nirmala said. "Will you be flying up
to Delhi from Goa? Just give me the date and the flight
number. A driver from our Delhi office will meet you at
the airport. Enjoy your tour." She smiled, and her long
red fingernails beat out a rhythm on the tabletop.

At the thought of the money I had unnecessarily
spent, a hot, nervous flush enveloped me. I tripped on
the front step of the tourist office and fell headlong into
the October sunshine. Brochures flew from my grasp
and fluttered to the ground. There they lay, a brilliant
collage of north India on the gray Mayfair pavement.

The doorbell rang. It was Brenda, wearing a sensible
cotton dress under her mackintosh and carrying an
almost empty suitcase. She looked at my overflowing
bag with disapproval, yawned and picked up the guidebook I wanted to read on the plane. It was the first of
many things that Brenda would need to "borrow" during our three weeks together.

"I need space in my suitcase for shopping," were the
only words that my companion, engrossed as she was in

my guidebook, uttered until our plane landed with a soft
bump on the runway of Madras airport.

It was the seventeenth of January. Brenda and I
were in India. Pushed, shoved, and jostled, our noses
assaulted by a mixture of aerosol room freshener, attar of
roses, sweat, and cigarette smoke, we emerged into the
damp heat of mid-afternoon Madras.

Something touched my leg. A small boy stood beside
me. He pointed to his mouth, rubbed his stomach, and
whined. Brenda found her voice.

"Now I suppose you see what it's like. I warned you,"
she said.

I saw. And in those first few minutes I was hooked.

I could not stop looking. Through the tinted windows
of the Ambassador, intriguing scenes unfolded. I suddenly
wished my eyes were bigger, my brain better able to absorb
the sights, smells and sounds that overwhelmed my senses.
We plunged through crowds of half-naked, spindle-legged
pedestrians, darted between motorcycles careering crazily
from side to side of the dusty road, passed sweating cycle-
rickshaw-*wallahs* pedalling stately matrons on shopping
sprees and clutches of clean-cut children walking home
from school for tea. Yellow and black three-wheelers
buzzed about like bees, overflowing with families, cargo,
and fumes. Terrifying tinselled lorries bore down on us.
"Give side. Blow horn," they blared in garish paint. "Use
dipper." An elephant plodded ponderously, his tiny eyes
alert in folds of flesh. Women in bright saris, like a swarm
of frightened butterflies, scattered before our honking
horn. Bullocks pulling mammoth loads, their blue- and
scarlet-painted horns held low, strained against wooden
yokes. Cows ruminated, chewed their cuds and munched
on indigestible cardboard boxes.

Filled with elation, I looked at Brenda. She stared ahead, neat and tidy in her straw *topi* and cotton dress. I forgot her and gave myself up to India.

But it was hard to forget Brenda completely.

On our first full day in Madras, we went looking for Brenda's adopted Indian "grandmother." Brenda had discovered a charity called Adopt-a-Granny in a magazine, and was sure that her granny lived near a place called Tirupati. We took a tour that went via Tirupati (where we just had time for breakfast and a change of bus) to Tirumala, and found ourselves waiting three hours in a narrow wire-netted passage for *darshan* along with thousands of shaven-headed pilgrims. "I'm not staying in here another minute. I might faint. Then what would you do?" demanded Brenda. "I've told you I'm not interested in temples. Where do I get out? And what about my granny?" Her irritation turned to hysteria. "I never wanted to come here. It's a filthy, terrible place. I'm catching a plane back to London tomorrow. If we'd only gone to Africa..."

We never found the granny. Brenda calmed down.

At Mahabalipuram I swam in the Bay of Bengal, walked along the beach to look at the rock-cut temples and decided I had arrived in Paradise, or come as close to it as I was ever likely to get.

Brenda lay in a hammock under the pine trees. "I never did like the sea; too many waves," she said. "Give me a swimming pool. And as I've told you at least twice, I'm not interested in temples, and I have a very delicate skin. Too much sun brings me out in a rash."

We lunched on lobster—sizzling, golden-brown, and tasting of salt water—and flew on to Cochin. Abu, a local fisherman, took us round the lagoon in his boat, and we stopped to see the Chinese fishing nets and the church where Vasco da Gama was buried. I chatted with Abu as he rowed us across the blue water, enjoying the ride, the company, and the sunshine. Brenda sat in stony silence. When we were again on dry land, her rosebud mouth pursed itself into a disapproving grimace, and spat out a sudden volley of fury that ricocheted across the water.

"Get rid of that man!" she barked at me, glaring at Abu. "You shouldn't become friendly with the natives. Pay him half the fee he asks. He's a crook. And you! I got very bored with your chat, I can tell you." She headed off in the wrong direction. I paid Abu and ran after her.

"And," she went on, when at last we were sitting by the hotel swimming pool with a cool drink, "we're seeing too much of each other. Why should we stick together like a pair of limpets? Unnecessary, I'd call it. I like my privacy. And another thing—I want my lunch and tea when I'm hungry. Do you think I can wait till eight o'clock at night for my tea? Well, I can't." She yawned and lapsed into silence.

After that, we never spoke unless we had to.

A night at Periyar Wildlife Sanctuary failed to produce Brenda's tigers. We traveled by train from Cochin to Mettupalayam, and at dawn we transferred to the little blue-and-white steam train. It chugged upwards through the Nilgiri hills past tea gardens and eucalyptus forests, awe-inspiring scenes that would have left me speechless even if Brenda had wanted to hear my comments, which, of course, she did not. At 2,268 meters above sea level we came to Ootacamund, queen of the southern hill stations. Our hotel gave us an introduction to the Ooty Club, a relic of the Raj and of bygone "Snooty Ooty."

Brenda looked with disapproval at the disjointed members of the fox family that decorated the walls. Her hackles rose. "Nasty barbarians, killing innocent little creatures. What's a 'point-to-point', anyway?" she asked with a sniff, studying a notice on a board behind the desk. I explained that a point-to-point was an informal race meeting for hunt horses; the races cover about two kilometers, from one point to another, of someone's private land. We had a hurried gin and tonic in the company of a talkative man propping up the bar, who puffed smoke rings from his briar pipe while his wife sat at a table polishing her riding boots. Brenda sniffed and coughed.

We left Ooty and, after another abortive hunt for tigers at Mudumalai Wildlife Sanctuary, came to Mysore.

Mysore is a clean and spacious city with wide, tree-lined streets, a spectacular nineteenth-century maharaja's palace and a bazaar of enormous and colourful proportions. Brenda bought striped Mysore silk for pyjamas for her Middle Eastern boyfriend. I bought wild silk for my daughters and went sightseeing.

The end was in sight. We traveled northwards to Goa, where we spent our two days in a chauffeur-driven car looking for a hotel swimming pool for Brenda.

Finally we flew to Delhi. Our three weeks were over.

My love for India had grown in almost equal proportion to my antipathy to Brenda. I hoped I would never see her again, with her yawns, her blinking gaze, her disapproval and her nagging. I am sure my feelings were reciprocated.

"You want taxi?" My suitcases were whisked off a whirling carousel and on to a trolley. There was no time for more than a perfunctory goodbye. Brenda held out her hand. I shook it and dashed after my disappearing luggage.

Her querulous cry followed me out of the airport building. "But where do I go? Can't you find out?"

"Ask someone else!" I yelled. "Goodbye, Brenda!"

જી જી જી

Jill Lowe was born into upper-class English society, but lost everything when her first husband went bankrupt. She worked hard as a travel guide for a decade to support her five children before deciding to travel to India. This story was excerpted from Yadav: Finding the Heart of India, *which is Lowe's book about meeting her Indian second husband and their life together. Lowe died in August 2004 of cancer.*

≈ ≈ ≈

Eruptions

In Sicily, a live volcano and a delightful
Frenchman stoke the author's internal fires.

I was going to Mt. Etna, the live volcano that rises up
more than ten thousand feet on the northeastern corner
of Sicily. I had just finished a weeklong tour studying sites of
ancient goddess worship on the island, but I did not realize
that the volcano, too, was once considered a goddess, she of
passion-heat who oozes molten fire from deep inside her
body. All I knew was that you could take a night trip all the
way up to Etna's peak and glimpse the red-hot throbbing of
lava inside her crater. This alone was enough.

Since it was early April, though, the snow still covering Etna's tip made a nocturnal excursion impossible. So
my hotel in Taormina had set me up with a day trip and
I would have to content myself with the view of the summit from three-quarters of the way up the mountain.

At 8 A.M. I boarded a bus near the hotel, which was half filled with Swedes. Tooling along the coastal road, we stopped fifteen minutes later in the little town of Giardini-Naxos to pick up a hoard of French tourists. One man of about thirty, with large eyes and a friendly, open face, chirped "'Allo evreebuddy!" as he popped up the bus stairs and made his way down the aisle to take a seat near the back. I smiled inwardly. How open southern Europeans seemed, so unlike Americans with their aloofness.

As the bus continued on, my gaze turned inland and there, suddenly, was Etna. Looming majestically on the horizon in blues and grays and whites, she seemed supernaturally imposed over what would otherwise have been a modest landscape of gently-rolling green hills. The tuft of steam at her summit seemed frozen in time, almost indistinguishable from the surrounding slate-colored clouds.

Driving through cozy towns at the base of the volcano, we began the winding climb up the mountain, passing long tongues of black lava that covered the hillsides from previous eruptions. Eventually we stopped at a tourist area filled with cheap-looking gift shops and restaurants. Some passengers headed indoors while others, like me, took the cable car farther up the snowy slope.

At the top, the air was wintry cold and I drew my coat closer around my body. Tourists and skiers milled about, some heading even higher up the mountain by snowmobile. From this distance, I could now see the slow-motion movement of milky white steam issuing from Etna's summit. The day seemed sunny and foggy in turn, as clouds passed over the landscape like ghosts moving through walls.

I struggled up a nearby incline to get a better view of Etna's tip. At the top of the hill, melting snow revealed a moonscape of brownish-gray volcanic rock beneath my feet. I sat on a lava boulder, watching Etna unfurl snaky coils of smoke in the distance. How I longed to go up to the crevice and peek into the black hole of her mystery. I imagined myself soaking in the energy of the earth's molten doings far beneath me, drawing it up through my body in great gulps of breath. The world was still and silent.

On a far slope, people skied. From this distance, they looked like fleas swooping and curving over a dog's back. Rushing headlong down the mountainside, they negotiated Etna's impossibly steep inclines flawlessly, fearlessly, without the benefit of prescribed trails or warning signs. Just watching them, I could feel my own pulse quicken and my insides began to tingle. Slowly the tingling spread, infusing me with a strange kind of desire. A desire that I could only interpret as sexual. I sat down between some boulders, feeling my own fire rising, mixing with the sharp bite of the air. It was as if I could feel the power of Etna shoot through me. Suddenly I was fire and air, ice and molten lava, clouds and steamy vapor, mountain and earth core, land and sky. It was as though I had made love to Mt. Etna.

I made my way down the hill, sputtering and sliding through the crunchy, granular snow. Taking the funicular back down to the tourist area, I headed for our group's restaurant.

Inside, a great hall echoed with the sounds of babel and loud, sentimental mandolin music played by a roving trio of men in colorful Italian peasant costumes. I spotted a young man sitting at a table. Wasn't that the Frenchman from the bus, the friendly one? He spoke

little English, so in sign language I asked if I might join
the group, which included a French woman in her fif-
ties and an older Sicilian couple. The young man indi-
cated, yes, of course, please, placed a menu in my hand
and rushed off to find a waiter. Again, the gesture of
European gentility, so simple and genuine.

When the man returned to the table, my lunch companions and I looked at one another stupidly, unable to
find a common language. I mentally reviewed the few
French words I knew: *croissant...beau...voulez-vous
coucher avec moi ce soir*. I focused on the mozzarella and
tomato salad the waiter brought, trying to make small
talk with the Italians at least.

Later, as we boarded the bus for the return, the
Frenchman stopped at my seat. "May I sit with you?"
he asked in his cheerful, easy way, speaking in halting
English.

"Yes, *oui*," I said enthusiastically, wondering how on
earth we would communicate.

As the bus made its way down the winding mountainside of Etna, the young man's English improved subtly
yet steadily, as though he were a self-charging battery.
"Who was the woman with you at lunch?" I asked.

"My mother," he replied. His father had not wanted
to go on holiday with her, so he had accompanied her
to Sicily. How different, I thought. How different from
America, where children break away from their parents
so early.

He was from Paris. I wanted to know all about
Parisian life. He said there was not enough work in
France, that the people were tired, afraid, cynical about
the government. What about the women, I wanted to
know, what were they like? They were very liberated,

the young man said, they were becoming more and more self-sufficient, independent, strong. How were the men taking all this? I asked. We are frightened, he smiled, only half joking. Women did not appreciate sensitive men, he said. His own girlfriend had mistreated him and then left him. They didn't know that under the flesh and blood is a heart that is beating, he said, sadness flashing across his face.

I looked at this gentle man whose large eyes were so honest and sincere. "What is your name?" I asked.

"Henri," he replied.

"Henri, speak to me in French."

He obliged and began a soliloquy. It was soft, penetrating. What was he saying? I sat primly, fixing my gaze out the window, trying to ignore the persistent tickling that the silvery syllables were creating throughout my body. Henri observed me closely and kept speaking. "You like French, eh?" he said finally in English.

"Yes," I said.

The driver stopped so we could admire two adjoining mountains of lava on the plain in the distance. Telling us in Swedish, Italian, and French, in turn, how they had formed, she ended each story with the same punch line: the locals called the two mounds "Gina Lolabrigida."

"Oh!" gasped Henri when she finished the French translation. He sputtered several inchoate syllables, breathing hard, flushing hot and red, smiling at me. There was no tinge of shame to his response, no showy macho pride at his own hair-trigger sexuality, only frank arousal, pure and natural. He had nothing to hide and nothing to prove.

I thought of what I had learned on the goddess tour I took the previous week: how thousands of years ago, some matriarchal cultures lived in harmony with each other and the rhythms of nature. How women were more respected and had less fear of sexual violence. Now, sitting beside this gentle yet virile man, something deep inside me relaxed. I glanced at Henri's muscular chest, his full lips, his thick hair, feeling my skin expand as though suddenly enveloped by a moist jungle breeze. This day was becoming something.

On the bus, were you aroused? he whispered to me later. Yes, I said. I was too, he smiled.

"What are you doing tonight, Henri?"

"Nothing," he answered, before I could even finish the sentence. He wrote down in deliberate European lettering the name of his hotel in Giardini-Naxos. I would meet him there after dinner.

Back in Taormina, I strode into the middle of the luxurious hotel room that the tour had granted me for one last night before I embarked on my own solo, penny-pinching journey of Sicily. From the large window I could see a craggy island covered with bushy trees that poked up just offshore like a tiny Eden. Water lapped against the sand below. The wind blew the curtains gently. A thrill ran through my body in wave after wave. I was a free woman in paradise. The world had suddenly become my duchy.

Voulez-vous coucher avec moi, ce soir? I wondered silently. And for the first time in my life I had no shame, no doubts, no fears about inviting a perfect stranger home with me. I simply knew that Henri and I would make love in the kingsized bed with fresh sheets that night. And when we were done we'd do it again in the one next to it. We'd bathe together, using the luxurious oils and soaps the hotel provided. Perhaps we'd run naked into the sea and roll in the sand. In the morning, we'd have brunch on the terrace overlooking the water.

"No," he said when I arrived at his hotel and opened up the cab door wide for him. "I can't go back with you tonight. My mother..."

I paid the cab driver and Henri and I found a quiet corner in his hotel lobby. Our chatter seemed meaningless now. He seemed less attractive, less intelligent than he had a few hours ago. Less romantic. Perhaps I had misunderstood his intentions. Perhaps I didn't like him after all. The chasm seemed to grow. Would we make the leap or not, the leap into love that always, for a split second, feels like a jump over thirty Grand Canyons?

"I am lost in your eyes," Henri said finally.

He agreed to come back to my hotel in Taormina. Just for a few hours, he said. The man at his hotel desk called us a cab. We waited in the corner of a couch, kissing behind a large plant. "Do you want to leave a message for your mother?" I asked.

"No," he said, it wasn't necessary since he would be returning soon. He mentioned something about getting documents out of his room, but then thought better of it. No, what documents, why would you need documents? I agreed. When the cab arrived, the driver assured us that Henri would be able to catch a taxi back to his hotel at any hour.

We were soon in my room in Taormina, on the bed, a tangle of clothes and motion and delirious Frenchness, Henri murmuring and gasping *oui! oui!* each time my lips caressed his neck, his chest, his back. Then, sitting upright and pulling me close to him he whispered fiercely in Italian, "*Fuoco, vulcano,* fire, volcano."

Ah yes, Etna.

Hours later, Henri decided it was time to return to his mother, to slip into the room without her knowing. I called the front desk. The clerk answered, gravely voiced. We would like a cab, I said. He told me he'd call back when it arrived.

In a few minutes he rang to say he couldn't get through to any taxi company; no one was answering. I suddenly knew we were in the middle of a classic Italian situation. Nothing, not an order from the president himself would get services running again. We would have to wait until morning.

Henri looked panicked when I told him, like a teen-ager who was suddenly in very big trouble.

Despite the hour, we decided to phone his mother at the hotel. Since the staff did not speak French, I put the call through. The desk clerk knew who I was immediately. Henri's mother had contacted them, he said, completely distraught, looking for her son. The best they could tell her was that they had seen him in the lobby with a woman.

As the clerk transferred the call to her room, I handed the receiver to Henri. "*Mammá*," he began, and was soon swept into a maelstrom of shouts and admonitions on the other end of the phone line. "No-no-no-no-no, *mammá*!" he kept exclaiming, "no-no-no-no-no!" After ten minutes of heated French dialog and what seemed to be intense negotiations, Henri finally extricated himself from the conversation and hung up the phone.

"She called the *carabinieri*, the police," he said, look-ing at me.

"The police?" I began to laugh.

"She wants me to come back as soon as possible."

It was now nearly 4:30 A.M. I roused the hotel clerk by phone once again. The best he could do, he said, was try the cab company at 6:30. I acquiesced, feeling a measure of relief now that we had a plan.

"Listen, though," the clerk interjected, "if he's going to stay, we'll need to see *i documenti*, the documents."

"The documents?"

"His identity papers," he said.

"But you see, that's just the problem, he left the documents in his hotel," I explained.

"Well, I don't know what to do. We need the documents," said the clerk.

"They need the documents," I said to Henri, covering the receiver with my hand. He wailed.

A sick feeling gripped my stomach. Until now, we had been dealing only with Henri's neurotic mother, but this was the government. Henri was a man without papers, and I was his accomplice. The police were already involved. I thought of the horror stories my guidebook recounted about unfortunate foreigners who had gotten caught breaking the law. Something about no immunity or relinquishing your rights. Nothing the American embassy could do about it.

"What can we do?" I pleaded with the clerk. "He simply doesn't have the documents."

He sighed. "Well, come to the lobby; he'll at least have to sign papers," he said resignedly.

Henri and I put our clothes back on. I tried to smooth my hair. Sheepishly, we made our way to the reception desk. Did I look like a woman of the night, I wondered, all smeared from her sexual escapade? "Hello," I called out tentatively. I could hear the jolt of cot springs as the clerk bounded unsteadily to the foyer. He rustled through some papers and handed them to us. Henri glanced through them helplessly and signed.

Back in the hotel room we got into bed with our clothes on.

We were roused by the sudden crash of the door being broken open as *carabinieri* in their elegant black uniforms entered, brandishing rifles. "*I documenti! I documenti!*" they shouted to Henri. Turning to me, they demanded, "What do you know about the Mafia? We know your father's family is from Corleone!" Behind them, three SS officers stormed through the door, rousting us roughly from the bed, telling us to get dressed. "*Schnell! schnell!*" they shouted, "Hurry up!" Visions of international headlines passed through my head: American Hussy Rendezvous With Young French Buck. Subhead: Just met him that day.

Henri and I shuddered with laughter at this fictional scene we had created together, hysteria the only remedy for our nervousness. And for our shame. *Carabinieri* or not, we had been found out.

Our laughter subsided. "Henri, you deserve to have your own life, separate from your mother," I said gently. There was silence.

"Come into my arms," he said.

Come into my arms? This was it. I had now made the total transformation into Catherine Deneuve in a French film. I slithered into Henri's embrace and nestled there, luxuriating in continental *je ne sais quoi*.

At 6:30 the alarm startled us both awake. Henri dressed, then kissed me as though wanting to drown. "I will wait for you in Par-ees," he said. We walked to the door and I closed it behind him with a little wave.

I sank back into the bed, thinking of a poem I once heard on the radio. "I know I'll never get to ride through Paris in a convertible with my hair whipping in the wind," went one of the lines. The women commentators talked about that line, about how it had grabbed them. Beneath their words you could hear the sadness and regret they felt over their own missed opportunities. I thought to myself how imperfect my life was, how I had endured more than my share of tragedy and sorrow. But how now, after today, I would not be one of those women who looks back on it all feeling that foreign romance and intrigue have passed her by. And suddenly I couldn't believe my luck in this world.

All that next week as I traveled in Sicily, I would scan the horizon for the snowy peak and smoky plume that was Etna, visible from much of the island. And I would smile in gratitude.

Marguerite Rigoglioso is a writer, researcher, and college instructor based in Northern California. She has published nonfiction stories in Voices in Italian Americana, Body & Soul *magazine, the anthologies* Women in the Wild *and* Travelers' Tales Spain, *among others, numerous feature articles in major magazines, and scholarly papers in books and academic journals. A doctoral student at the California Institute of Integral Studies, she has also written a book on the ancient oracular center to Demeter and Persephone at Enna and Lake Pergusa in Sicily. Visit her website at http://womenvisionaries.com/Marguerite.*

ॐ ॐ ॐ

The Slaying of the Yabbies

In a cooking school in Australia, a traveler faces her
fears—and a six-inch-long crustacean.

I have no business being in culinary school. I'm slow,
clumsy, uncoordinated. Not chef material. Here I
am anyway, slogging through a Commercial Cookery
course in Sydney, Australia. We've covered soup through
dessert in just ten weeks, skipping over the main courses.
But now the party's over. No more frilly stuff like canapés
and Chantilly cream. We're in the throes of the Fish and
Shellfish module. Crustaceans are on the menu, and we're
staring down a tub-load of live yabbies.

So far, the seafood module has been less distress-
ing than the previous one, Hot and Cold Desserts. By
and large, fish dishes don't *collapse,* as do soufflés and
Bavarian creams. The slumping mounds I presented
as "Bavarois Rubane" didn't earn me top marks on the

desserts exam. I have yet to master gelatin. But, during the Fish and Shellfish Module, I've become reasonably skilled at deboning. I've learned how to glide the slender filleting knife along a fish's skeleton to release the flesh.

I'm apprehensive, though, about the crustacean portion of the Fish and Seafood module. I've spent enough time around prawns to know I don't like them. After backpacking in Asia for a year, I found myself in Malaysia apprenticing with a Chinese chef. Grilled tiger prawns were one of his specialties. That apprenticeship lasted all of two months. Prior to coming to Sydney, I had "volunteered" on and off at other Malaysian restaurants. Mostly off. In order to get a decent—and legal—restaurant job in Asia, I would have to earn a chef's qualification, which is why I enrolled in this Sydney school in the first place.

The Australian yabby is the subject of today's Shellfish class. Yabbies are a type of crayfish that grow to roughly six inches in length. With longish tails and claws, they look like baby North American lobsters. I'm hoping they'll be less nasty to prepare than prawns. After only five minutes of peeling prawns, my fingers start to itch. Mantis shrimp are another nightmare. They have grasping front legs that clasp at their chests, like praying mantises. In my book, prawns and shrimp are the roaches of the ocean, gobbling up refuse that more dignified sea creatures wouldn't touch. I've come to loathe their wiggling legs and waving tentacles. Live or dead, shrimp give me the willies.

The teacher, Chef Richard, begins the yabby demonstration as a dozen students in white jackets and toques gather around his stainless-steel worktable. He's standing beside a large plastic tub he just removed from the refrigerator. Reaching into the container, he grabs one of the critters by its back and holds it aloft.

"What we have here, class, are live yabbies. They're like miniature lobsters, but they live in fresh water. We are *not* going to drop them headfirst into a pot of boiling water. No, no, no. Some chefs kill them like that; they drop yabbies directly into boiling water. But if you do that, you lose all that good yabby flavor. No, no, no. Place your chef knife between their eyes and push down hard, one time. Slice neatly through their brains before cooking them. It's much more humane that way. They die a quicker death."

The chef puts four yabbies on his chopping board. Snicker-snack, he makes a quick cut through each of the heads and slices each body in half from head to tail. Crunch, crunch. He scoops out the guts with a spoon. Once all our yabby bodies are halved, we are to sauté them for a couple of minutes, extract the meat from the shells and use the shells to make a cream sauce.

"I don't want to see you boys torturing these animals," adds Chef Richard. "If you do, it will make me *very* angry."

"Oh, no, Chef," I tell myself faintly, "the torture is all mine."

I had prepared for the day's events by reading carefully over my lesson, as I do for every class, but nowhere in the terse description does it say we have to *slay* the yabbies. The recipe merely reads, "Cut the yabbies in half and discard the sac from the carapace."

Despite my thorough investigation of the chef's profession, nothing prepares me for tasks such as these. It's dawning on me that just because I love to eat, it doesn't mean I love to cook. And if you want to be a chef, you have to *love* to cook. You're on your feet toiling away, for too many hours at a stretch, for too little pay to do it otherwise. In interviews, celebrity chefs claim to love what they do. At least the Western chefs do. All the Malaysian chefs I've met say they cook, not out of passion, but to survive. "Must *cari makan*, *lah*," they say, which literally means, "Must search for food," but with the broader sense of "earning a living." Whether or not you enjoy killing or cooking live animals is irrelevant. Your livelihood may depend on it.

Storing the yabbies in cold conditions had put them in a sedated state, but when Chef Richard took the tub out of the fridge, the beasts had awoken from their slumber. The yabbies remained tranquil for the chef, but by the time I come to collect my yabbies from the tub, they've revived in the warm kitchen air. They're starting to panic. They're doing their yabby dance of fear, curling and uncurling their tails and flailing their claws. What a horror show. It's like a Chinese dragon dance, only these dragons are live and lunging for fingers, not pearls.

The chef gingerly picks up three and puts them on a plate for me. He starts reaching for more, but I say, "That's O.K. That's enough, Chef, thank you. That's *enough!*" I take the plate over to my chopping board and look down at the yabbies kicking and flopping. Suddenly, I start to scream. As soon as I hear the noise coming out of my mouth, I shut myself up. It's too late. I've humiliated myself.

I run the crawling plate back to the fridge and shove it inside. I slam the door shut so hard the fridge starts rocking. To steady the tall silver box, I spin around and push my back up against the door, my arms fully extend-

ing from both sides. I stand there quaking, drawing and
expelling huge breaths.

Where did I get the crazy notion I could even be a
chef? Somewhere in India. After a twenty-year career
in publishing, I became restless and quit my job in the
States to travel. During the trip, it had seemed that I
wasn't traveling so much as *eating* my way around Asia.
Sightseeing was secondary to finding good food. If I
found something delicious to eat for lunch or dinner,
then the day was a success. Food was my true calling. In
India I met a couple of Western chefs who had it made.
They were in demand. They could choose when and
where to work and take time off to travel in between
cooking gigs. They were happy and free.

Couldn't I do that, too? I had never shown the slight-
est predilection for cooking, but maybe I had never
given it a fair shake. As a child, whenever I would wander into the kitchen to see what my mother was up to,
she'd say, "Get out of here. Go read a book." So I would.
The kitchen remained terra incognita to me.

I should have known early on that cooking isn't my
forte. At age sixteen, I was fired from a deli for failing
to cut the signature strawberry cheesecakes into twelve
even pieces. When my first Malaysian chef stopped
speaking to me, I found other, more patient chef-men-
tors. Even under their tutelage, I can't say I've improved
much.

Now, it's halfway through the semester, and I still
have grave doubts about my culinary aptitude. I don't
advertise the fact that I have restaurant experience. If
I did, my classmates would wonder why I'm so poky. I
bring up the rear in nearly every class. During the exams

at the end of each module, I complete my dishes a good fifteen minutes after everyone else. I sweat out my last presentation, racing back and forth between my stovetop and workbench, as the other whitecoats finish cleaning the kitchen around me and sashay out the door.

I imagine that the other students have the right stuff. They must've been cooking since they were old enough to peek over the edge of a chopping board. They probably wielded huge cleavers in their chubby little hands and mastered precision cuts quicker than most humans learn to use a remote. As teenagers, they probably hosted gala garden parties for their families and friends. They would have heaved whole pigs onto spits to roast, while stirring great gallons of barbecue sauce in enormous pots. Their sated guests would have run their thumbs around uncomfortably tight waistbands, leaned back in their chairs and declared, in whatever language, "That kid sure has a bright future ahead of him."

Most of my classmates are from Asia and Europe. I'm the sole North American and twenty years older than almost everyone else. The largest contingent is the Chinese Indonesians. There are three of them. They break off into jovial huddles, cracking jokes in Indonesian. I envy their camaraderie. I can't relate to the sulky German woman who's the only woman in the class besides me. David—a Jewish, white South African—offers moral support when it's painfully obvious I'm lagging behind.

Unlike me, most of my classmates already have part-time restaurant jobs in Sydney. Robi, one of the Chinese Indonesians—and the tallest Chinese guy I've ever met—is the most accomplished cook. He's been apprenticing at an Italian restaurant for three years. Tareq, a Bangladeshi, works fast and smart. He's a commis cook for a yacht club. Pachi, from the Canary Islands, is working front-of-house, as a waiter and a maitre d', but he's a natural in the kitchen and *never* loses his cool in class.

As I stand there trembling, splayed across the refrigerator, I suddenly remember I'm not alone. How are these culinary prodigies handling *their* yabbies? I quickly scan the kitchen. Despite my outré behavior, no one is looking at me. Most of the whitecoats are looking down at their chopping boards with impassive expressions. Some are already at the stovetops with their extinguished yabbies, firing up their saucepans. No one is screaming or gesticulating wildly. No one is storming the exits. Peace prevails in the room.

Where the hell is Anica, that miserable German girl? How is *she* coping? Recently, she announced that she *detests* commercial cookery and that next semester she's going to switch to Web design. She's only eighteen, but she has more sense than I have. *She's not here.* She's conveniently absent on Crustacean Day.

I can't get out of the slaughter. No one comes to my rescue. Chef Richard doesn't say, "That's O.K., Lucy, you don't have to do it. Ask one of the boys to kill them for you." I fight to regain my breath, realizing I have to go through with the deed. A real chef would not waver. A real chef would do it and do it fast. I push back my revulsion, turn and open the fridge door. I won't look at them. I just won't look. I grab the plate and rush it back to my cutting board. I had thought that if I put them back into the fridge, they would settle down. They're still riled, but a little less so than before.

I run over to the paper-towel dispenser, yank a few sheets and run back to my cutting board. I cover one of the bodies with a paper towel, leaving its head exposed. I pick up my chef knife. My hand is shaking so hard, I might as well be clutching a chainsaw. I bring the knife down over and over, until I make mincemeat of the head. Then I quickly cover the next body and whack at the next head. Then, the third. Paper towels off. I sever the remaining bodies in two while they're still convulsing. It takes the rest of my will power to keep from bursting into tears.

I'm way behind everyone else—as usual. I run the mutilated yabbies over to the stovetop, slap them into a pan with sizzling butter and fry their still twitching bodies until they turn pink and die for good.

The weekend comes and goes, and my composure returns. We're back to fish for the next couple of classes. At lunch break, I make a point of heading over to the canteen to find my classmates. Usually by the time I clean up my workbench, I don't have enough of a lunch break left to buy food at the canteen. I'll eat a sandwich I bring from home in the quiet of the women's locker room. But, today I have to find out if there's any fallout from the yabby debacle. Robi, Pachi, Jimmy, and a couple of the others are seated at a picnic table in the courtyard outside the canteen.

I join the table, unwrap my sandwich and ask as casually as possible, "Hey you guys, what did you think of Friday's class?

"What was Friday's class?" asks John-Paul, the Dutch guy.

"You know...the yabbies." I look around at their faces. They glance at each other and shrug.

At last, David, the South African, turns to me and says, "Once you put those yabbies in the fridge, I never thought you'd take them out again. I don't blame you. Killing those things was distasteful. Then again, I don't like seafood, any seafood."

I check out Robi. "What about you, Robi? How'd you do?

"No way, I had Pachi do mine." *Pachi?* How'd he get away with that? I look at Pachi. He purses his lips together and blows out a *pppfft* of air.

"Nada, no big thing."

"How many did you kill?" I wonder if he had killed the yabbies for all four students at his workstation without Chef Richard noticing.

"I don't know, lots of them."

I let it drop. Later, after class, I mull over Robi's confession. Astounding. A *Chinese* couldn't go through with the slaughter. Aren't the Chinese second only to the Japanese in their fetish for fresh seafood? Aren't Chinese chefs famous for yanking whole, live fish out of tanks and butchering them to order? A *Chinese* with three years restaurant experience—O.K., in an Italian restaurant—couldn't kill a puny yabby? At least I didn't hand off my yabbies to someone else to kill. Does this mean I have the mettle to be a chef, after all? If I do, then why am I such a nervous wreck in the kitchen? This whole cooking venture has been more harrowing than gratifying.

If I give up on being a chef—if I throw in my tea towel—I'll spare other living creatures, and myself, further torment. Maybe I can be a vegetarian chef someday. I have a better rapport with plants than animals, anyway. There's no chance of exploring that now. The Meat

Butchery modules—beef, veal, pork and lamb—follow in the wake of Fish and Shellfish. I've been dreading those meat modules. For lamb butchery, we have to hack apart a whole side of lamb.

I console myself that at least the lamb will already be dead.

❦ ❦ ❦

Lucy Friedland abandoned her brilliant surfing career (see Travelers' Tales Australia) *for another dubious career as a cook. She did finally earn her Commercial Cookery Certificate I in Sydney, Australia. Since then, she has been waiting tables and making tea at a South Indian vegetarian restaurant in Malaysia. Her "true" calling continues to be writing and editing.*

✍ ✍ ✍

Cold Front

A car trip from Iowa to Florida redefined for this
author the term "family vacation."

When I was a young woman in Iowa, one quality
I considered indispensable in a prospective mate
was the willingness to drive to a coast. Over the years,
there were trips to every conceivable coast, including
Puget Sound, Niagara Falls, and Santa Barbara. Thus it
was that, in January, 1984, when my daughters were five-
and-a-half years and fourteen months, it did not occur to
me to worry about our journey by car all the way from
Ames, Iowa, to the southern tip of Florida and then back
up the coast to Sag Harbor. We just told several friends we
were heading their way, threw some things into the back
of the Chevy Cavalier wagon, and strapped the girls into
their seats. We didn't look at the weather report. Perhaps,
therefore, we should not have been surprised when we

were overtaken by sleet and snow an hour later and forced
to stop far too soon at a Holiday Inn only a hundred miles
or so from our house (twenty-nine hundred miles to go).
When we got up in the morning and went out to the
parking lot, the sun was suspiciously bright, but to us it
seemed that Florida was just over the horizon.

There was snow all the way to Nashville, where we
stayed with my uncle. In gratitude for his hospitality, my
husband shoveled my uncle's two-hundred-and-twenty-
foot driveway. The neighbors came out to watch, and
we soon discovered why—Nashvillians didn't mind
being snowed in, and, anyway, as soon as the sun came
out in the morning the snow began to melt. But we were
Iowans, and Florida was just over the horizon.

Crossing into northern Alabama, we admired the
ice-covered trees, the graceful sweep of the highway
through the hills, and the bright grass by the roadside
that seemed to be strewn with shattered glass. We were
alone on the highway with our snow tires. Not even
road crews had come out with sand. We didn't intend
to be reckless—it simply never occurred to us to stop.
At the end of a very long day, we reached Montgomery,
where we pulled off into the parking lot of the first
motel we saw.

Once we got some food, and unpacked a few things
from the car, and visited with some friends who lived
there, it was midnight. At this point, the fourteen-month-
old decided that she was going to learn to walk. She staggered back and forth from one end of our motel room to
the other for two hours, before falling over in her sleeper.
Right about then, I noticed that the doors of the motel
rooms kept slamming, and that lots of big semis were
idling in the parking lot. We were up by six.

We smiled and made pleasant conjugal conversation. His job was to drive, and mine was to keep the peace. In the Florida Panhandle, we finally relaxed—no more snow. That was probably why the children started to fuss. It was also probably why he said, "Can't you do something to shut them up?" and why I took a bag of small wrapped soft candies out of the glove compartment and tossed them over the back of the seat to shouts of joyful disbelief. When I looked around, I saw it was the best game ever—unwrapping each piece and having the bliss of abundance melt in their mouths. I knew this stopgap offended him, though, so that's probably why I said, "So, if something happened to both of us, who would they go to?"

He said, "My sister, of course."

And I said, "Oh, not her. My—"

I don't clearly remember that argument, except that it went on for five days and had many branches—down the sunny west coast of Florida (Me: "She's twenty-two! Him: "Her B.A. is in education!"), through tight lips at his sister's apartment in Boca Raton (Me: "Yeah, right!" Him: "Say what you really think, I want to hear it"), and all through Washington D.C., where we were supposed to stop for dinner with friends. We were getting along so badly by then that when he missed the exit I didn't dare say anything. When I called my friend from a hotel in Trenton to apologize, she informed me that only two days before she had fallen down the stairs and broken her arm but she had cooked dinner anyway. I apologized again. I didn't try to explain; she didn't have any kids. But years later, when she had two boys of her own, she said to me, "I was angry then, but I understand now. You were on a family vacation."

ॐ ॐ ॐ

Jane Smiley's works include the novels Moo, Ordinary Love, *and the Pulitzer Prize-winning* A Thousand Acres, *as well as nonfiction books such as* A Year at the Races *and* Thirteen Ways of Looking at the Novel. *Her essays have appeared in magazines including* Vogue, The New Yorker, Practical Horseman, Harper's, *and the* New York Times Magazine.

⟋⟋⟋ ⟋⟋⟋ ⟋⟋⟋

Other Types of Wealth

In Havana, a visitor attends a Cuban no-frills wedding—
cake and honeymoon courtesy of the State.

O n my first trip to Cuba, I fit everything I needed
into my trusty old camping backpack. But on my
second visit, to accommodate all the presents I had for
my new friends, I bought a fancy, fashionable wheeled
suitcase. Despite its supposedly comfort-enhancing pull-
out handle, I had calluses on both hands after wheeling it
from the airport entrance to the check in terminal where
the agent promptly informed me that, at ninety-five
pounds, my suitcase was a whopping fifty pounds over
the limit.

For the past several months, I had been stocking up
on the things I wished I'd brought before, for others and
for myself. My suitcase now contained multi-vitamins
and ibuprofen, toilet paper, an assortment of power bars

and dehydrated bean soups, twine for impromptu laundry lines, automatic laundry detergent for my friend Dinora, bed sheets for my friend Liudmila, and running shoes for my boyfriend Alfredo, who I had met on my first trip.

Once I'd run out of money to purchase more gifts, I'd begun scavenging through the lost-and-found at the bookstore where I worked. With its multitude of misplaced and never retrieved cell phones and watches and palm pilots, the bookstore drawer contained more electronic gadgets than Alfredo had seen in his lifetime.

Aside from the useful domestic goods I'd collected, most of my items were impractical, space mongers that I couldn't bear to abandon. I wanted to make Alfredo some of the food I ate at home, so I brought a package of Thai noodles and seasonings and one of macaroni and cheese. And even though I feared a penalty for fruit violations, I'd bought a half-dozen different colored apples. Eight months after a schoolgirl had befriended me at a pizza stand in Havana, I still remembered her delight as she'd bitten into a polished, red apple I'd bought her that day, a seventy-five-cent delicacy, which Cuba imported from colder countries.

Among my other unessential items, I had a bottle of California red wine, a mixed tape of the music I listened to in the U.S., photos of the trail I ran on, of my dogs, of my parents and friends. I had a copy of the newspaper I used to write for even though I doubted Alfredo would be able to understand anything in it.

I doubted, too, that Alfredo would understand the words to the music I listened to. And I had a feeling that he might balk at the idea of eating pasta out of a box that included a dusty, pre-packaged, pseudo-cheese sauce.

But the truth is it almost didn't matter, so great was my need to share the details of my world with him.

Alfredo and I had met through a mutual friend on my third night in Cuba and, during the four months that followed, he had introduced me to his large, extended family, invited me to jazz and folk and classical concerts at the National Symphony where he worked as a light and sound technician, and, on one of our first dates, taught me how to bribe the police to bypass the long line in front of Coppelia, Havana's popular two-story ice cream parlor.

With its dizzying array of contradictions—its crumbling buildings, vibrant street life, and lingering sense of hope—Alfredo had introduced me to his world. And now I wanted to do the same for him.

Unfortunately, because of the politics between our homelands, our only option for being together in the U.S. was a fiancé visa, which we were in the process of applying for. If our papers were approved, Alfredo could visit for three months, after which we would either have to marry or he would have to return to Cuba with no real possibility of visiting me again. The decision, which was too great for me to fully grasp without knowing how we might be as a couple in my country or even if Alfredo would be granted a visa, loomed large before us, a permanent presence in my thoughts.

At the San Francisco International Airport, I spent half an hour weeding out my weightiest gifts and several more minutes trying, without success, to convince other departing travelers to take them. The airline attendants also refused and one even directed me to a trash can, explaining that, in the newly opened terminal

I was departing from, there were not even storage lockers I could rent. Unwilling to throw out my presents, I abandoned them in a dark corner of the airport, an altar to the material goods that were—and would now still be—lacking in Cuba.

On my second day back in Havana, I trudged over to Alfredo's grandparents' house with a book bag that, despite my previous purging, still overflowed with gifts.

As if to spotlight my excesses, the early evening sun beat relentlessly onto my book bag. It sent rivulets of sweat down the black evening gown I had unwisely donned for my hike—rather than keeping it clean and dry in my bag—so that Alfredo and I could go directly to a wedding party after our dinner with his grandparents.

More sensibly dressed, less-encumbered Cubans walked languidly by as I approached the asphalt desert of Plaza de la Revolución. I worried suddenly that maybe Alfredo's grandparents and sister would be overwhelmed by my offerings of coffee and tea and chocolate, t-shirts and tank tops and aspirin and fruit-scented soaps and, for Alfredo's newborn nephew, a small, caramel-colored stuffed lion.

There was much more I'd wanted to get for the baby, but before I'd returned to Cuba, Alfredo had quickly dismissed my desire, telling me, "There'll always be someone around to hand down whatever Bruno needs and, besides, he's so young now that he doesn't really need anything yet."

"Are you sure?" I asked. Cubans had a reputation of doting on their children with lavish *quinceañera* festivities and annual Day of the Children and Day of the Adolescents celebrations, which were marked by parties and presents and, in Havana, family trips to play in Parque Lenin. It surprised me that in such a country, no one would expect me to bring presents, especially as a foreigner who could afford them.

I thought of all my pregnant friends in the U.S. who sent out baby shower invitations with the words, "gifts optional," written above the names of the stores at which they had registered. And I wondered if maybe there wasn't also a subtext to what Alfredo was saying.

"This isn't one of those cultural things where you say 'don't' when you really mean 'do,'?" I asked Alfredo.

"No," he said laughing at my skepticism. "It's not. Trust me."

True to Alfredo's word, when I met up with him at his grandmother's house, not only did the stuffed animal prove to be enough for Bruno who, at just under three months, could do little more than drool on it, but the little lion also appeared to be more than anyone had anticipated.

"*¡Ay, qué rico!*" Alfredo's sister said, stroking a drool-free patch of the lion's fur as gently as if it were a living, breathing cub, liable to wake from a deep slumber any minute.

"*¡Qué lindo!*" exclaimed Alfredo's grandmother when it was her turn to touch the lion. "It's been a long time since I've seen such a handsome *muñequito*."

"We used to have stuffed animals in the ration shops when I was little," Alfredo's brother-in-law explained. "But all that changed after the Soviet Union, our main ally, collapsed."

Alfredo's grandmother nodded thoughtfully. *"Muchisimas gracias, Lea,"* she said.

I laughed, embarrassed by all the attention my present had yielded.

Only Alfredo's grandfather, the quiet one in the family who always addressed me with the formal, *"usted"* form of "you," seemed capable of containing his excitement. He sat in his rocking chair, silently surveying the scene with an air of detached amusement.

I decided to hold off revealing the rest of my presents until after dinner, but still, much of our mealtime talk centered on the lion and Cuba's missing *muñequitos.* After I finished my rice and beans and tomato salad and everyone else polished off their plates, we moved on to our dessert of chilled papaya cubes. And from here the conversation branched out into a discussion of everything—including cigarettes and clothing—that had disappeared from the ration shops since their long gone glory days.

I dealt out the remainder of my gifts with Alfredo's sister, brother-in-law, and grandmother huddling in front of me on the living room sofa and Alfredo standing attentively at my side. Like a magician's assistant pulling rabbits out of a hat, Alfredo made his own magic, transforming each gift I silently gave into a fully-formed, albeit heavily-accented, English word.

He did fairly well with chocolate and aspirin, but once he got through these cognates, he stumbled on soap, and pronounced it as "soup."

I grinned at the mistake, but his sister, who spoke fluent English, mimicked a game show buzzer going off at a wrong answer.

"Alfredo has been so diligent about studying his

English. He must really be in love with the language," she said to no one in particular and then, winking at me, added, "or maybe it's just Lea."

I looked at Alfredo who smiled shyly back at me.

After his sister and grandmother had their fill of sniffing the fruit-scented soaps, Alfredo asked me to describe for them, as I'd done once before for him, the dozens of different soaps sold in the U.S. His grandmother and sister exchanged wistful glances. But when I searched Alfredo's grandfather's face, again I found only a calm, distant look, devoid of longing.

As I wondered what enabled Alfredo's grandfather to remain so detached while surrounded by everyone else's excitement, I recalled Alfredo once telling me that his grandfather was the most revolutionary member of his family. And I also remembered, on another occasion, watching his grandfather excuse himself in the middle of a conversation so that he could attend a CDR meeting. Committees for the Defense of the Revolution were neighborhood watchdog groups. In the U.S., I had heard them described as Fidel's spies who made sure no one was engaging in any counter-revolutionary activities. From what I'd seen in Cuba, the CDRs appeared to be more like apartment managers, collecting money to set up communal gardens and taking complaints about faulty electrical wires and much-needed house repairs. My friend Dinora's husband was his neighborhood's CDR president, and his job reminded me of that of a college RA. Once a week, from 10 P.M. to 2 A.M., he paced his surrounding streets, making sure all was safe.

Now, after the initial soap euphoria had subsided, Alfredo's grandfather finally spoke.

"You know," he said slowly, like the end of a long

sermon that had been going on in his head. "There are other types of wealth than the material. There is cultural wealth and emotional, and spiritual, and intellectual."

Alfredo and I walked to his coworker's wedding party beneath the dark, starlit streets of Nuevo Vedado.

"Why didn't we go to the wedding ceremony?" I asked as we stepped cautiously between potholes.

"Oh, the ceremony," Alfredo said, sounding surprised. "Well, I guess we could have gone. Usually only those who feel they're obligated to go, like the family, attend the ceremony. I've heard it's really boring, just a lawyer at the *Palacio de los Matrimonios* dictating the vows."

"You've never been to one?" I asked. "What about when your sister got married?"

"No one really went to that," Alfredo said. "They just wanted it to be the two of them. Don't people ever do that in the U.S.?"

"Sometimes," I said. "But usually weddings are a really big deal. People prepare for them a year in advance, maybe more."

"Why?"

"They have to decide who they're going to invite, where the wedding will be held, where the reception will be, how to decorate the dinner tables, and who will sit where. And then they have to save up money to pay for it all."

"What a complicated life," Alfredo said, shaking his head in disbelief.

The wedding party was in full swing when we arrived, the second-floor apartment's tiny living room transformed into a salsa floor with children and grandparents and Alfredo's coworkers from the National Symphony. Like every other Cuban social function I'd attended, the music at Soyla and Argeo's party was so loud that just entering the living room felt like stepping into another dimension. It was a world comprised solely of sound and movement where language existed only if it could be sung, and people spun by too quickly to be identified.

Alfredo and I edged our way over to a back table with munchies where we each took a cardboard deli-style takeout box, pre-packed with a slab of frosting-heavy cake. I followed Alfredo's example as he picked through the remaining refreshments and deposited a handful of popcorn in his box. I passed on the *ensalada fria*—a salad with macaroni, pineapple, mayonnaise and bits of ham. There were several cans of Tropicola, but the rum bottles were all empty.

I looked around for a place where we could sit to eat and talk. But, unlike parties back home where conversations struck up everywhere from the line outside the bathroom to the overcrowded living room sofa, here there was neither a space to sit nor a place quiet enough to carry out a conversation. Unlike wedding receptions in the U.S., there was also no table overflowing with presents.

"You give a present if you can," Alfredo told me. "So most people don't, except for the couple's family. They try to put together a little money."

"Man, they've got the worst of both worlds," I said, laughing. "They have to sit through the ceremony, and then they have to give money, too."

Alfredo smiled at my joke and moved in closer to me along the wall we had settled against to eat, balancing our boxes on our palms, the oil from the cake frosting seeping through the cardboard and staining it a deep, muddy gray-brown.

I scanned the room to see who the bride and groom were, but I failed to find anyone in a wedding gown or tuxedo.

"Which ones are Soyla and Argeo?" I yelled at Alfredo, but I had no luck here either, receiving only a baffled expression in response.

"What?" Alfredo yelled back. "I can't hear you."

I tried once more, leaning in closer this time, but it was still no use.

Alfredo took my hand, and we worked our way back through the crowd and out the front door onto a tiny balcony. Alfredo pulled out his *panuelo* to sop up a streak of sweat dripping down his cheek, and I fanned my face with my hand while posing my question once more.

"I don't know where they are," Alfredo said. "They must be in another room."

He pointed to the living room wall where a sepia-toned photo of a ballerina hung, only a triangle of her silhouette visible from behind the half-open front door.

"Soyla's a dancer," Alfredo said. "This is her mother's house."

"Will she and her husband live here?" I asked.

"Probably," Alfredo said. "It looks like there's enough room."

"Will they go on a honeymoon?" I asked. "Do people do that here?"

"Of course, everyone gets two nights at a hotel, but not any hotel." Alfredo paused, thinking. "I'm pretty sure you can't stay at Habana Libre. You have to pick one from the list."

"What list?"

"When you buy your marriage certificate, you get a list. You pay $12, maybe $15, and then the government gives you a hotel room and rum and several cases of beer and this cake," Alfredo said, dramatically dropping the final crumb of his into his mouth. "This is the official Cuban wedding cake that you'll see at every wedding you attend."

Before I could move it out of his line of vision, Alfredo looked down at my box with its slice that I'd been poking at and reshaping with my fork for the past several minutes.

"Don't you like it?" he asked.

"It's just a little too sweet for me."

"*¡Ay, a mi me encanta!* I love it," Alfredo said. "It's very popular here." Lowering his voice, added, "Sometimes Cubans get married just for the cake."

"What?"

"Well, really for the whole package—the cake and the alcohol and the honeymoon room," Alfredo said. "The government gives them to newlywed couples for so much less money than anyone else could buy them for, so people get married and then they sell everything for a profit and then, a few days or a few weeks later, they get divorced."

"Really?" I asked, fascinated by this underworld of Cuban coupling.

"Is it common to marry like this?" I asked.

"It was more common when times were tougher right after the Soviet Union collapsed," Alfredo said. "But it still happens. There's even a Los Van Van song about it where they sing, '*La gente se está casando para vender la cerveza,*' People are getting married to sell the beer."

"Do you think the government is aware that this is going on?"

"I'm sure they are, but what can they do? Tell you that you have to stay married for a year before you get your cake?"

When we reentered the party, I spotted one of Alfredo's coworkers scanning the dance floor with the Symphony camcorder, and the thought of having my clumsy salsa moves so formally recorded was nearly enough to make me walk back out. Fortunately, another of Alfredo's co-workers motioned for him to dance with her and, relieved to be off the hook, I quickly nodded for him to go ahead, motioning that I was stepping outside. I walked onto the balcony and then down the steps into the front yard where I found Orestes, one of Alfredo's fellow light technicians, leaning against a jag-üey tree. We talked—about upcoming concerts at the symphony, about his mother's health, about his Mexican girlfriend—and then we walked back into the house together.

To my surprise, the party had transformed itself in our absence. The front door, which had been trembling from the vibrations of the stereo when I'd left, was now still, and a musky incense wafted through the air, which felt several degrees cooler than it had before. The flashing fluorescent lights overhead had been replaced with a half-dozen candles laid out in a circle in the center of the living room floor. Inside the circle, a couple, whom I assumed were the bride and groom in street clothes, danced a fast-paced salsa to the song, "*La Vida es un Carnaval,*" performed live by an outer circle of impromptu musicians seated on a combination of chairs and tabletops. About a dozen members of the party comprised the chorus while one of Alfredo's coworkers beat out the rhythm on the wicker underside of an overturned chair and Alfredo stood tapping out the time with a spoon on the back of a frying pan.

I stood, awed by the beauty of the moment and amazed by the way this spontaneous version of the song so closely resembled the original, which I'd heard countless times before on radios blasting through the streets of Havana.

With a wave of his frying pan, Alfredo motioned for me to come over, and the chorus circle parted accordingly to absorb me.

"I was just about to go look for you," Alfredo whispered in my ear as he continued playing his frying pan.

I felt like I had entered into the middle of something magical, and soon I found myself singing along without any of my usual self-consciousness about being off-key. But after just one round of the chorus, a light from a beaded bamboo chandelier flickered on and flooded across the room. And then, almost simultaneously, the fluorescent lights returned, and the stereo blared back on and everyone clapped as though this, rather than the a cappella musical performance, had been the real showstopper.

"*Fue una apagón.* It was a blackout," Alfredo said, reading the confusion on my face.

I watched as the newlyweds stepped outside of their candlelit circle and the groom switched off a miniature flashlight that adorned his belt loop where a cell phone or pager might have hung in the U.S. Within minutes, everyone was dancing again, the silent spell of the blackout quickly forgotten.

When the newlyweds headed outside for their getaway, I stood with the Symphony staff to watch. Like a master of ceremonies, a friend who had lent Soyla and Argeo a fancy cherry-red Chevy for the occasion presented the key through the driver's side window. Argeo turned the ignition while everyone poised their hands for applause. But after an initial rumble, the engine choked and then died.

The air echoed with disappointed cries of "*¡Pinga!*" and "*¡Coño!*" followed by a flurry of other angrily yelled-out private parts.

Alfredo ran over to help the owner of the car and several other men inspect the engine. Each amateur mechanic took a turn at poking his head under the hood, but after about fifteen minutes, Alfredo returned to me, shaking his head.

"It's not going to turn on," he said. "They'll have to walk."

"Do you think we should go out to a main street and get them a taxi?" I asked.

Alfredo shook his head once more. "Look, they're going to walk," he said, pointing as the bride kissed her mother goodbye and then joined hands with her new husband, followed by a procession of guests who cheered them on.

I thought about the simplicity of this wedding reception without a band, without presents, without a bar of endless drinks for the guests, without tables to sit down and eat at, and, for a while, without electricity. And I thought about what Alfredo's grandfather had said in response to my plethora of presents.

"*Me encanta mi vida aquí.* I love my life here," Alfredo said, looking into the distance thoughtfully as the newlyweds and their entourage disappeared around a corner. "It's peaceful in my country, and I have a good job and good friends. The only thing that's missing," he said as casually as an afterthought, "is that I don't have any money."

I smiled at Alfredo's sentiments, silently wondering about this other life—my country's capitalist life of money and possessions—that I was inviting him to join me in. I worried that perhaps I should have brought something more significant than just macaroni and cheese and scented soap to prepare him for the transition. And then I worried that, like a trip to the moon, there was no real way to prepare Alfredo for life in the U.S. No way to protect him from the complex and often cruel realities of capitalism. No way to preserve the sincerity and simplicity I so loved about him and, which, in many ways, existed because of his lack of experience with my world and its other, very different types of wealth.

Lea Aschkenas has written about travel, literature, and life at large for The Washington Post, San Francisco Chronicle, Los Angeles Times, San Francisco Bay Guardian, *and Salon. com. She has also contributed stories to the books* Travelers' Tales Central America, Travelers' Tales Cuba, The Unsavvy Traveler, *and* Two in the Wild. *This story was excerpted from her book,* Es Cuba: Life and Love on an Illegal Island. *She lives in Northern California with her husband, Alfredo. Her web site is www.leaaschkenas.com.*

NIKKI FINKE

❦ ❦ ❦

Only Real Castles Will Do

Childhood travels with her mother
were memorable indeed.

On my childhood trips, there was First Class, Deluxe Class, and Mother's Class. My mother didn't just arrange a meal in Rome; she reserved fettuccine at Alfredo's. She collected hotels the way other women collect jewelry, racking up holidays at the George V, Carlton, Claridge's, Hassler, Cipriani, Costa Smeralda, Voile d'Or, La Reserve. In her view, travel was a privilege not to be squandered by booking stingily or mechanically. And to my lasting gratitude, she believed firmly in taking along the children.

Parents may think children won't remember much of anything after being taken on holiday, but I recall every detail. Mother made our trips unforgettable—even if that required, as it frequently did—torturing the concierge.

My sister and I learned about foie gras and Champagne aboard the *France*. Mother arranged a private trek for us to the oracle at Delphi. We played vicious croquet on the green lawns of Barbados and sipped Swiss hot cocoa on a balcony with a 180-degree view of the Alps. In Spain, Mother induced the hotel chef to show us how to make a small-batch version of his tasty gazpacho Andaluz, a dish I still make today.

When we came home from school, our mother, surrounded by travel brochures, would be talking too loudly on the phone to Paris, Rome, the Algarve, or the Galápagos, and in a foreign language comprehensible only to her, a cockeyed combination of French and Italian and smatterings of other languages in which she also had no fluency. Our father often went abroad on business, and she saw her job as making sure each trip was as luxurious and expensive as humanly possible—and also included her and, when possible, my sister and me.

Mother gleaned the most from every moment, as she showed most graphically the day in Paris when she lost track of time and we arrived at the Louvre less than an hour before closing. Instead of turning away, she took my sister and me by the hand and literally ran with us through the rooms and hallways. "Don't look! Don't look!" she ordered breathlessly. "These paintings are not important."

An artist herself, she knew the Louvre layout, and she put on the brakes only for Tintoretto or the "Venus de Milo" or the "Mona Lisa." From then on, "Don't look!" became something of a catchphrase in my family. But to this day I never suffer museum fatigue. I don't even try to see every treasure; in advance, I track down the most important works and map the quickest route to them.

When I begged to be taken to Disneyland to see Cinderella's castle, my mother responded, "Why do you want to see fake castles when you've seen the real ones?" She reminded me of the palaces we had visited or stayed in: Hampton Court, Chambord Chateau, Montreux Palais in Switzerland. She wanted the genuine. And after spending fantastic sums, she also wanted her money's worth.

"Don't touch the luggage!" she would bark to the porter who dared put a hand on the family's set of Louis Vuitton as we entered a hotel. While the rest of us encamped in the lobby, she would ask the bewildered desk staff for five different room keys on a variety of floors and inspect the rooms. Under her intense scrutiny, this room smelled of mildew, that room had a stained rug, those bathrooms didn't have enough marble. Success was achieved if she came back down and pleasantly told the bellman that now it was time to take up the luggage. Failure was when she asked in an icy voice for another five room keys.

When my sister and I were teenagers, we skipped a lobby encampment in the Bahamas, stripped down to our bikinis and went to the beach. Several hours later, when we returned to the hotel and asked for our room key, the clerk informed us, "I'm sorry, but your family has checked out." This was a first: Mother had not only left us stranded in our bathing suits with no clothes or money, but had not even thought to leave a forwarding address. When we finally found her at the hotel next door, she was gleefully unpacking and chatting about how much "nicer" this hotel was.

But nothing compared with our trip to Majorca, where Mother took one look around the suite she had reserved and swore she saw bugs. She scampered into a taxi, with us teenagers in tow, and said in her best Spanglish, "*Por favor*, take us to a new luxury hotel. *¡Nuevo, NUEVO!*" After some aimless driving around the island, then still mostly undeveloped, Mother spied a sign at the entrance to a modest promontory. "There!" she told the driver. "Go there. Hotel. HOTEL!"

"No, no, no!" the taxi man replied.

Needless to say, Mother got her way. But when we entered the hotel, we found it absolutely empty—no doormen, bellmen or clerks; no guests. After fifteen minutes of wandering, we found the skeleton staff dining at a faraway table in the cavernous dining room. Catching the manager in mid-bite, my mother politely but firmly demanded to check in. He said he would be delighted—but only in two weeks, when the hotel officially opened.

Not for a minute did my sister and I doubt our mother's ability to get us into the hotel. And she did. We were not just the first guests, but also the only guests for those two weeks. It was weird and wacky and wonderful. Every day, something new would arrive to complete the rooms, like soap and shower curtains, and my mother happily spent her time instructing the staff on how to run a luxury hotel. We had a glorious summer in Majorca.

It was only after I had started supporting myself that I arrived at a very rude awakening about travel. My paltry beginner's salary made Motel 6 barely affordable, so when my parents invited me to accompany them to the Hôtel du Cap, I soaked up the fabulousness, from the splayed homard at Eden Roc to the sparkling pool perched cliffside. My parents headed off to another paradise, and after a few days solo, I went to check out. Of course, my room had been paid in advance. But the clerk, knowing nothing about this arrangement, presented me with a bill that gave new meaning to the term astronomical.

I panicked. Regulars know the Hôtel du Cap takes only cash, not credit cards, and I had $100 in my wallet. Finally, the hotel manager recognized my name and whisked the bill out of my hands, saying in halting Franglais, "Please don't tell your *mère* about this." How nice to know the effect my mother had on people when she traveled hadn't changed in my absence.

Now, as I spend a portion of every day on the Internet planning my next imaginary vacation, I think of my mother, who requires round-the-clock care and rarely leaves her room. It's a far cry from the dotage she had predicted for herself: driving a white convertible Rolls-Royce Corniche through the winding roads of the French Riviera with a small dog on her lap. Which is why I'm so determined to go where she no longer can, and so glad she took all those trips when she was well. It comforts me to imagine that, during those many hours she spends neither alert nor awake, she returns in her mind to those marvelous hotels and gives orders to the staff.

Nikki Finke is a freelance writer for publications such as The LA Weekly *and the* Drudge Report.

SARA B. FRASER

Hands Full of Kiwis

Life in a Spanish village offers one family
new definitions of abundance.

A patchwork of vineyards stands on either side of
the road—rows of vines like soldiers in orderly
files—built into the hills and divided by stone walls
put together years and years ago, perfectly, without any
kind of cement. Vineyard staircases, with fluffy green
grapevine carpet laid on each step. Like one of my great-
grandmother's quilts: soft squares, all of a similar tone,
but each slightly different from the others, tossed in a
heap onto the surface of the planet. Tufty forest growth
springs up between each vineyard, but the vineyards
themselves are relentlessly tended: the weeds plucked so
that the ground between the rows is like beach sand, the
color of coral, but a little coarser.

I buzz open the window of the rental car and shut off

the AC. How can the air feel so soft? Is it something in the pine trees, the mimosas, the honeybees, the grapes that releases a softening agent—like a dryer sheet or fabric softener? Or is it a psychological trick of my mind—a culmination of the effects of returning to my beloved As Regadas, in the south of Galicia, Spain, on summer vacation, content to be where I am always more calm, more relaxed, saner? No, the air really is softer here, and I feel it on my skin like clean cotton sheets, or immaculate fresh water in a river or a lake at that moment when you dive in. I let it wash across my arm and my face as my husband, Colin, guides our car up the hills. We are nearly there.

The flight took us here overnight and we have arrived at lunchtime. People are coming back from the fields for lunch: mostly old women, carrying bales of *verdura* home on their heads for the pigs. When they smile you can see that they may not have a single tooth in their heads. Or they may have one or two and you wonder at their lack of vanity. Is Americans' obsession with dental hygiene all that necessary? I mean, look at these people: A happier crowd you'd seldom encounter. "*HOLA!*" they shout, because they are hard of hearing (I have always assumed—though it's possible that they just like to shout when they speak), and they stop, bend under the weight of vegetables to squeeze my baby's cheeks. There are some old men as well, but it seems that the women far outnumber the men. We always offer them a ride home and they laugh and shake their heads.

We take a left off the main road, stop and say *hola* to Carmen and Manolo, whose house is smack in the center of the village. Carmen and Manolo are the main organizers of the big yearly fiesta that we'll attend in a few weeks. Their house is like town hall—they are the president and first lady of Regadas. They used to have a bar in their kitchen and we'd stop in and have a glass of wine with the two or three old men who would be there watching the *futbol* match. Now that they have renovated their dining room, the closest thing to a shop or a café is the water fountain just outside, where, throughout the summer, we will go for our drinking water and a chat with whoever is about. Manolo's father, an angelic man with a distended goiter, has told me that the fountain is where the young men and women used to do all of their flirting. None of the houses had running water, so everyone would have to come to the fountain to collect water for everything from drinking to washing to cooking.

Carmen, in her apron, is drying a dish out on the road. She leans dish-glove forearms into the window of our car. "We've just arrived," we say. "Welcome back," she tells us. "*Me alegro mucho.*"

The roads get narrower and narrower as we ascend until we have to pull in the mirrors on our rental car to fit through. We have scraped the paint off the mirrors of one car and nearly exploded another by trying to get it, with its standard-shift, to climb slowly enough through the crowding granite walls. Our nerves are steadier now; we're getting used to the intricacies of life in a Galician village: the tiny roads, the illustrious lunchtime siesta, the strangers—tourists and neighbors' relatives—who show up and want to come inside, having heard about the view from our window.

We're the first foreigners to have bought a house here. The villagers find it curious; they find us curious. Neither Colin nor I have any relatives in Spain. He's Irish; I'm

American. So what on earth are we doing with this big stone house in tiny As Regadas, population twenty-nine and declining, a pinprick of a village in the south of Galicia, just north of the Portuguese border? And it is curious, when I stop to think about that. But for Colin, for me, for our kids, it feels anything but strange. It feels like a home. I'm surprised to find that it feels, at times, more like home than home does. I guess it's because the evolution of our being here came in such a natural and unhurried way: We met Carmen, the daughter of a village couple, Tobo and Laura, when we were teaching ESL in Santiago de Compostela. After returning to the U.S. for graduate school and money earning and other necessities, we invested a small amount of money in a ruin in this village. We had fallen in love with the place and the prices were affordable, so why not? At first we camped on the land. Then, when the house was cleaned out, we camped on the floor.

Now the house is nearly finished. Even though the roof and the inside walls and floors had completely collapsed, the granite was in great condition: three feet thick, and each stone two feet high by four feet long. We had to burn down the trees that were growing up through the center of the house before we could start reconstruction. The last people to inhabit it lived on the second floor while the musty barrels of wine and the pigs and the chickens lived on the first floor. It's customary in Regadas to build a lot of tiny rooms, but we decided to leave the whole thing open. Because we usually come in the summer, we don't need to conserve the heat. The main room is huge, with windows all across the front sporting a view of the village below and the knuckled hills all around, a fireplace on one side and the kitchen area on the other. Above has been left open all the way to the tile roof and with the original chestnut beams stuck across even though we know our older son, Aidan, is going to beg us to hang him a swing, or that Emmet, the climber, will get himself up on top of one of them sooner or later.

We're exhausted from the flight and the boys fall asleep immediately and even though we're beat from traveling with two small children, Colin and I open a bottle of *vino blanco* and settle in on the balcony, watch the bats veer madly around the lone streetlight—the last light at the edge of the village.

In the morning we walk down the winding road, up again, and through one of Tobo's and Laura's vineyards; we arrive at their door. Living in a village like this, where there are so few people, Tobo and Laura look forward to our arrival each summer, because we are their closest neighbors up here, on the hill above the village. Laura is almost seventy. Tobo is sixty-seven. From our height, Tobo and Laura look like country gnomes. Perfectly rounded, hardened, wrinkled from the sun like raisining grapes. Both have very few teeth. When either of them speaks to me I study their features, imagine what a beautiful portrait I could paint if I were a good enough painter. I can't muse too much, focus too intently on the shadows that lay along the folds of weathered skin, the shining, passionate eyes, because they are usually yelling something at me in half-Castellano, half-Gallego and, especially at the beginning of the summer, Gallego, spoken loud and very fast, is nearly impossible for me to follow. I am out of practice even with Castellano and Tobo and Laura don't usually speak that either so we have to work fairly hard to understand each other.

Emmet was only three months old when we were
here last summer. Now he's like a tiny SUV, an avalanche of boulders. I've started calling him "Bam Bam."
Aidan is closing in on four years old and Tobo asks me,
his gaze ferocious, whether he still loves to collect stones.
"No," I tell him. "Not so much. He likes flowers better
now." Tobo roars. "Well we knew he wouldn't go into
the army, that Aidan."

Laura emerges from the smokehouse, her hands full
of kiwis. "*Toma,*" she says, putting them into Emmet's
stroller. She breaks one open and gives it to Aidan.
Another to Emmet. They are as soft inside as a palmful
of shaving cream, the end of last season's harvest.

We sit at the outdoor granite table and Tobo pushes
his dirty straw hat back on his head, leans forward. "Tell
me," he says, "Is it as bad as it seems over there?" We
relate the details of life in America: the American flags,
the protests. The cowboy. "It's all true," we tell him. He
shakes his head in disbelief. Laura tells us we should
live here, in Spain, for the kids. It's better for the kids.
"Yes," we wag our heads. "You're right. But how would
we live?" Tobo sucks air in through his teeth, raises an
eyebrow. His eyes are like fire. "Well you're right," he
says, "It's tough here. And no one wants to farm grapes.
But what do you need? What do you really need?"

This is the question we keep asking ourselves when
we are here: What do we really need? In Boston, money
seems to evaporate, our house fills up with stuff as if it is
breeding like bacteria, and we run blindly from one thing
to another, trying to fulfill our obligations to our jobs, our
schedules, the kids' activities, time together as a family.
Something seems to get lost in the bustle. I think I can
understand a little bit of that loss when Laura shows me

the begonias that have bloomed and the herbs that have sprung up and the kiwis that hang small and hard from the vine. We walk slowly from one part of the yard to the next, observing plants and trees, talking about the rainfall and the winds. Laura cuts up some homemade chorizo sausage (last year's pigs) and Tobo pours tumblers of his best white wine (last year's grapes).

Finally, Emmet gets tired and needs to go home for his nap. Laura is rocking him back and forth, singing to him, as nurturing with him as she is with her own grandson, Nicolá. I can't get Aidan to come with me; he wants to stay with Nicolá. I push Emmet along the path to the winding road that loops down and then up again, through mossy walls and abandoned stone houses, hydrangea bushes peeking out of windows, blackberries soaking in the sun, their bushes replacing the fallen roofs. I imagine what it used to be like here, when there was a school for the children and all these houses were full of people. Tobo and Laura have told us what it was like years ago, when there were six people living in a small two-room stone house and each house that stepped on the toes of the next was full like that. During the civil war, many people died and later, many people emigrated, mostly to South America. Then in the years that followed, the young people moved out, to the cities, to work. Now there are few people left, and I would guess their median age to be about sixty-eight.

I think about our role here, and feel a little like a voyeur, that I've stumbled onto something that I don't deserve to enjoy because it isn't mine. But the locals would think I was being silly if I told them that; they seem to understand that we are all just people who are living our lives as best as we can. I'm embarrassed by our comparative wealth. Materially, we have so much—a vacation home in Spain? Who do we think we are—Hollywood stars? But in this village, no one judges us, which, after having been in so many tourist-addled destinations where locals are understandably resentful, is a blessing. Once, Mercedes, Laura's eighty-eight-year-old sister-in-law, grabbed my arm and pulled me close to her. "I am so happy to look up on that hill and see your lights on," she told me. "*La vida es mas alegre con gente,*" Tobo said once, when we were all gathered in their courtyard for dinner. Life is happier with people around you.

Colin finishes laying the tiles in our courtyard and Tobo is going to plant kiwi trees along a ditch by the wall for shade; they have to be planted in the fall and we'll be back in Boston by then. Tobo has already planted a number of trees for us, and throughout the winter, when we were trying to save enough money to spend another summer in Regadas, he watered them every couple of days. Hazelnut, walnut, apples, pears. He is hardly ever indoors. He shakes his head at you, "*¡Coño!*" he says. "Damn! What the hell are you thinking? You can't plant a tree in the summer! You silly tourist, you need to have your head examined."

No matter what it's about, Tobo is often laughing at us. I've finally gotten used to this treatment but as an American it was a tough transition from Thank you very much and Have a wonderful day. Colin on the other hand is from Ireland and slips into this banter easily.

One year, we brought Tobo and Laura slippers. Nice sheepskin ones. They nearly killed us for it. "We have slippers!" they yelled. "What the hell are you wasting your money for?" "But your slippers have holes." We pointed to their feet. Laura in a wraparound housedress pinned together in front of the bosom with a safety pin; Tobo's pants mended in ten or fifteen places. Their big toes had pushed through the worn plaid of their slippers. "*Coño,*" they said, and put the slippers on the couch, brought out chocolates and licor *de café*, which they make themselves. "Don't waste your money."

We cannot help but feel grateful to them, and to struggle for ways to pay them back for all they've done for us. If we hadn't befriended their daughter, Carmen, when we were living in Santiago de Compostela, we would never have seen As Regadas or met her parents; if not for Tobo's help, we wouldn't have been able to buy the house. He took us to meet the owners, helped us negotiate a price, and helped us at every stage. But Tobo's philosophy is quite simple: you do what you can for others. This year, we bring them maple syrup, reasoning that it is something they have never tried, and they seem to accept that. Still they look at us curiously and push the syrup into the cabinet.

This year we'll be here for the fiesta—Dia de Bon Xesus. Every village has, on its patron saint's day, a surreally elaborate fiesta. It usually lasts two or three days, with a *churrascada*, or pig roast, one day and every night two or three different *orquestas*, complete with dancers, smoke machines, and costume changes, until the sun rises.

Before the fiesta, Tobo and Laura, along with Carmen, her husband Ivan, and Nicolá come to our house carrying the makings for a *queimada*. Into a big ceramic bowl, Ivan pours about a liter of pure alcohol: *aguardiente*. It's made from the stuff that's left over after making wine and it's like liquid fire. Into that he adds a whole bunch of sugar and fruit, some spices, and sets it on fire. The fire is like water, rolling up out of the bowl like a waterfall in reverse. It's water made from electricity: neon blues, oranges, reds. So the water is the fire and the fire is the water and it's flowing up toward heaven and even though I should probably be a little worried that the world is upside down, I'm not. You can stick your finger into the fire and take it to your mouth and put the lump of flame right in there and it tastes sweet, fruity, and warm.

We head to the fiesta, down the hill and across to the field behind the church. The party lasts all night—kids, old people, everyone is there, the teenagers on the church steps cracking sunflower seeds between their teeth, too cool for those few adolescent years to be a part of it all. Carmen and I see our sons' very near futures in their huddle. Looking at the teenagers, at us parents, at the grandparents, I realize another thing that makes this place special for me, and comfortable, and sane. Life is for everyone, not just the twenty-somethings. Every age takes part, has a role to play. At home I feel a tacit expectation, as I approach forty, that I should hide out in my house in the suburbs and devote my life to ferrying my children from one play-date to another, my social life satisfied by attending meetings of the PTO. But here there's a place for me. And I can still party, and will party—*si Dios quiere*—well into my golden years.

When Carmen's son Nicolá begins to get frustrated and Aidan cries because some dancing couple plowed down one of the dirt houses he'd been making in front of the stage, we know it is time to head home. But Laura and Tobo won't let us leave. They want us to have the time of our lives and are getting tired themselves so they take the children back to their house to sleep. Carmen and Ivan try to teach Colin and me to dance—no easy feat with the two of us—until we are too tired to keep going. When we leave, there are still whole families at the fiesta. The old people put us to shame with their endurance. Finally, we cut through a vineyard on our way home. The sun is about to rise and the sky is pink. The grapes are becoming fuller, the sugar inside them developed by sunshine: green globes and purple globes, tiny universes of grape planets heavy with the weight of earth.

In another few weeks it will be time to go home, to work, to school, to save the money to come back. I'm sad that we'll miss the harvest, miss the kiwis as they come off the vine and the chestnuts that get collected and roasted in the smokehouse, their flavor burned into the legs of ham and the chorizos, the figs that aren't ripe until October. But we'll have to make do with this—our month and a half of summer—to restore our sanity. We'll try to hold onto it as we reenter the crazy American battlefield.

Leaving is more difficult every year, as we become closer to our friends here. Tobo takes the morning off on the day when we depart; he has put on a fresh shirt and combed his sparse hair to say goodbye. Aidan and Nicolá, having learned a few words in each others' language, hug and say goodbye, *adiós*. Laura tries to shove chorizos and bottles of wine into our luggage; they don't taste the same when we are home, I tell her. The *taste* is the same, but somehow it feels different as it enters your body. Perhaps it's because in Boston, that soft air is missing. And missing too is that sense of plenty, of abundance found in the simplest things: in the scent of the vineyards that fills the air; in the elegant gesture of an old woman offering you kiwis.

ॐ ॐ ॐ

Sara B. Fraser teaches at the University of Massachusetts, Boston, writes stories and essays, and lives in Medford, Massachusetts.

ঞ ঞ ঞ

Oaxaca Care

In a Mexican village, a traveler fulfills
a promise to herself.

*M*y forehead rests against the window of the bus
bound for San Bartolo Coyotepec, a village in
southern Mexico. Longing to see the view beyond the
dirty bus window, I make several unsuccessful attempts
to lower it. My effort results in a torn fingernail and a
nasty cut from the rusty metal hinge. I scrounge in my
pack to find a band-aid and wonder how long a tetanus
shot lasts. I press my nose against the window and peer
through the grime and recall the long months of rehab
to reclaim my weakened body and the vow I made to
visit this tiny pueblito in Oaxaca. *Por fin*, yes, finally, I
am going to see the lustrous black pottery that I covet,
made by the indigenous artisans of this village.

But the dream of the Valley of Oaxaca that made

me feel better when I was sad is hidden from view by a mud-caked window. The undulating forms outside can only be seen in my mind's eye. The pattern on the glass resembles a miniature alluvial fan at the mouth of a tiny canyon—thin layers of rain-spattered dust spread across the surface depositing fine sediment in the metal groove at the bottom edge—almost an inch deep.

I determine that on the way back, I *will* have a working window. *But—a clean bus window that works? Is there a clean second-class bus anywhere in Mexico?* Smiling, I visualize a fleet of kaleidoscopic colored buses lined up at an American-style car wash. Yes, a traveler in rural Mexico had better bring along a sense of humor.

The bus driver's raspy voice startles my reverie, *"¡Cinco y media, regresamos a Oaxaca!"* he shouts. The brakes groan to another tortured stop. I look at my watch—1:30—four hours until the bus returns to Oaxaca City at 5:30 P.M. Standing up, I segue into the line of passengers. *"Muchas gracias,"* I say to the driver as I descend the stairs. Only a person *mal educado* (ill-mannered) forgets to thank the bus driver in Mexico.

Once off the bus, I realize I have no idea where to catch the return. Leaning back into the doorway to ask, I sense that the driver is in a hurry.

"¿Por favor, dónde tomo el autobús para devolver a Oaxaca?"

"Aquí, pero en el otro lado," he says tersely and shuts the door.

This street on the other side, I repeat to myself. Looking across the street, I note the small market on the corner that must be the bus stop. I check my watch again. I can't afford to miss the last bus—there isn't another until Sunday—and there are no accommodations in the village.

The other passengers wander off into the *pueblito*—native women with tightly wrapped bundles balanced on their heads, one arm holding a nursing infant, the other clinging to the tiny brown fingers of their children. Weathered *campesinos* wearing straw hats trudge along the roadway—their backs bowed with the weight of several cardboard *cartones* tied together with hemp. The *zócalo* is quiet—shops closed for siesta. Three scraggly, dun-colored dogs lie in the shade of a huge cypress tule tree, dozing in the sultry afternoon heat. The only sound I hear is the empty bus as it clatters across the cobblestone placita.

Suddenly, the blare of the bus horn followed by squeals and squawks pierces the stillness of the afternoon. I look up to see pigs, goats, and chickens scatter in every direction. A gaggle of barefoot children run behind the bus, playing their dangerous game of tag with the back bumper. No matter how many times I witness this scenario, it always makes me shiver. I shake my head and worry that life in the third world often seems like a cheap commodity.

Ambling along the narrow streets, I notice that many of the vendors display a black ceramic pot outside their simple adobe homes. Some even have lean-to "showrooms" attached to one side. I select one with a hand-carved sign that reads, "Doña Rosa, Alfareria." Because it is customary to walk right in, I find myself in the middle of Doña Rosa's family activity—several old women are shelling peas—I hear the crisp *tink, tink* as they drop into the pan. A young mother looks up, smiles and continues to nurse her baby. Because privacy is such a sacred concept in the U. S., I have had to learn to overcome my *Yanqui vergüenza* (embarrassment) so that I don't miss any wonderful cultural exchanges.

Stunning black pottery—clay hauled from the valley floor, burnished and smoothed to perfection by the hands of Zapotec descendents—fills the tiny *sala*: huge *ollas* (urns) with curved handles, Virgins de Guadalupe with long necks and slender fingers, tiny sets of dishes, and pierced clay lampshades studded with cat's-eye marbles. A delicate pot the size of a small melon catches my eye. Serpentine ropes coil at the base, each sinuous spiral hand-tooled—tiny flecks of mica sparkle in the light. A stoop-shouldered old woman wearing the ubiquitous *delantal* (apron) rises from a rickety wooden stool in the corner. Her hair hangs down her back in a long gray plait laced with red and yellow ribbons that identify her Zapotec clan ancestry.

"Doña Rosa?"

"*Si, señora, soy yo,*" she says, smiling broadly, a gold tooth flashing.

She picks up the small pot and cradles it in her hands—hands that have molded clay into art for a lifetime. "*Mi nieta hizo esta olla, ella sólo tiene catorce años,*" she says.

Her granddaughter created this beautiful piece. Only fourteen years old and her talents are already contributing to her family's survival.

"*Es preciosa, la tomará,*" I say, handing her a fifty-peso note. *La Doña* wraps the pot in newspaper, places it carefully into a *cartone*, and ties the box with a frayed piece of hemp. I tell her it will look beautiful in my home in Colorado. We clasp hands briefly and I leave, walking in the direction of the bus station.

I glance at my watch—5:00 P.M.—thirty minutes early. At 6:00 P.M., I check again and then I begin to worry. There is no one else waiting and nothing in the village remotely resembles a hotel. I walk into the market and ask a shopkeeper about the bus to Oaxaca, saying I thought there was supposed to be one at 5:30.

"*Sí, hay normalmente, no sé lo que pasó,*" the shopkeeper says.

No one seems to know what has happened to the bus. I feel like every pair of brown eyes in the market is staring at me. My heart starts to thump and the blood pulses in the tip of my injured finger. *Stay calm,* I tell myself and silently begin to recite my travel mantra—*what is the worst thing that can happen? Will this experience kill you? If the answer is no, then think of it as a story you can tell your grandchildren.* I buy a bottle of water, a chunk of Oaxacan cheese, two freshly baked *bolillos* and a ripe mango, take a deep breath and stride out of the market.

Hoisting the heavy pack onto my shoulders, I aim straight down the dusty road—Highway 175—to Oaxaca City. I wonder if the customers in the market are watching me, but I dare not turn around. A mile or so down the road, I see a huge *tule* tree outlined against the purple haze of twilight. It stands in a *milpa* surrounded by corn almost fifteen feet high. At the edge of the Oaxacan cornfield, I am transported back to an Indiana farm thousands of miles away. *It is a hot and humid August night and my brothers and I are chasing lightning bugs through the cornfield, our skin damp and itchy from the sweet-smelling sap. We have dragged our blankets from the stifling heat of the attic to the edge of the field where we will watch the stars twinkle through the tasseled stalks.*

The warm childhood memories comfort me. I look

around to see if anyone has followed—nothing but silence. I slip silently into the row that leads to the *tule* tree.

The scent of moldy corn mingles with other strange odors that my nostrils can't identify. I remember how Midwestern farmers spray their corn with chemicals to prevent this black smut fungus. In Mexico this fungus is an Aztecan culinary treat called *cuitlacoche*. Indigenous peoples believe it is a gift of the gods. Drooping corn leaves tickle my face and block out the wan light of the rising moon. I stumble over the gigantic root system that spreads across the field and anchors the *tule* to the earth. Hunching into a semi-crawling position, I work my way blindly toward the massive trunk. I giggle softly to think that I'm going to sleep in a cornfield once again. When I finally reach the tule, I stretch my arms out as far as I can around its enormous girth and inhale the spicy aroma. *Por Dios, I feel so small.* I drop my pack and dig around in the pocket for the mango. I bite into the ripe fruit—the sweetness of its flesh surprises me. I spit out the skin, the sticky juice dribbles down my chin and neck. I pray there will be no fire ants living in the tree.

Except for the chirping of the crickets, the night is silent. Too tired to eat anything else, I lean back against the smooth bark and close my eyes.

"Ruth, Ruth, wake up," says the nurse patting my cheek. "Dr. Jones will be here soon to talk with you."

"I'm awake," I murmur, and try to open my eyes, but there are heavy weights pulling down on the lids and little blue waves are washing gently back and forth.

A man's face is looking down at me. It is grave and knowing. "I'm so sorry Ruth," says the voice as a warm hand takes my cold one. "The biopsy was malignant. You have breast cancer."

I jump up, hitting my head on a low hanging branch. *Where am I? Not the hospital. Oh yes, the dream again.* Straddling a root, I plop down and the sadness I've carried inside for months finally escapes. The tears come— slowly at first and then violent racking sobs from a place deep within me. My shoulders heave and I gasp for breath. It feels like a fishhook has been pulled out of my soul. But the flare-up is short-lived—there is a little click of recognition and I understand why I am here. *I am alive.* I suck in a long draught of the mysterious odors that permeate the night. I wipe my eyes, blow my nose, and turn my tear-streaked face to the velvet blackness of the Oaxacan sky. Thousands of stars wink beyond the canopy of the *tule* leaves and the goddess moon peeks into its branches. I nestle deeper into the wide crevasse between the sturdy roots of the tule—the long arms of Mother Earth.

"I'm so happy," I say to the *tule*, "*Finalamente, yo estoy contenta.*" *Gracias*, IxChel, goddess of the moon, goddess of the corn and goddess of healing. Thank you for giving me this adventure—the one I promised myself if I were allowed to survive.

Somewhere in the distance I hear a coyote yip.

Ruth Kear, a restaurant designer for over twenty-five years, recently returned to college to complete a Master's Degree in English as a Second Language. She told her family and friends that she wanted to give something back to the Mexican people for the wonderful life experiences she acquired traveling the backroads of their country. She teaches English to Mexican immigrant mothers,

sharing stories about a culture she has come to love with women who understand what it is like to be a stranger in a foreign land. She continues to travel, solo and on a shoestring, taking photos and chronicling the experience.

☙ ☙ ☙

Point, Shoot, and Remember

The best photographs you ever take may
well be the ones you'll never see.

*M*inding my own business on the Bridge of Sighs,
I am suddenly the most popular traveler in
Venice. "Excuse me," says a German fellow. "Would you
mind...?" Two Japanese girls, giggling and blushing,
communicate their request with gestures. An Italian man
pulls his sweetheart over. "This is my new wife. We are
just married. Can you...?"

Certainly, I say. My pleasure. And then I take the
proffered Olympus point-and-shoot, the Nikon digital,
the hefty Cannon EOS, and go to work. I position my
new friends in flattering light, compose a shot that has
a panoramic vista of water and gondolas in the back-

ground—the memory of Venice I imagine they'll want to hold in their hands twenty years down the road.

Click! Click! Click! Smiles all around. I hand back the equipment and return to my wanderings.

The role of Good Samaritan travel photographer is not something I ever thought I'd play. It seems to have been thrust on me by a combination of circumstances. I usually travel alone, look pretty approachable, and—the key factor—I carry a retro-looking black 35mm camera (a Contax) with a couple of lenses and a tripod, which fools other travelers into thinking I must know what all those f-stops do.

If only my subjects knew that for about the first ten years of my travels, I refused, as a matter of principle, to carry any camera on my trips at all.

Photography—or so I thought then—was a traveler's trap, a technology that got in the way of real experience, creating barriers between me and the local people I yearned to get to know. What I really wanted was to live all my travel moments, rather than spend that time collecting them to take home. I did not need trophies to prove that I'd prowled the narrow streets of Old Havana or circumnavigated the spooky giant red rock Uluru (Ayers Rock) in Australia.

One night in a bar in Sydney, several beers along, I blurted out my anti-camera manifesto with great gusto and conviction to poor Jake, the professional travel photographer I'd made friends with on a group tour to the Outback.

He did not get insulted. Instead, he bought me a whiskey and quietly said, "I think you need to relax."

Photography didn't have to be a trap, he explained gently. It could be fun. He pulled out a few shots he'd taken of my back while we tromped through the Outback—showing my white shirt covered by hundreds of black flies.

"You could tell your friends about how thick the flies were in Uluru, or you could pull out this snapshot—which would make them laugh more?"

Then, devilishly, he told me about a new model of point-and-shoot camera, small and cheap, that had, in his opinion, a superb lens and took flawless pictures. I never saw Jake again after that trip, but I still have the little Olympus that I bought on his recommendation.

Talk about a pendulum. In just a few years I went from anti-camera snob to equipment geek, prowling the camera shops in search of specially tinted lens filters and joining Internet news groups populated with like-minded fanatics, photographers still glum about the invention of the auto-focus lens.

My fear that holding a camera would keep me from making local friends evaporated the moment I set foot in Asia. There I discovered a world in which taking pictures is not only a gesture of friendship, but a required activity in any happy social situation. No Japanese dinner or Chinese banquet would be complete without a round of giddy picture-taking, followed by the pleasure days or weeks later—of receiving a slew of images on the computer or in the mail from your new buddy.

In my first flush of enthusiasm for capturing images (preferably with old, hard to use, very hip equipment), I went overboard and almost became my worst nightmare. You've seen the person in the khaki multi-pocket jacket, huffing and puffing under the strain of heavy shoulder bags. She is the traveler who wakes at five A.M. to catch the "good light" of early morning, and who blows off the pleasant late-afternoon tea or cocktail in order to elbow for position in the pack of other tripod-hefting travelers who absolutely must catch that perfect sunset shot in Angkor Wat.

One afternoon, in the courtyard of an old Buddhist temple in Laos, I let go of my obsession with getting everything picture perfect. I'd just convinced a reluctant monk to pose for a portrait. As I fiddled and fussed with the lens, the tripod, and my exposure settings, another traveler burst in on my scene. Smiling at me and my subject, he aimed his Sony digital camera, grabbed a shot of the monk, and walked over to show him his own image on the camera's display screen.

The monk, astonished and overjoyed, turned to the Sony-toting traveler and burst into the biggest smile I'd seen in Laos. He posed, again and again, for his new friend. He entirely forgot about me.

I got annoyed. And then I went out and bought my own digital camera.

It's hard to beat the thrill of sharing your pictures, instantly, with the people you photograph on the road. In fact, there's only one better thrill I can think of: the feeling I get when I hand the camera back to the couple on the bridge in Venice. I cross my fingers that their pictures come out well. That someday they will turn the page of an album, or leaf through a long-forgotten box, and find themselves back in Venice, remembering the afternoon they handed their camera to a stranger, and smiled.

Some of my favorite travel photographs are the ones I will never see.

☙ ☙ ☙

Daisann McLane is a contributing editor for National Geographic Traveler. *She is at work on a book about learning Cantonese in New York and Hong Kong.*

ACKNOWLEDGMENTS

Anthologies are the result of not one editor's work but rather many people's labor and care, including hour upon hour of reading, formatting stories, and seeking permission to use the stories. Thank you for all the labors of love provided by Travelers' Tales founding editors James O'Reilly and Larry Habegger, as well as Sean O'Reilly, Christy Harrington, and Melanie Haage. Special thanks to Susan Brady, Travelers' Tales' production manager extraordinaire, for her consistently excellent rendering of every aspect of these books from start to finish.

I would like to add a special note of appreciation, in this book that honors women's voices, to all the women in my life who support and sustain me, including my mother and my sister, my niece Nikki McCauley, my daughter Hannah, and my dear women friends in Dallas and Cambridge. Blessings upon you all.

Romantic Education by Patricia Hampl. Copyright © 1989 by Patricia Hampl. Reprinted by permission of Marly Rusoff & Associates, Inc. Literary Agency and the author.

"Traveling Heavy" by Susan Orlean excerpted from *My Kind of Place: Travel Stories from a Woman Who's Been Everywhere* by Susan Orlean. Copyright © 2004 by Susan Orlean. Reprinted by permission of Random House, Inc.

"What They Taught Me" by Amy Wilson published with permission from the author. Copyright © 2006 by Amy Wilson.

"The Barber's Beads" by Deborah J. Smith published with permission from the author. Copyright © 2006 by Deorah J. Smith.

"Rudolph for Newlyweds" by D'lynne Plummer published with permission from the author. Copyright © 2006 by D'lynne Plummer.

"To Dresden with Tears" by Hannelore Hahn published with permission from the author. Copyright © 2006 by Hannelore Hahn.

"Tibetan Truths" by Stephanie Elizondo Griest published with permission from the author. Copyright © 2006 by Stephanie Elizondo Griest.

"A Tale of a Journey Deferred" by Judy Copeland reprinted from Issue #14 of *New Millenium Writings*. Copyright © 2006 by Judy Copeland. Reprinted by permission of the author.

"Aunty Mame Learns a Lesson" by Sophia Dembling published with permission from the author. Copyright © 2006 by Sophia Dembling.

"In the Hamam" by Sharon Balentine published with permission from the author. Copyright © 2006 by Sharon Balentine.

Passage Out of Madagascar" by Gisele Rainer published with permission from the author. Copyright © 2006 by Gisele Rainer.

"Awash in the Jungle" by Kari J. Bodnarchuk published with permission from the author. Copyright © 2006 by Kari J. Bodnarchuk.

"Bandit Territory" by Faith Adiele published with permission from the author. Copyright © 2001 by Faith Adiele. This work previously appeared in *A Woman Alone: Travel Tales from Around the Globe* and *Crab Orchard Review*, Volume 7 #1, Fall/Winter 2001.

About the Editor

Lucy McCauley's travel essays have appeared in such publications as *The Atlantic Monthly, The Los Angeles Times, Harvard Review*, *Science & Spirit*, and Salon.com. She is series editor of *Best Women's Travel Writing*, and editor of three other anthologies—*Travelers' Tales Spain* (1995), *Women in the Wild* (1998), and *A Woman's Path* (2000), all of which have been reissued in the last few years. In addition, she has written case studies in Latin America for Harvard's Kennedy School of Government, and now works as a developmental editor for publishers such as Harvard Business School Press.